Microsoft®
Outlook 2002
fast&easy®

Check the Web for Updates:

To check for updates or corrections relevant to this book visit our updates page on the Web at **http://www.prima-tech.com/support.**

Send Us Your Comments:

To comment on this book or any other PRIMA TECH title, visit our reader response page on the Web at **http://www.prima-tech.com/comments.**

How to Order:

For information on quantity discounts, contact the publisher: Prima Publishing, P.O. Box 1260BK, Rocklin, CA 95677-1260; (916) 787-7000. On your letterhead, include information concerning the intended use of the books and the number of books you want to purchase. For individual orders, turn to the back of this book for more information.

Microsoft® Outlook 2002

fast&easy®

Lori J. Swan
C. Michael Woodward
Diane Koers

A Division of Prima Publishing

A Division of Prima Publishing

Prima Publishing and colophon are registered trademarks of Prima Communications, Inc. PRIMA TECH Fast & Easy is a registered trademark of Prima Communications, Inc., Roseville, California 95661.

Publisher: Stacy L. Hiquet

Associate Marketing Manager: Heather Buzzingham

Managing Editor: Sandy Doell

Acquisitions Editor: Debbie Abshier

Project Editor: Elizabeth A. Agostinelli

Technical Reviewer: Jacqueline Harris

Copy Editor: Kate Givens

Interior Layout: Argosy Publishing

Screen Imager: Diane Koers

Cover Design: Prima Design Team

Indexer: Kelly Talbot

Proofreaders: Daryl Kessler and Jeannie Smith

ISBN: 0-7615-3422-9

Library of Congress Catalog Card Number: 2001-086690

Printed in the United States of America

00 01 02 03 04 GG 10 9 8 7 6 5 4 3 2 1

To Corwin Michael Woodward,
the man who taught me not to fear change
or brilliant challenges. Thanks for sharing
more than your "Outlook" with me.

And to Joseph John Swan,
the man who has shared his lifetime with me
and reminds me by experience
that love and beauty and art are passions of the soul.
You feed mine with your spirit.

—Lori J. Swan, March 10, 2001

Contents at a Glance

Contents

PART V
STAYING ON TOP OF THINGS WITH TASKS....... 303

PART VI
TRACKING YOUR TIME WITH THE JOURNAL 339

Acknowledgments

To all the people at Prima Publishing: thanks for making your magic happen. With special thanks to Senior Acquisitions Editor Debbie Abshier, whose support did not go unnoticed when tasks were tough. Thanks to the unending list of editors and taskmasters that make this book happen, especially project editor Elizabeth Agostinelli. To Michael Woodward, my partner, friend, and mentor on this book and many other interesting and challenging collaborative efforts. I thank you for expanding my horizons, keeping my "outlook" optimistic, reminding me to use my tools, and having the patience to see this project through with me to the end. You're an amazing example of "yes you can" and I admire the magic in you. Also thanks to my friends and family for understanding my absence during this project, especially to my son Joey for being my strongest supporter and encouraging me on when times were tough; to my folks who now have two authors in the family; to Christine and Adrian, my angels; to my brother Bruce who really "gets it"; to Kim and Julie for never giving up on me, and to Vicki, for whom a thank-you will never be enough.

About the Authors

Lori J. Swan is a Branch Manager for PIP Printing, a Dynamark Graphics Group company in Indianapolis, Indiana. She is a founding partner of Artemis, Inc., a company providing software, support, and training to medical and dental practices. Lori is also an experienced development and technical editor, and worked for more than 16 years as a corporate trainer and financial systems analyst at General Motors. Away from the computer, Lori has an extensive community-theatre resume, enjoys all types of music and dancing, and currently sings with the Indianapolis Women's Chorus. She also likes to doodle. This is her first published title.

C. Michael Woodward recently moved to Tucson, Arizona after spending the first 37 years of his life in Indianapolis. He is a Senior Technical Writer for Analysts International, Inc., and is the founder of Echelon Editorial and Publishing Services, which provides freelance writing, editing, and project management services to the technical publishing industry. Michael has authored or contributed to more than a dozen computer books, including *Create FrontPage Web Pages in a Weekend, Adobe Illustrator 9 fast & easy, Microsoft Outlook 2000 fast & easy, Create FrontPage 2000 Web Pages in a Weekend, Microsoft Windows 2000 fast & easy,* and many others. He's currently spending all his free time exploring his new home state, which is a full-time job in itself.

Diane Koers owns and operates All Business Service, a software training and consulting business formed in 1988 that services the central Indiana area. Her area of expertise has long been in the word processing, spreadsheet and graphics area of computing as well as providing training and support for Peachtree Accounting Software. Diane's authoring experience includes 14 other Prima Publishing Fast & Easy books including *Windows Millennium fast & easy, WordPerfect 9 fast & easy, Paint Shop Pro 7 fast & easy, Office 2000 fast & easy, Office XP fast & easy,* and has co-authored Prima's *Essential Windows 98.* She has also developed and written software training manuals for her clients' use. Active in her church and civic activities, Diane enjoys spending her free time traveling and playing with her grandson and her three Yorkshire Terriers.

Introduction

This new fast & easy guide from Prima Publishing will help you unleash the power of Microsoft Outlook 2002. Outlook is a messaging and contact management program that will allow you to do all the things that other Personal Information Management (PIM) programs do, and it will also make it easier than ever to make your information work together. For example, you can make your contact information work seamlessly with your e-mail messages in Outlook.

Microsoft Outlook 2002 fast & easy provides you with all the information you need to begin using the powerful features of Outlook 2002 today. As you read this book, you'll tackle many of the features Outlook has to offer. You'll learn at a record pace with the step-by-step approach, clear language, and illustrations of exactly what you will see on your screen.

WHO SHOULD READ THIS BOOK?

Microsoft Outlook 2002 fast & easy is ideal as a learning tool or as a step-by-step task reference. The easy-to-follow, highly visual nature of this book makes it the perfect learning tool for a beginning computer user. Veteran computer users who are new to this version of Outlook will also find this book helpful.

Current users of Outlook 2002 can utilize this book when they need occasional reminders about the steps required to perform a particular task. It is designed to cut straight to the chase to provide the information you need without having to sort through pages of dense text.

ADDED ADVICE TO MAKE YOU A PRO

As you use *Microsoft Outlook 2002 fast & easy,* you'll notice that it focuses on the steps necessary for a task and keeps explanations to a minimum. Included in the book are some elements that are designed to provide additional information, without encumbering your progress through the steps:

- Tips provide helpful hints and suggestions for working with features in Microsoft Outlook 2002.

- Notes give you information about a feature, or comments about how to use a feature effectively in your day-to-day activities.

As a bonus, the helpful appendix will give you additional tips on working with shortcut keys. Finally, the glossary is designed to take the mystery out of Microsoft Outlook 2002 by providing definitions of key terms used throughout the book.

Read and enjoy this book! It is certainly the fastest and easiest way to learn Microsoft Outlook 2002.

PART I

Getting Started with Outlook 2002

1

Welcome to Outlook 2002

If you're working in a corporate environment, chances are Outlook may already be installed on your computer. But if you're among the ever-growing number of small business and home users, it might not be. Because Outlook is only available as part of the Microsoft Office XP suite, installing Outlook really means installing (or adding to a previous installation of) Office XP. But don't worry—installing Office is typically very quick and easy. In this chapter, you'll learn how to:

- Install Office XP on your computer
- Choose which Office components you want to install
- Detect and repair problems
- Reinstall Office
- Add and remove components
- Uninstall Office XP completely
- Install content from other Office CDs

Installing the Software

The installation program for the Office XP programs is almost entirely automatic. In most cases, you can simply follow the instructions onscreen and let it run.

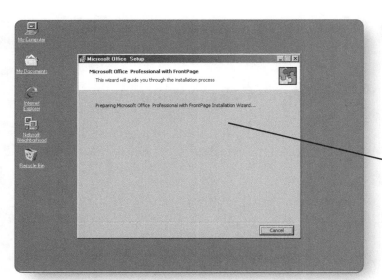

1. Insert the **Office XP CD-ROM** into your computer's CD-ROM drive. The Windows Installer will start and the Microsoft Office Setup, User Information dialog box will open.

NOTE

When you insert the Office XP CD for the first time, you may see a message that the installer has been updated, prompting you to restart your system. Do so, and when you return to Windows after restarting, remove the CD and reinsert it so that the Setup program starts up automatically.

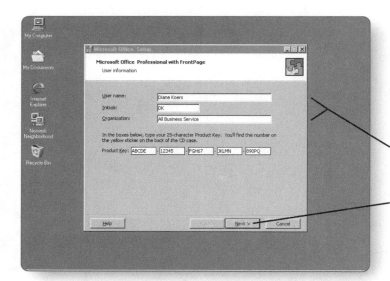

2. Type all of the **information** requested.

3. Click on **Next**. The End User License Agreement will appear.

NOTE
You'll find the CD Key number on a sticker on the back of the Office CD jewel case.

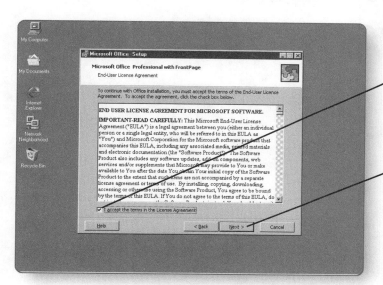

4. **Read** the **License Agreement**.

5. **Click** on the **I accept the terms in the License Agreement option button**. The option will be selected.

6. **Click** on **Next**. The Ready To Install dialog box will open.

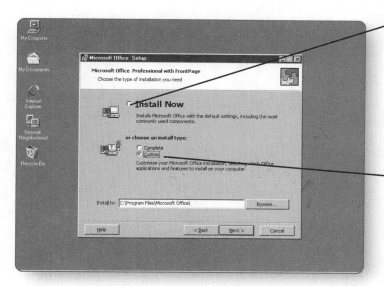

7a. **Click** on the **Install Now button**. Use this option to install Office on your computer with the default settings. This is the recommended installation for most users.

OR

7b. **Click** on the **Customize button**, if you want to choose which components to install or where to install them. The Installation Location dialog box will open. Then see the next section, "Choosing Components," for guidance.

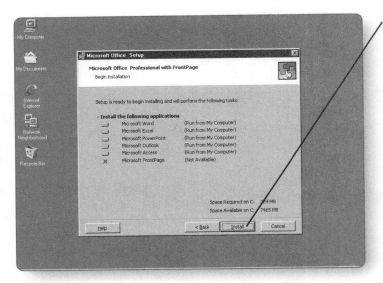

8. **Click** on **Install** when you reach the end of the wizard. The installer will begin copying files and setting up Office XP on your computer.

9. **Wait** while the **Office software** installs on your computer. When the setup has completed, the a message box will appear.

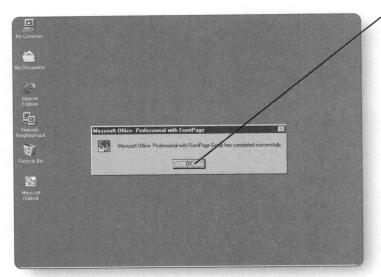

10. **Click** on **OK**. The Setup Wizard will close.

TIP

After the installation is complete, it's not a bad idea to restart your computer. Click on Start, Shutdown, and then choose Restart from the drop-down list that appears.

Choosing Components

If you selected the Custom install option in the previous section, you have the choice of installing many different programs and components.

NOTE

For a custom installation, you have the option of placing Office in a different location on your computer. It is recommended that you use the default installation location. If you want to install Office in a different directory, type the directory path in the text box or click on the Browse button to select a directory.

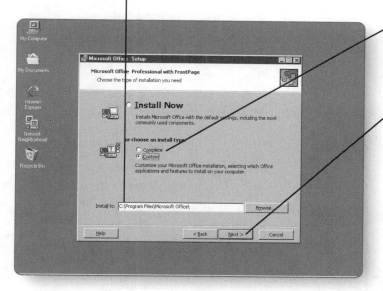

1. **Click** on **Custom**. The installer will give you options for choosing individual programs and features.

2. **Click** on **Next**. The wizard will present the list of available Office programs you can install.

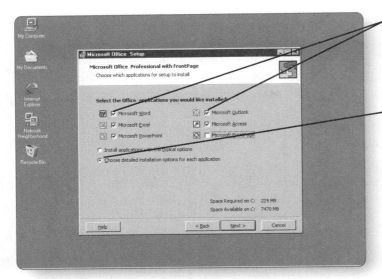

3. **Click** on the **program check boxes** to select the ones you want to install. The indicated boxes will show a check mark.

4. **Click** on **Choose detailed installation options for each application**. The installer will let you control which components and add-ons within the various applications you want to install.

5. **Click** on **Next**. The wizard will progress to the next page.

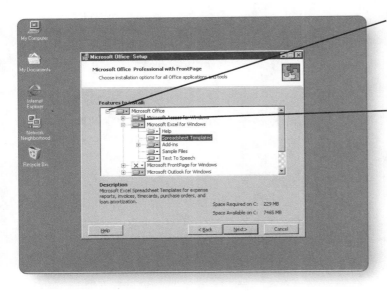

6. **Click** on a **plus sign** to expand a list of features. The features listed under the category will appear.

7. **Click** on the **down arrow** to the right of the hard drive icon. A menu of available installation options for the feature will appear.

8. Click on the **button** next to the individual option, and choose a setting for that option:

- **Run from My Computer**. The component will be fully installed, so that you will not need the Office CD in the CD-ROM drive to use it.

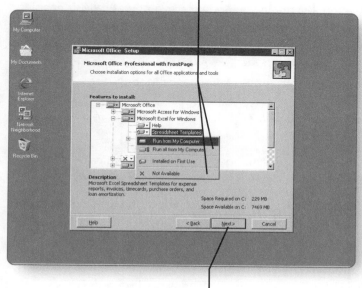

- **Run all from My Computer**. The selected component and all the components subordinate to it will be fully installed.

- **Installed on First Use**. The first time you try to activate the component, you will be prompted to insert the Office CD to fully install it. This is good for components that you are not sure whether you will need.

- **Not Available**. The component will not be installed at all.

9. Click on **Next**. The Installing dialog box will open.

Working with Maintenance Mode

Maintenance Mode is a feature of the Setup program. Whenever you run the Setup program again, after the initial installation, Maintenance Mode starts automatically. It enables you to add or remove features, repair your Office installation (for example, if files have become corrupted), and remove Office completely. There are several ways to rerun the Setup program (and thus enter Maintenance Mode):

- Reinsert the Office XP CD. The Setup program may start automatically.

- If the Setup program does not start automatically, double-click on the CD icon in the My Computer window.

- If double-clicking on the CD icon doesn't work, right-click on the CD icon and click on Open from the shortcut menu. Then double-click on the Setup.exe file in the list of files that appears.

- From the Control Panel in Windows, click on the Add/Remove Programs button. Then on the Install/Uninstall tab, click on Microsoft Office XP in the list, and finally, click on the Add/Remove button.

After entering Maintenance Mode, choose the button for the activity you want. Each option is briefly described in the following sections.

Repairing or Reinstalling Office

If an Office program is behaving strangely, or refuses to work, chances are good that a needed file has become corrupted. But which file? You have no way of knowing, so you can't fix the problem yourself.

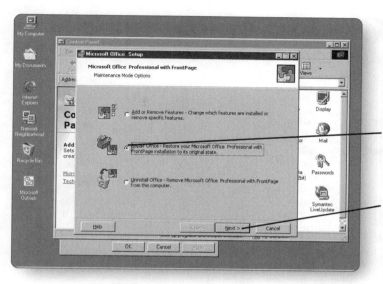

If this happens, you can either repair Office or completely reinstall it. Both options are accessed from the Repair Office button in Maintenance Mode.

1. **Click** on the **Repair Office button** in Maintenance Mode. The option will be selected.

2. **Click** on **Next**. The wizard will progress to the next step.

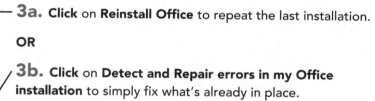

3a. **Click** on **Reinstall Office** to repeat the last installation.

OR

3b. **Click** on **Detect and Repair errors in my Office installation** to simply fix what's already in place.

4. **Click** on **Install**. The process will start.

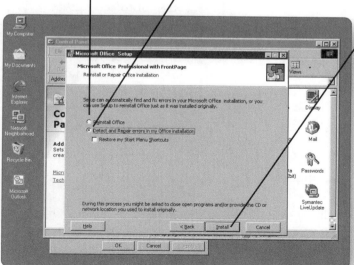

TIP

You can also repair individual Office programs by opening the Help menu in each program and clicking on Detect and Repair. This works well if you are sure that one certain program is causing the problem, and it's quicker than asking the Setup program to check all of the installed programs.

Adding and Removing Components

Adding and removing components works just like selecting the components initially.

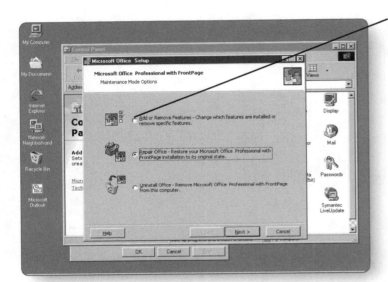

1. Click on the **Add or Remove Features button** in Maintenance Mode. The Update Features window will appear. This window works exactly the same as the window you saw in the "Choosing Components" section earlier in this chapter.

NOTE
Some features will attempt to automatically install themselves as you are working. If you have set a feature to be installed on first use, attempt to access that feature. You will be prompted to insert your Office XP CD, and the feature will be installed without further prompting.

Removing Office from Your PC

In the unlikely event that you should need to remove Office from your PC completely, click on Uninstall Office from the Maintenance Mode screen. Then follow the prompts to remove it from your system.

After removing Office, you will probably have a few remnants left behind that the Uninstall routine didn't catch. For example, there will probably still be a Microsoft Office folder in your Program Files folder or wherever you installed the program. You can delete that folder yourself.

> ### CAUTION
>
> If you plan to reinstall Office later, and you have created any custom templates, toolbars, or other items, you may want to leave the Microsoft Office folder alone, so that those items will be available to you after you reinstall.

Installing Content from Other Office CDs

Depending on the version of Office you bought, you may have more than one CD in your package. CD 1 contains all the basic Office components, such as Word, Outlook, PowerPoint, Excel, Access, and Internet Explorer. It may be the only CD you need to use.

The other CDs contain extra applications that come with the specific version of Office you purchased. They may include Publisher, FrontPage, a language pack, or a programmer and developer resource kit. Each of these discs has its own separate installation program.

The additional CDs should start their Setup programs automatically when you insert the disc in your drive. If not, browse the CD's contents in My Computer or Windows Explorer and double-click on the Setup.exe file.

2

Finding Your Way in Outlook

Outlook has many features that are identical to those used in other Windows-based applications, especially Microsoft Office applications. If you are familiar with these applications, you may already know how to use many of these features. What's more, the way you use Outlook may not be the same way someone else uses the program. Fortunately, Outlook has several options for displaying information. In this chapter, you'll learn how to:

- Use toolbars
- Move with scroll bars
- Use dialog boxes and menus
- Work with the Outlook bar and Outlook Today
- Display the Folder list
- Use the Preview pane
- Understand the Outlook icons

Understanding the Outlook Environment

When you first start Outlook, you see the Information viewer. By default, the Information viewer displays the contents of the Inbox. The Inbox stores your incoming e-mail messages.

The data displayed in the Information viewer will change depending on your selection.

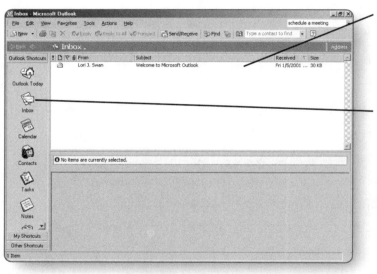

- **Information viewer**. The display area for e-mail messages, calendar items, contacts, tasks, journal items, or notes.

- **Folders**. Outlook's primary folders are displayed as icons on the Outlook bar. The selected folder's contents will be displayed in the Information viewer.

Using the Outlook Toolbars

Toolbars are located at the top of the Outlook screen. Each toolbar contains a collection of buttons; each button represents a commonly used command. You'll find these same commands within Outlook's menus, but the toolbar buttons are easier and faster to use.

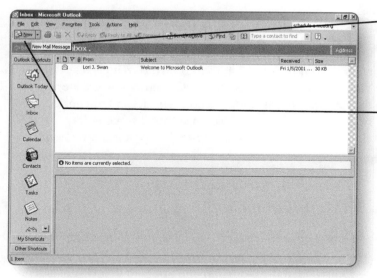

1. **Move** the **mouse pointer** over any toolbar button. The toolbar button's name will display in a ScreenTip.

2. **Click** on a **toolbar button**. The command associated with the toolbar button will be executed.

Moving with Scroll Bars

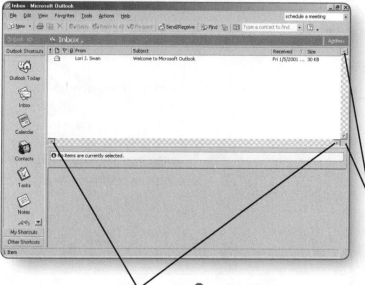

Scroll bars allow you to change the contents of your screen when there is more information than can fit on one screen. The vertical scroll bar appears on the right edge of the screen, and the horizontal scroll bar appears on the bottom of the Inbox window.

1. **Click** on the **up arrow** or the **down arrow** on the vertical scroll bar to move up or down on the screen.

2. **Click** on the **left arrow** or the **right arrow** on the horizontal scroll bar to move to the left or right on the screen.

NOTE

If you don't have a horizontal scroll bar, automatic column sizing might be turned on. To turn it off, click on View, Current View, Customize Current View. Click on the Other Settings button, and then click in the check box next to Automatic column sizing to remove the check. Click on OK until all open dialog boxes are closed.

Using Menus

If you look above the toolbar, you'll see the menu bar. The words on the menu bar are called commands. When you click on a command, a drop-down menu appears that contains several other commands.

1. **Click** on **File**. The File menu will appear.

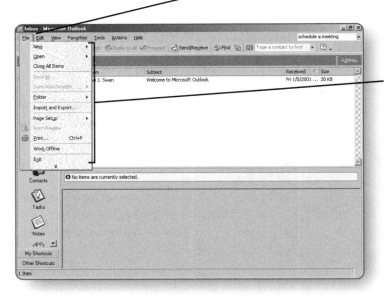

Some things to note about menus include the following:

- **Common commands**. Your most commonly used items appear first. The others remain hidden out of the way, giving you easy access to the commands you use most.

TIP

To see the full, expanded menu, you can click on the arrow at the bottom of the menu, or just wait a moment for the menu to expand automatically. Alternatively, double-click on the menu name (such as File) to open the expanded menu immediately.

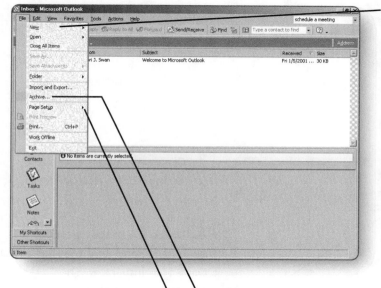

- **Expanded menu.** If you hold the pointer over the arrow at the bottom of a dropdown menu, the menu will expand to show all of the commands available.

- **Unavailable commands.** Any menu may include some commands that appear light gray, or dimmed. This means that these commands are not available at this time. For example, you can't choose Print Preview if you don't have an item selected to print.

- **Ellipsis.** If a command in the drop-down menu is followed by three periods, called an ellipsis, a dialog box will open when you click on the command.

- **Extended menus.** Some of the commands on the Outlook menus have an arrow to the right of the command. This indicates that another menu will appear when you place your mouse over or click on the command. These additional menus are sometimes called cascading menus or submenus.

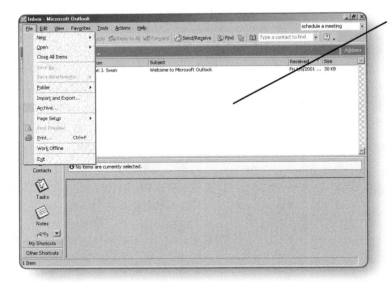

2. Click anywhere in the Information viewer. The menu will close.

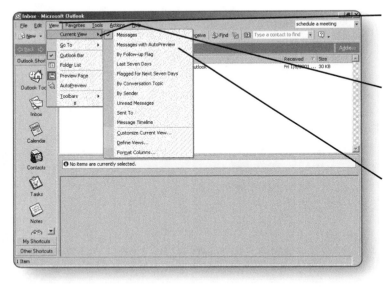

3. Click on **another command** on the menu bar. A drop-down menu will appear.

4. Move the **mouse pointer** down to a command that has a right-pointing arrow. The submenu will appear.

5. Click on the **command** you want to perform. The associated action will occur.

TIP

You can use the keyboard rather than the mouse to select a command. Simply hold down the Alt key on the keyboard and press the letter corresponding to the underlined character in the command. For example, to open the Format menu, press and hold down Alt and O on the keyboard.

Also, you can use the keyboard's arrow keys to move within the menu and submenus, and then press Enter to make your selection.

Exploring Dialog Boxes

Dialog boxes are windows that appear on the screen asking for more information.

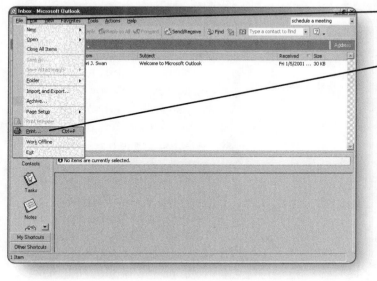

1. Click on **File.** The File menu will appear.

2. Click on **Print.** The Print dialog box will open. The Print dialog box is typical of those you will encounter in Outlook.

● **Click** on a **down arrow** to make a selection from a *drop-down list*.

● **Click** on the **up or down arrows** to increase or decrease a number. This type of control is called a *spin button*.

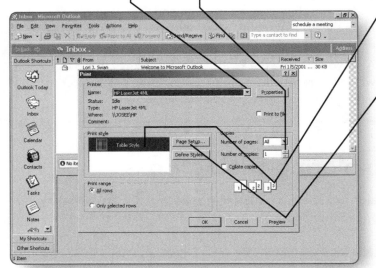

● **Select** a **Print style** to define a selection to print. This "visual" type of option group is known as a *palette*.

3. Click on **Page Setup**. The Page Setup dialog box will open. Any time a menu or button label includes an ellipsis (...), a dialog box will open when you click on it.

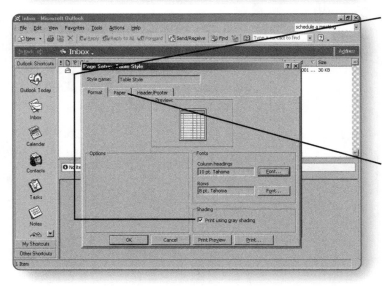

4. Click in the **check box** to turn on or off the Shading option. A check box works like a toggle switch. When a check appears in the box, the option is selected. If the box is empty, the option is not selected.

5. Click on the **Paper tab**. The tab will come to the front. Like tabbed index cards, a dialog box tab helps organized sets of options into groups that make sense to you, the end user.

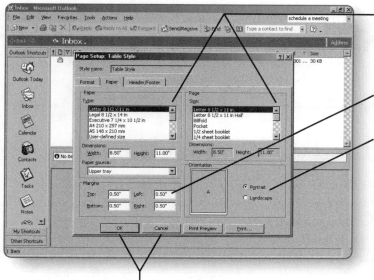

- **Scroll** on **Paper Type** and **Page Size** and click on an item in the list to change your selections.

- **Click** in a **text box** to edit specific settings.

- **Select Portrait** or **Landscape** to change the print layout. These two choices represent option buttons, sometimes also called radio buttons. You can only select one option within a group (in this case, the Orientation group). Clicking on one button selects that choice and deselects any option in the group that was previously selected.

6. Click on a **command button** to execute the desired command. In this case, click on OK. The settings will be saved and the dialog box will close.

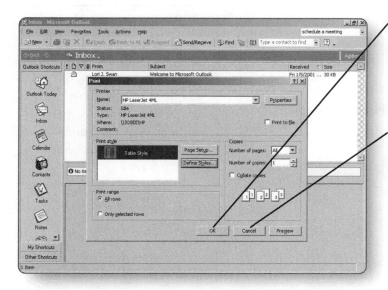

7a. Click on **OK** to close the original dialog box and execute the command.

OR

7b. Click on **Cancel** to exit the dialog box without executing the command or saving changes.

TIP

Press the Esc key on the keyboard to cancel a dialog box, or click on the Close button in the upper-right corner of the dialog box.

Using the Outlook Bar

The Outlook bar is the gray column located on the left side of the screen. The Outlook bar contains icons that represent shortcuts to folders. You can click on an icon to change what is displayed in the Information viewer quickly. Each icon represents a shortcut to a folder. When you first start Outlook, the Information viewer displays the contents of the Inbox folder.

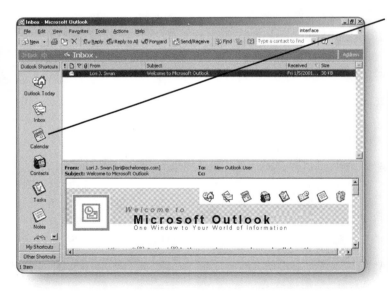

1. Click on **any icon**. The folder associated with the icon will appear in the Information viewer.

NOTE

The Outlook bar can be toggled on or off. If you do not see the Outlook bar, click on View, and then click on Outlook bar. A check mark will appear next to the Outlook bar if it is displayed.

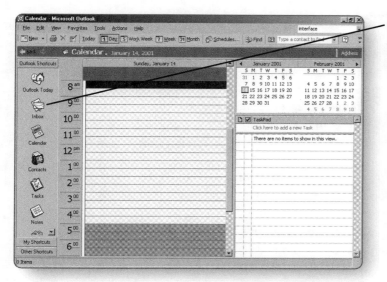

2. Click on the **Inbox icon**. E-mail messages will appear again.

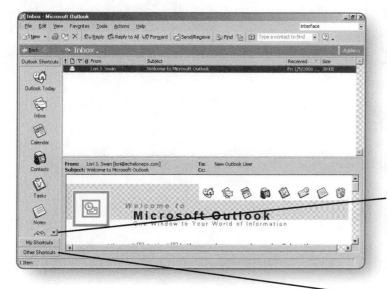

There are many icons on the Outlook bar that are not immediately visible. You can click on the scroll bar arrows to see more icons, or switch to a different Outlook group. The default Outlook groups are Outlook Shortcuts, My Shortcuts, and Other Shortcuts.

- **Outlook scroll bar arrows**. Click on the up or down arrow at the top or bottom of the Outlook bar to scroll up or down.

- **Outlook bar group buttons.** Click on an Outlook group button to display different icons.

NOTE

An Outlook group is a way to organize folders on the Outlook bar. You can add, delete, or rename the Outlook groups by clicking the right mouse button on the Outlook bar and clicking on one of the options on the shortcut menu.

You can make the icons on the Outlook bar larger or smaller, depending on your preference.

3. **Click** the **right mouse button** in a gray area of the Outlook bar. A shortcut menu will appear.

4. **Click** on **Small Icons** with the left mouse button. The Outlook bar icons will change to a smaller size.

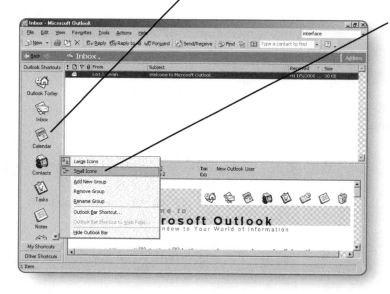

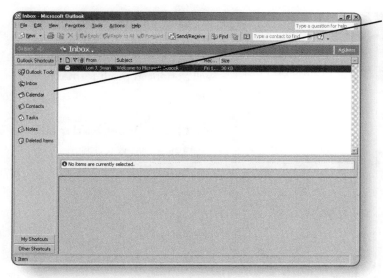

5. Repeat steps 3 and 4, but this time **click** on **Large Icons.** The icons will be restored to their default appearance.

Displaying the Folder List

The icons that appear on the Outlook bar are actually shortcuts to the Outlook folders. Whether you choose to display the Outlook bar, you can always use the folder list to navigate in Outlook.

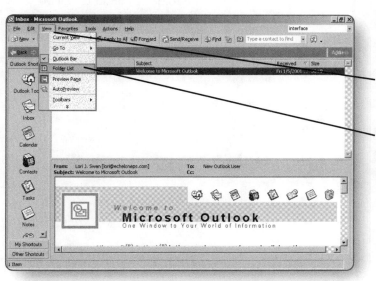

1. Click on **View.** The View menu will appear.

2. Click on **Folder List.** A pane will open next to the Outlook bar that will allow you to navigate your folders.

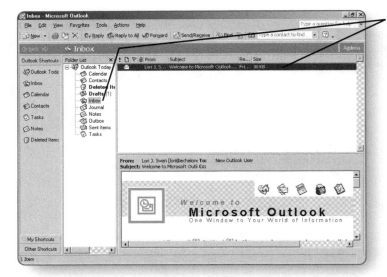

3. **Click** on **any folder** that appears in your folder list. The contents of the selected folder will appear in the Information viewer.

4. **Click** on **View, Folder List.** The folder list will close.

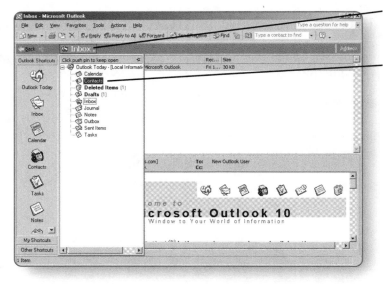

5. **Click** on the **folder title**. A pop-up Folder list will appear.

6. **Click** on any **folder name**. The folder's contents will be displayed in the Information viewer and the Folder list will close.

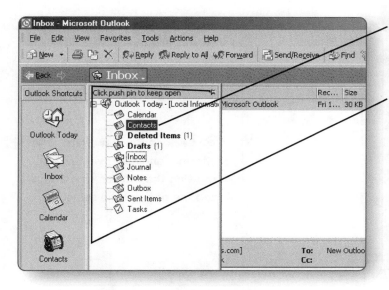

7. Click on the **Folder title** again. The pop-up Folder list will reappear.

8. Click on the **thumbtack**. The Folder list will remain open.

9. Click on **Close**. The Folder list will close.

Using the Preview Pane

The Preview Pane divides the Information viewer in half—you can see the header on the top half of the screen and the actual content on the bottom half of the screen. This tool might already be activated when you click on your folder. I find this tool particularly useful when reviewing the messages in my Inbox, but it is accessible from most Outlook folders.

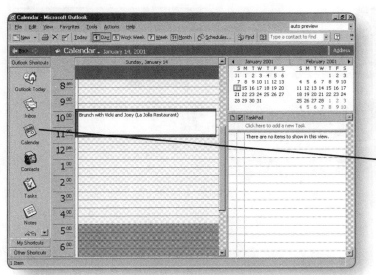

1. Select a **folder** from the Outlook toolbar. The folder will open.

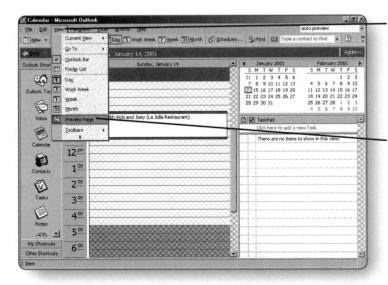

2. Click on **View**. The View menu will appear.

3. Click on **Preview Pane**. The Information viewer will split, showing the regular view above and the body of the selection below.

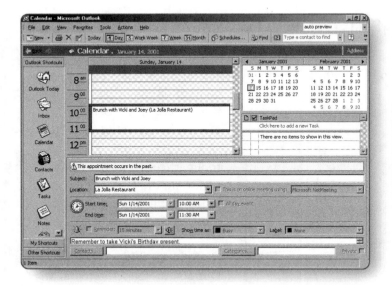

TIP
Repeat steps 2–3 to toggle your Preview Pane on and off.

Using Outlook Today

One of the icons on the Outlook bar is labeled Outlook Today. Outlook Today displays a snapshot of all the items you need during the day. You can open any folder or event directly from Outlook Today just by clicking on its link.

1. Click on the **Outlook Today icon.** The Information viewer will change to display the Outlook Today page.

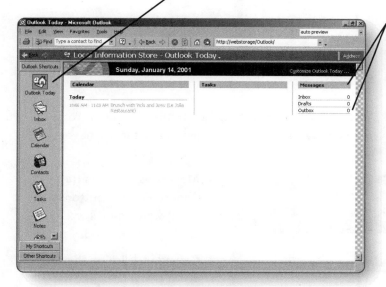

2. Point to **any item** in the Outlook Today page. An underscore will appear below any linked items.

3. Click on the **desired link.** Outlook will open the selected folder in the Information viewer.

Customizing Outlook Today

You can customize Outlook Today to display the folders you need, or to adjust the display of the calendar or task list. You can even designate Outlook Today as the default page that appears when Outlook starts.

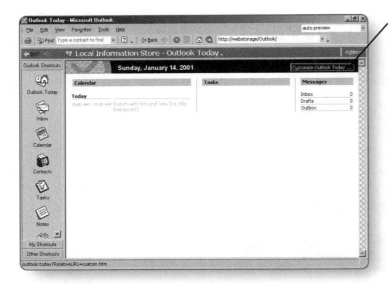

1. **Click** on **Customize Outlook Today** in the Information viewer. The Customize Outlook Today options window will appear.

● **Startup.** Click on this check box to make Outlook Today your start page. Your start page will appear whenever you start up Outlook.

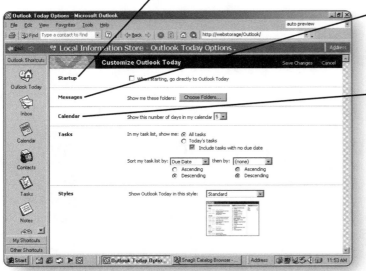

● **Messages.** Click on the Choose Folders button to select which e-mail will appear on the Outlook Today page.

● **Calendar.** Click on the drop-down arrow to select the number of days to appear in the calendar.

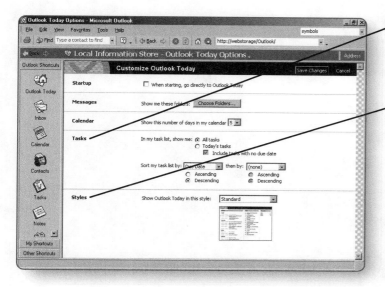

- **Tasks.** Click on an option button to select today's tasks or the complete task list.

- **Styles.** Click on the drop-down arrow to select a layout style for the Outlook Today page.

2. **Click** on **Save Changes** at the top of the Customize Outlook Today screen. The Outlook Today folder will reappear with the new settings applied.

3. **Click** on **any icon** on the Outlook bar. The Outlook Today page will close and the selected folder will appear in the Information viewer.

Understanding Outlook Symbols

Outlook uses numerous symbols to represent different types of items. For example, a red exclamation point is used for high priority items, whereas a blue down-pointing arrow is used to identify low priority items. Symbols appear next to e-mail messages in the Inbox. You can learn more about the symbols in Outlook Help.

TIP

For complete details on the Office Help system, see Chapter 3, "Getting the Help You Need."

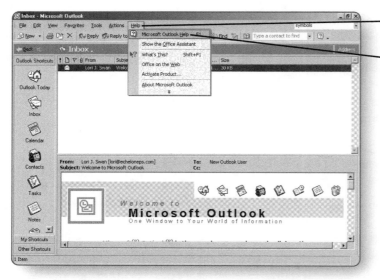

1. **Click** on **Help**.

2. **Click** on **Microsoft Outlook Help**.

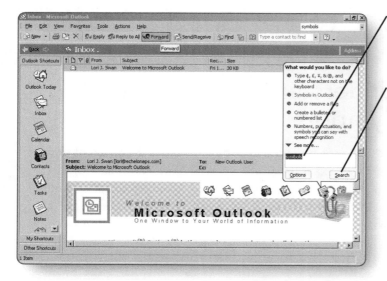

3. **Type** the word **Symbols** in the text box. The word will appear in the text box.

4. **Click Search.** A list of topics will appear.

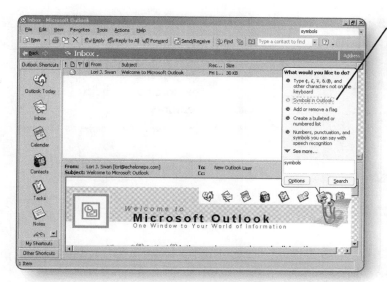

5. **Click** on **Symbols in Outlook**. A Help window will open.

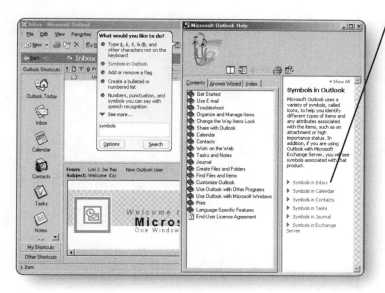

6. **Click** on **any topic** in the Microsoft Outlook window. The symbols used in Outlook will appear.

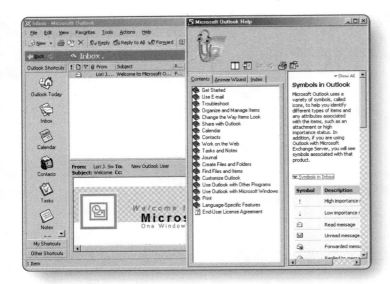

NOTE

Outlook's help feature is a very useful tool. Chapter 3 explores other help features.

3

Getting the Help You Need

Outlook has so many features that you may need occasional assistance when you are first learning the program. Even after you learn to use Outlook, you'll find yourself checking the application's help when you get stuck. Fortunately, Outlook gives you several ways to get help while working with the application. In this chapter, you'll learn how to:

- Use Ask a Question
- Use the Office Assistant
- Search Contents and Index
- Get help on the Web

Introducing Ask a Question

Microsoft has provided a quick question-and-answer option that simplifies your search for help, for those "tell me now!" moments. A guided resource of options appears when you type your question. The Ask a Question box is conveniently located on most screens in Outlook. You can ask Outlook plain-English questions about any feature or procedure.

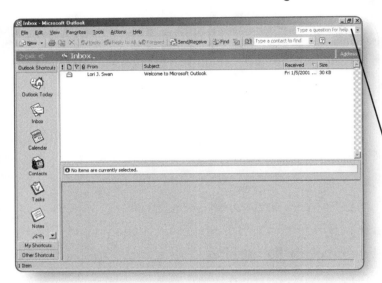

1. **Click** in the **Ask a Question box**. The existing text will disappear and the insertion point will be in the text box.

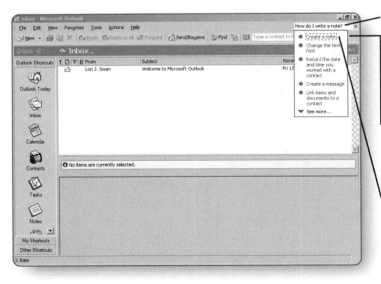

2. **Type a question**. The question will appear in the text box. You can use complete sentences or just a few key words related to your question.

3. **Press Enter**. A list of topics corresponding to your question will appear.

4. **Click** on a **help topic**. A detailed answer will appear.

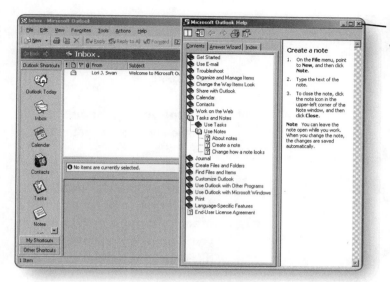

5. Click on **Close**. The help window will close.

Introducing the Office Assistant

If you have used recent versions of Microsoft Office, you may already be familiar with the Office Assistant. The Office Assistant is a tool that provides an animated character that interacts with you to answer your questions about the application. The Office Assistant can be completely customized; in fact, if you get tired of the current one, you can even choose a different animated character (sometimes called an actor) for your Office Assistant.

1. Click on **Help**. The Help menu will appear.

2. Click on **Microsoft Outlook Help**. The Office Assistant will appear and present a message box asking what you want to do.

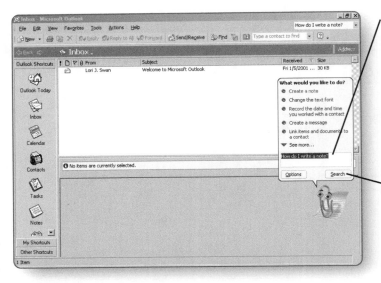

3. **Click** in the **text box**. The existing text will disappear and the insertion point will be in the text box.

4. **Type your question**. The question will appear in the text box.

5. **Click** on **Search**. The Office Assistant will respond with a list of topics that match the words in your sentence to answer your question.

TIP

You can type natural language questions, such as "How do I print?" to find help on a specific topic. You do not need to type punctuation or proper capitalization in your help queries.

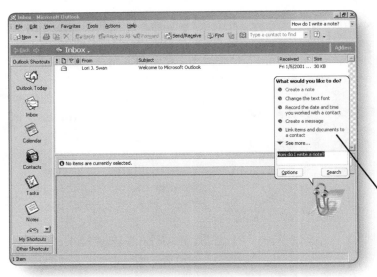

6. **Click** on **any topic** to get further help. A window will appear that expands on the topic that you've selected.

7. **Click** on the **Close button** when you are finished. The window will close.

Selecting an Office Assistant

When you start Outlook, you will meet Clipit, the default Office Assistant. If you get tired of this character, there are other assistants that you can choose from if they were installed during your installation of Outlook. Each assistant has its own personality, so you can pick the assistant that you will learn from the best.

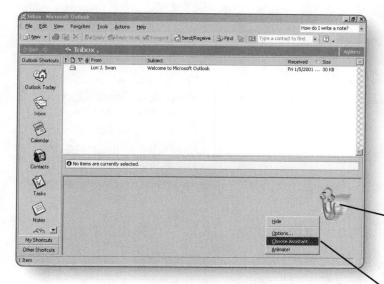

The Office Assistants are a shared component of the Microsoft Office XP suite. If you would like to change your Office Assistant and you do not have the Office XP CD-ROM on hand, you can download additional Office Assistant characters from Microsoft's Web site at http://www.microsoft.com.

1. Right-click on the **Office Assistant**. A shortcut menu will appear.

2. Click on **Choose Assistant**. The Office Assistant dialog box will open.

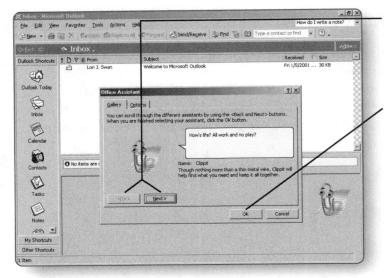

3. Click on the **Back** or **Next button**. As you continue clicking on the Next button, the available assistants will appear.

4. Click on **OK**. The dialog box will close and your Office Assistant will change to the one you've selected.

NOTE

You may be asked to insert your Office XP CD-ROM so that Office can install the files needed to use the Office Assistant you select.

Customizing the Office Assistant

As you work in Outlook, the Office Assistant will give you tips and suggestions to make your work easier. As you become more familiar with the application, you may need these tips less often. You can customize the Office Assistant so that it gives you only the information you need.

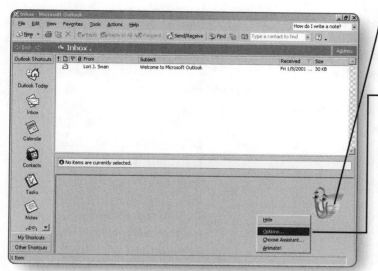

1. **Right-click** on the **Office Assistant**. A shortcut menu will appear.

2. **Click** on **Options**. The Office Assistant dialog box will open.

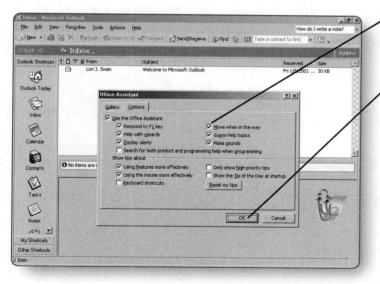

3. **Click** in the **check boxes** to select the options you want. The boxes will be checked.

4. **Click** on **OK**. The dialog box will close and your changes will be saved.

Hiding the Office Assistant

Sometimes the Office Assistant pops up when you don't really need it, or you just find the character distracting from the matter at hand. If so, you can hide the Office Assistant until you are ready to use it again.

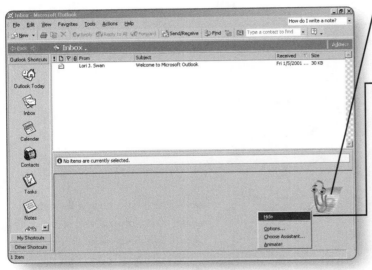

1. **Right-click** on **Office Assistant**. A shortcut menu will appear.

2. **Click** on **Hide**. The Office Assistant will perform an animated exit and disappear.

TIP

Right-click on the Office Assistant and click on Animate! to watch the Office Assistant's built-in animation effects. The effects appear in random order each time you select Animate!

Searching Contents and Index

Another way to get help is by using the online Help system provided with Outlook. You can either search through this reference guide by using the Index, or browse through the Table of Contents.

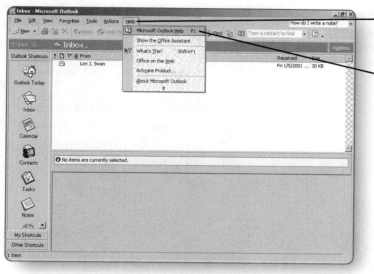

1. Click on **Help**. The Help menu will appear.

2. Click on **Microsoft Outlook Help**. The Office Assistant will appear.

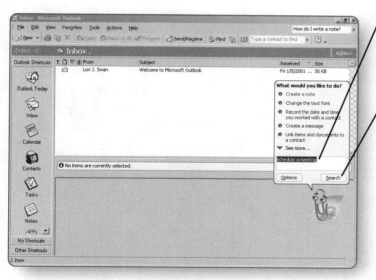

3. Type a question in the **Office Assistant text box**. The question will appear in the text box.

4. Click on **Search**. The Office Assistant will respond with a list of topics to answer your question.

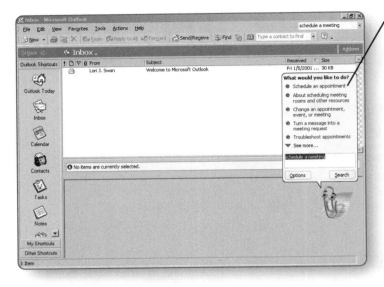

5. **Click** on any **topic**. The Microsoft Outlook Help window will appear, displaying details on the topic that you've selected.

6. **Click** on the **Show button**. The Help window will expand to show the Contents, Answer Wizard, and Index tabs.

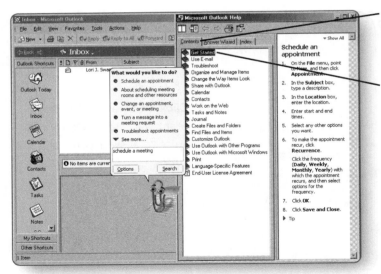

7. **Click** on the **Contents tab** if it is not already selected. The tab will come to the front.

8. **Double-click** on any **topic**. You can continue until you find the item you want. If there are subtopics, more items will appear.

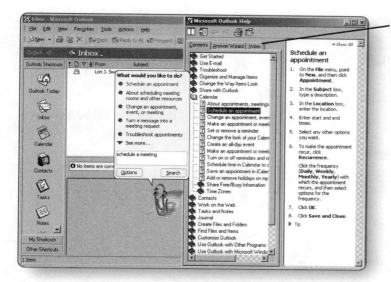

9. **Click** on the **Index tab**. The tab will come to the front.

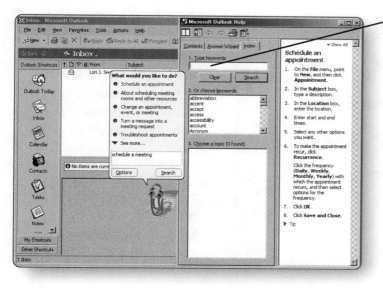

10. **Type** the first few **letters** of the topic for which you are searching in the first text box. The list will scroll to any words that begin with the letters you type.

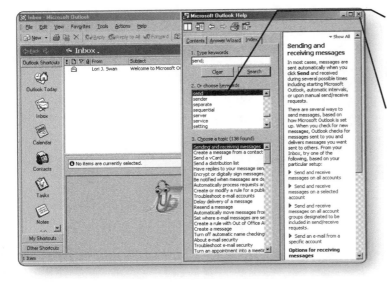

11. **Double-click** on the **index entry** you want to view. The corresponding help topic will appear.

12. **Click** on the **Close button** to close the window. The Help window will close.

Getting Help on the Web

If you have access to the Internet, you can get help by using the Web and visiting Microsoft's Web site. Some topics available are frequently asked questions for Outlook, free stuff, and product news about Outlook.

1. **Click** on **Help**. The Help menu will appear.

2. **Click** on **Office on the Web**.

Your Web browser will appear and will point to the Outlook support Web site.

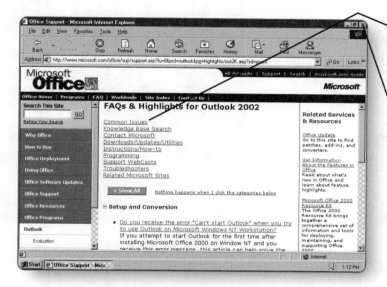

3. **Click** on any **topic**. Details on the selected topic will appear in your browser.

4. **Click** on the **Close button** in your Web browser when you are finished. Your Web browser will close and Outlook will reappear.

4

Setting Up Accounts

If you're on a corporate network that runs Microsoft Exchange, chances are that your messaging accounts have already been set up by the network administrator. On the other hand, maybe you're using Outlook at home or in a small business—which usually means *you are* the network administrator! If that's the case, you'll need to get Outlook set up to send and receive e-mail messages through your server or that of your *ISP* (Internet Service Provider). Outlook also lets you tap in to Internet directory services, which are essentially online "white pages" you can use to look up the e-mail addresses of people not on your own network. In this chapter, you'll learn to:

- Set up an e-mail account
- View or change existing e-mail accounts
- Add a new directory service
- Edit a directory service account

Creating a New E-mail Account

Even if you are on a corporate network that runs Microsoft Exchange for business e-mail, in most cases you also can read and reply to messages from an Internet e-mail account you might have through an Internet Service Provider or from a free Web service such as Hotmail.

NOTE

Keep in mind that the mail from all the accounts will come into the same Inbox. If you share your computer with other users, each user should have a separate profile configured, including individual passwords. That will help to ensure that your mail isn't getting mixed in with someone else's messages.

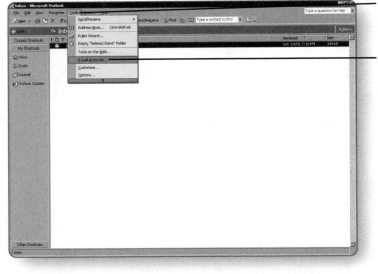

1. Click on **Tools**. A drop-down list will appear.

2. Click on **E-mail Accounts**. The E-mail Accounts Wizard will open.

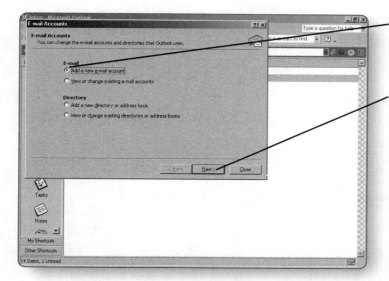

3. **Click** on **Add a new e-mail account**. The option will be selected.

4. **Click** on **Next**. The E-mail Accounts Wizard will continue, and a list of server types will appear.

NOTE

The next steps will depend on which type of account you're creating. See the appropriate section for further instructions.

The account types you're most likely to use include the following:

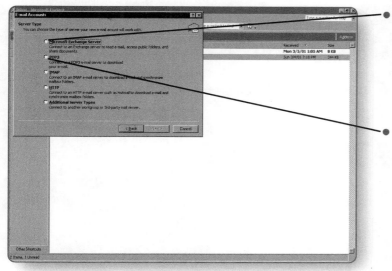

- **Microsoft Exchange Server**. A server-based network application that essentially acts as a server to access public folders, read e-mail, and share documents.

- **POP3**. If you're using Outlook to get your mail from an Internet Service Provider account, you probably have a POP3 account (sometimes called an SMTP account). You can set up multiple POP3 mail accounts in Outlook.

● **HTTP.** Web-based e-mail services are growing exponentially in popularity. If you use a service such as Hotmail or Excite for your e-mail, you can now use Outlook to download and read your mail, saving you lots of time—no more piddling around in those slow, inflexible Web mail interfaces.

In the following sections, we'll walk through the rest of the E-mail Accounts Wizard, exploring the steps connecting you first to a POP3 server, then to an HTTP server, which seem to be the most commonly used servers among the non-corporate arena. (Check with your systems administrator if you need help configuring a Microsoft Exchange Server account.)

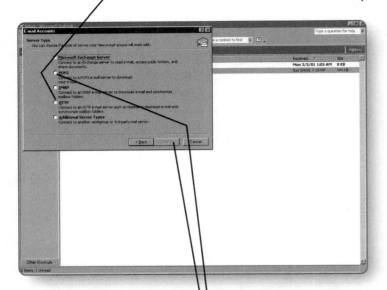

Connecting to POP3

If you need to access a POP3 server to get your mail, follow these steps.

5. **Click** on **POP3**. The option will be selected.

6. **Click** on **Next**. The E-mail Accounts Wizard will continue.

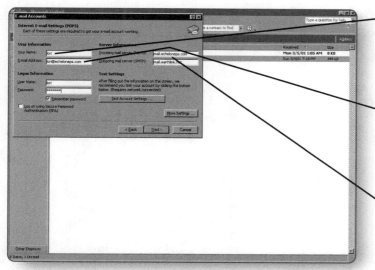

7. **Click** in the **box** to the right of Your Name: and type your username. Your username will appear.

8. **Click** in the **box** to the right of E-mail Address: and type your e-mail address. Your e-mail address will appear.

9. **Click** in the **box** to the right of Incoming mail server (POP3): and type your incoming mail server name. The name will appear.

10. **Click** in the **box** to the right of the Outgoing mail server (SMTP): and type your outgoing mail server name. The name will appear.

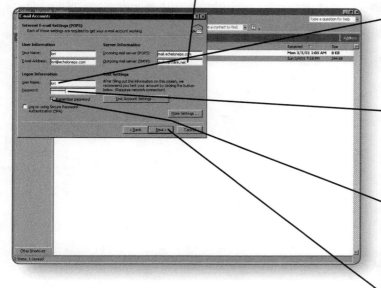

11. **Click** in the **box** to the right of User name: and type your username. The name will appear.

12. **Click** in the **box** to the right of Password: and type your password. Asterisks will appear as you type.

13. **Click** in the **check box** next to Remember password. A check mark will appear and your password will be remembered.

14. **Click** on **Next**. The E-mail Accounts set-up will be completed.

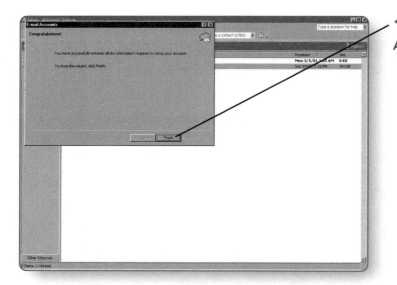

15. Click on **Finish**. The E-mail Accounts Wizard will close.

Connecting to HTTP

If you use a Web-based e-mail service such as Hotmail, you can also get your mail in Outlook. Just follow steps 1–4 earlier in this chapter, and then continue with the following steps.

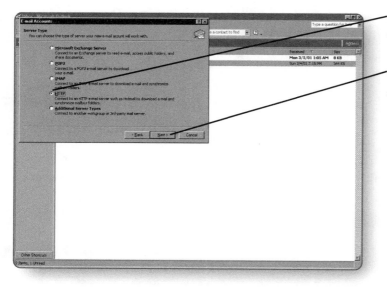

5. Click on **HTTP**. The option will be selected.

6. Click on **Next**. The E-mail Accounts Wizard will open.

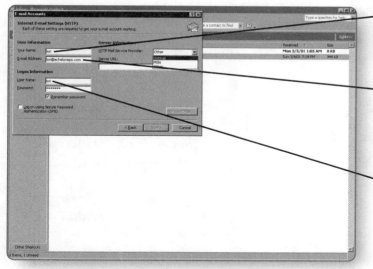

7. **Click** on the **box** to the right of Your Name: and type your username.

8. **Click** in the **box** to the right of E-mail Address: and type your e-mail address. Your e-mail address will appear.

9. **Click** in the **box** to the right of User name: and type your username. The name will appear.

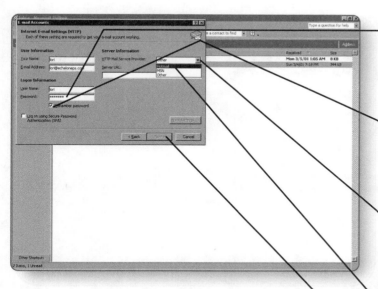

10. **Click** in the **box** to the right of Password: and type your password. Asterisks will appear as you type.

11. **Click** on the **check box** next to Remember password. A check mark will appear and your password will be remembered.

12. **Click** on the **down arrow** to the right of HTTP Mail Service Provider. A drop-down list will appear.

13. **Click** on a **server**. Your selection will be displayed.

14. **Click** on **Next**. The Internet E-mail server choice will open.

NOTE

Because Hotmail is a (free) service from Microsoft, Outlook was programmed to recognize the hotmail.com domain name in your address and automatically enter the server information for you.

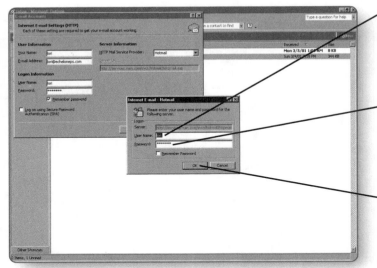

15. **Click** in the **box** to the right of User Name: and enter your username. The name will appear.

16. **Click** in the **box** to the right of Password: and enter your password. Asterisks will appear as you type.

17. **Click** on **OK**. The Internet E-mail – Hotmail window will close.

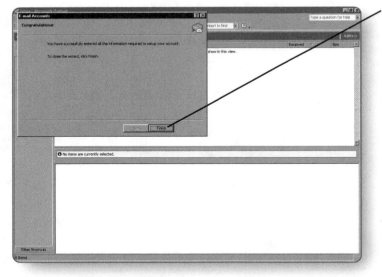

18. **Click** on **Finish**. The E-mail Accounts Wizard will close.

Editing an Existing E-mail Account

If you entered any information incorrectly, or you want to change something in the account settings (such as how your name appears on outgoing mail), just run the wizard again.

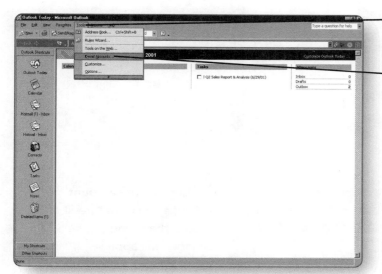

1. Click on **Tools**. A drop-down list will appear.

2. Click on **E-mail Accounts**. The E-mail Accounts Wizard will open.

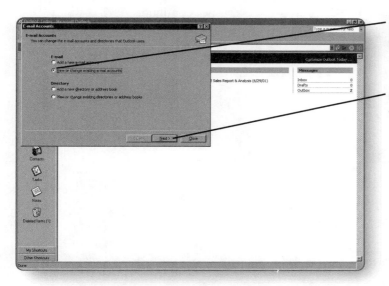

3. Click on **View or change existing e-mail accounts**. The option will be selected.

4. Click on **Next**. The wizard will continue.

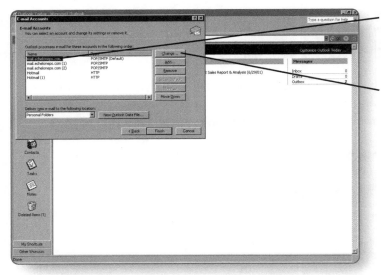

5. Click on the **e-mail account** you want to edit. The account will be highlighted.

6. Click on **Change**. The wizard will continue.

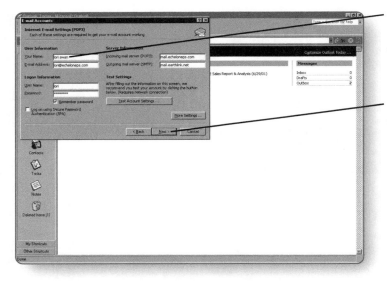

7. Click on the **account settings** you want to edit and type in the changes. The changes will appear.

8. Click on **Next**. The wizard will continue.

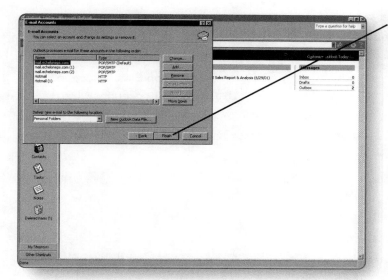

9. **Click** on **Finish**. The E-mail Accounts dialog box will appear.

Adding a Directory Service

How many times have you wished for a way to find someone's e-mail address like you can do with phone numbers in a phone book? Directory services are exactly that—directories of e-mail addresses.

1. **Click** on **Tools**. A drop-down list will appear.

2. **Click** on **E-mail Accounts**. The E-mail Accounts Wizard will open.

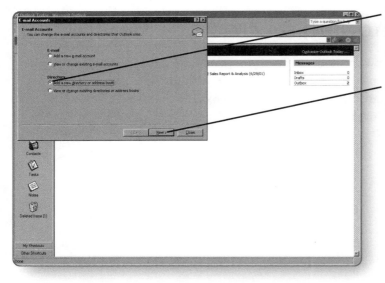

3. **Click** on **Add a new directory or address book**. The option will be selected.

4. **Click** on **Next**. The E-mail Accounts window will continue.

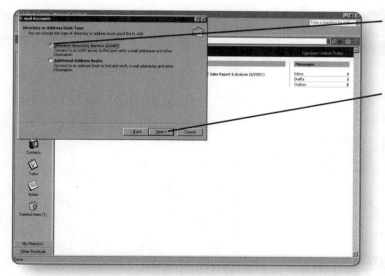

5. **Click** on **Internet Directory Service (LDAP)**. The option will be selected.

6. **Click** on **Next**. The E-mail Accounts window will continue.

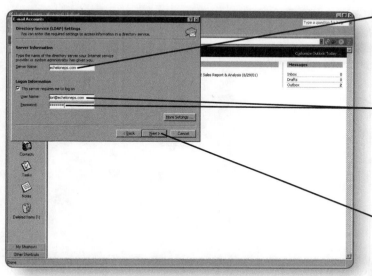

7. **Click** in the **box** to the right of Server Name: and type your new server name. The name will appear.

8. **Click** in the **boxes** to the right of User Name: and Password: and type in the information. Your username and asterisks will appear.

9. **Click** on **Next**. An Add E-mail Account window will open. You will be advised that the new account will require you to restart Microsoft Outlook.

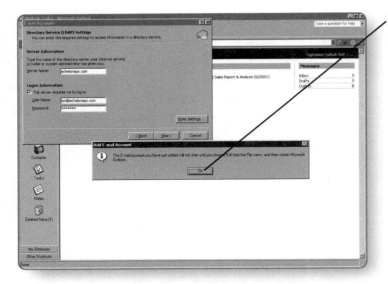

10. **Click** on **OK**. The E-mail Accounts window will continue.

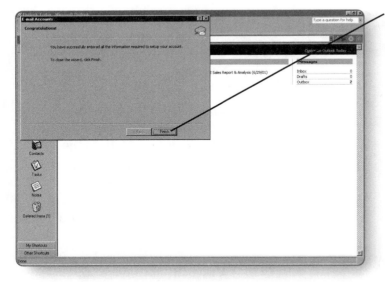

11. **Click** on **Finish**. The E-mail Accounts window will close and the directory service will be added to the account list. Outlook will include this directory as a resource the next time you search for an e-mail address.

Editing a Directory Service

Making changes to your directory service settings is very easy.

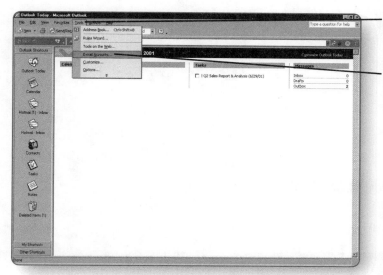

1. Click on **Tools**. A drop-down list will appear.

2. Click on **E-mail Accounts**. The E-mail Accounts window will open.

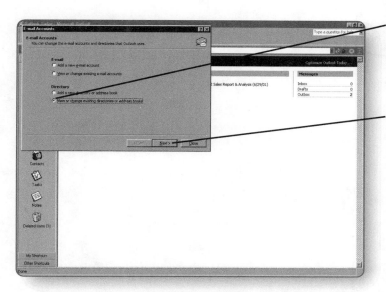

3. Click on **View or change existing directories or address books**. The option will be selected.

4. Click on **Next**. The E-mail Accounts Wizard will continue.

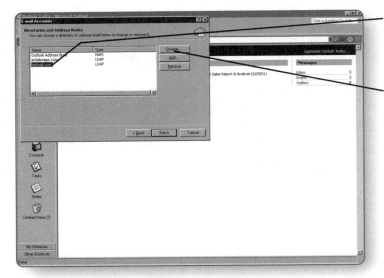

5. **Click** on a **directory** you would like to change. The directory will be highlighted.

6. **Click** on **Change**. The E-mail Accounts window will continue.

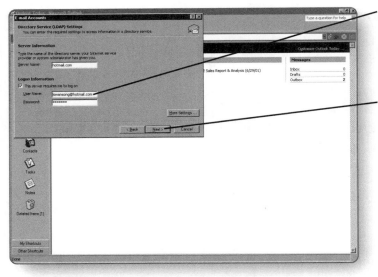

7. **Click** in the **box** where the change is to be made and type the change. The change will appear.

8. **Click** on **Next**. The E-mail Accounts window will continue.

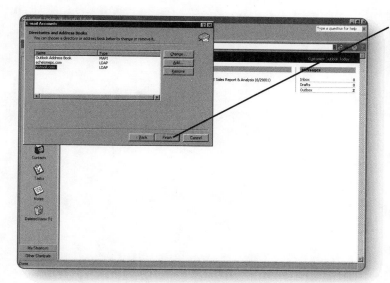

9. **Click** on **Finish**. The changes will be updated and the window will close.

5

Working with Address Books

Outlook offers several tools to help you organize your collection of names and numbers, and address books are among the key players. Outlook supports address books from Exchange Server, Internet directory services, the Outlook Contacts folder, and a handful of other network services. You also can create your own address books for personal or business use, so you can store names, addresses, phone numbers, e-mail addresses, and notes for large and small groups of contacts. In this chapter, you'll learn how to:

- Create a Personal Address Book
- Add new e-mail addresses to your address book
- Use the Contacts folder as your address book
- Use Personal Distribution Lists
- Edit Personal Distribution Lists
- Delete Address Book entries

Creating a Personal Address Book

If you are sending an e-mail message to some people and think that you may need to write to them again, it's a good idea to add the addresses to your address book. If you work for a company, many e-mail addresses may already be stored in your corporate server's Global Address List (you don't create those as a user; they are set up by your network administrator). In this section, you'll learn how to create a Personal Address Book.

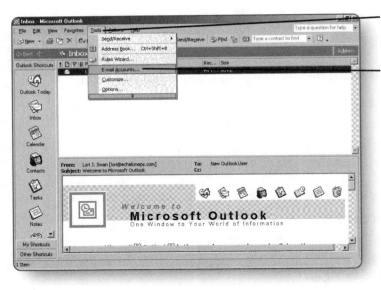

1. Click on **Tools**. A drop-down list will appear.

2. Click on **E-mail Accounts**. The E-mail Accounts dialog box will open.

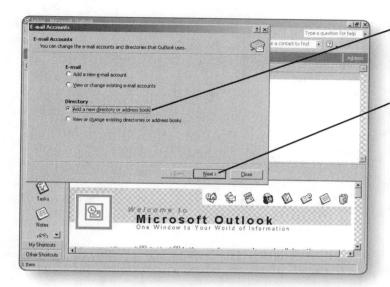

3. **Click** on **Add a new directory or address book**. The option will be selected.

4. **Click** on **Next**. The Directory or Address Book Type Wizard will open.

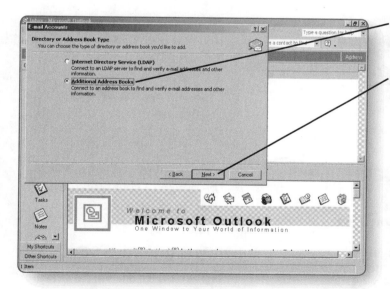

5. **Click** on **Additional Address Books.** The item will be selected.

6. **Click** on **Next**. The wizard will continue to the next step.

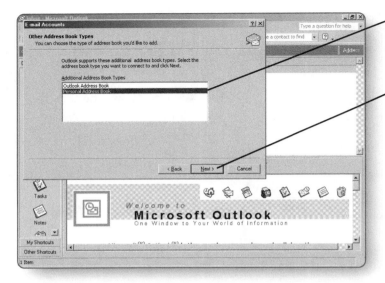

7. **Click** on **Personal Address Book**. The selection will be highlighted.

8. **Click** on **Next**. The Personal Address Book dialog box will open.

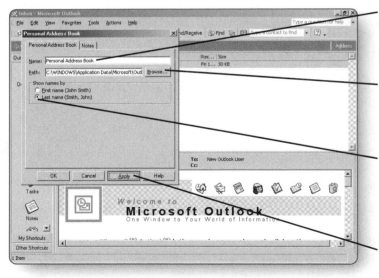

9. **Accept** the **default** or **click** in the **Name box** and type a new Personal Address Book name.

10. **Accept** the **default** or **click** on **Browse** to select a different path.

11. **Click** on the **Show names by** option of your preference. Names will be stored as you choose.

12. **Click** on **Apply**. Your screen selections will be saved.

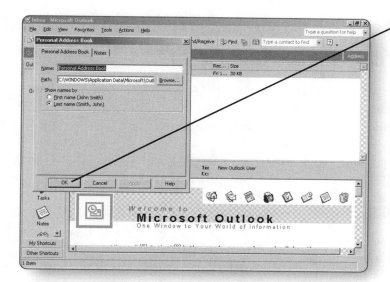

13. **Click** on **OK**. The Personal Address Book dialog box will close. A message box will appear informing you to exit Outlook and restart your computer.

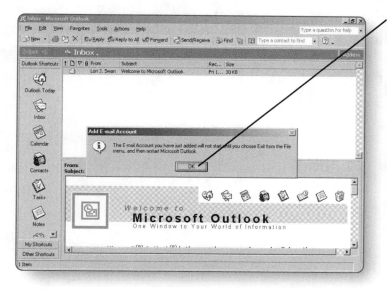

14. **Click** on **OK**. The message box will close.

15. **Exit** and **restart Outlook** following your proper shut-down procedures. When you reopen Outlook, your Personal Address Book E-mail account will be activated.

Adding New Addresses to Your Personal Address Book

Now that you have your Personal Address Book set up, you're ready to fill it with names! In this section, you'll learn how to add an address to your Personal Address Book.

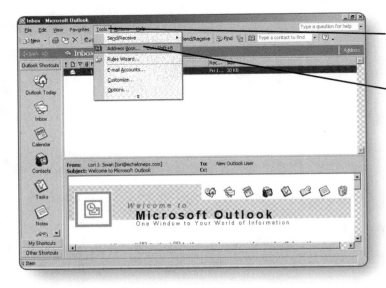

1. **Click** on **Tools**. A drop-down menu will appear.

2. **Click** on **Address Book**. The Address Book dialog box will appear.

TIP

Alternatively, just click on the Address Book button on the Standard toolbar.

3. Click on the **drop-down arrow** to select your address book. A drop-down list will appear, listing all the address books available to you at this time.

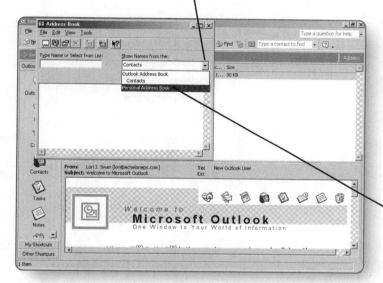

NOTE

The list is likely to include your Contacts folder as well as any corporate address books provided on your company's network.

4. Click on **Personal Address Book**. Your selection will be highlighted.

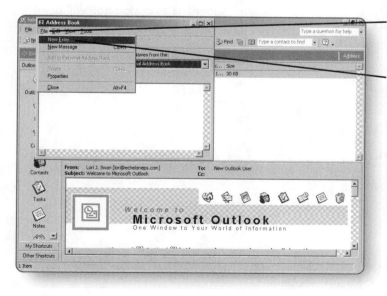

5. Click on **File**. A drop-down menu will appear.

6. Click on **New Entry**. The New Entry dialog box will open.

TIP

Alternatively, just click on the New Entry button on the toolbar.

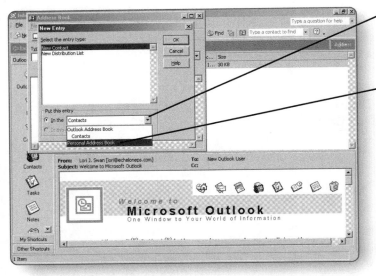

7. Click on the **Put This Entry down arrow**. A drop-down list will appear.

8. Click on **Personal Address Book**. The Select the Entry Type list options will change to Other Address and Personal Distribution List.

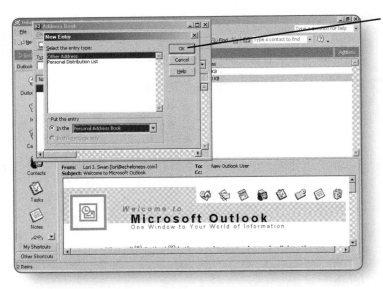

9. Click on **Other Address** (if needed) and then **click** on **OK**. The New Other Address Properties dialog box will open with the New – Address page in front.

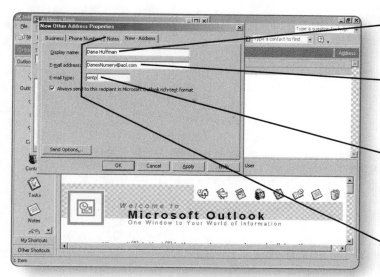

10. **Click** in the **Display Name text box** and **type** a **name**.

11. **Click** on the E-**mail Address text box** and **type** the new **e-mail address**.

12. **Click** in the **E-mail Type text box** and **type** an appropriate **message format** such as POP3, SMTP, or HTTP.

13. **Click** on the **Notes tab**. The Notes page will come to the front.

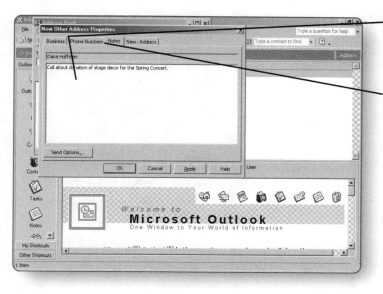

14. **Click** in the **Notes** text box and **type** any **comments** you care to add.

15. **Click** on the **Phone Numbers tab**. The Phone Numbers page will come to the front.

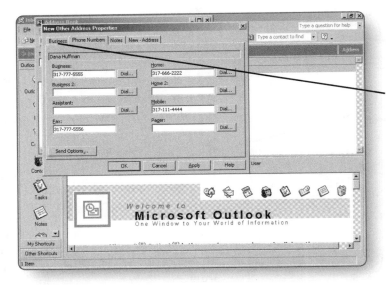

16. Enter the appropriate **phone numbers** in the text boxes.

17. Click on the **Business tab**. The Business page will come to the front.

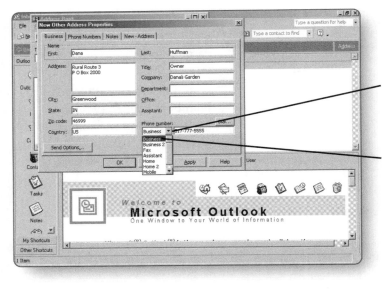

18. Enter the appropriate **business information** in the text boxes.

19. Click on the **Phone Number down-arrow**. A drop-down list will appear.

20. Select the appropriate **phone number label**. Your selection will be highlighted.

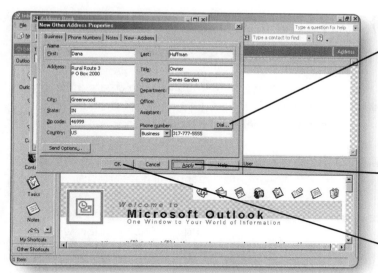

NOTE

If you use your modem on the same line as your voice calls, you can autodial the selected number by clicking Dial.

21. Click on **Apply**. The new e-mail information will post to the Personal Address Book.

22. Click on **OK**. The Properties dialog box will close and save the information.

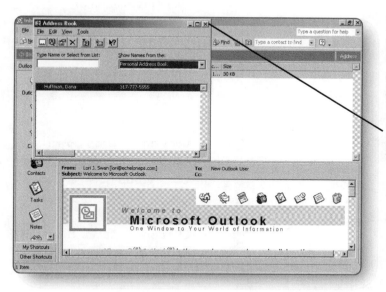

Your new e-mail address appears as a listing in the Address Book. To review, add, or change the contents of your e-mail address, double-click on the entry.

23. Click on **Close**. The Address Book will close.

Using the Contacts Folder as Your Address Book

In the previous section, you learned you can create a Personal Address Book to store entries. Optionally, you can use the Outlook Contacts Folder as your address book.

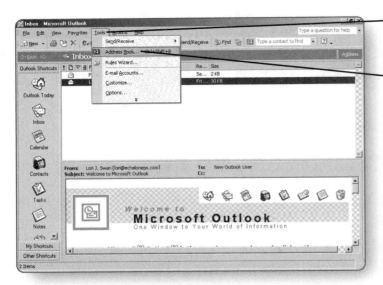

1. Click on **Tools**. The Tools menu will appear.

2. Click on **Address Book**. The Address Book window will appear.

NOTE

If your installation of Outlook is configured for Corporate and Workgroup use, your Address Book may look different.

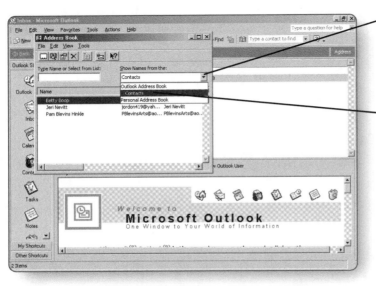

3. Click on the **drop-down** arrow of the **Show Names from the** box. A drop-down list will appear.

4. Click on **Contacts**. The Contacts Address Book will be highlighted.

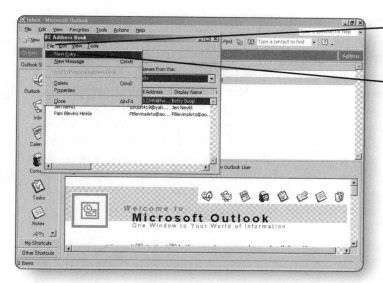

5. Click on **File**. The File menu will open.

6. Click on **New Entry**. The New Entry dialog box will open.

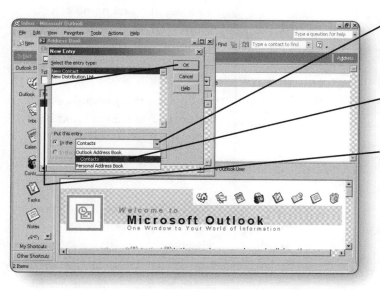

7. Click on the **Put This Entry down arrow**. A drop-down list will appear.

8. Select Contacts. Contacts will be highlighted.

9. Click on **OK**. The Contact window will open.

NOTE

The Contacts new entry window looks different than the Personal Address Book new entry window. In case you were suspicious—yes, this is the same Contact window you see when you open a contact entry in the Contacts. Any new entries posted in the Outlook Contacts Address Book will also appear in the Contacts list when selected from the Outlook Tool Bar. This is true for any other Microsoft-supported address books. Your Personal Address Book entries will not, however, appear in your Outlook Contact list unless you manually direct them there via the Windows Mail control panel.

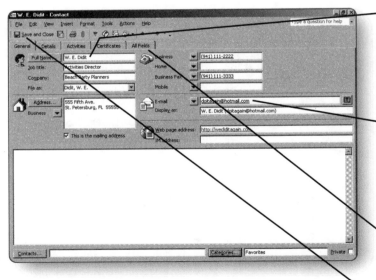

10. Type the **person's first, middle, and last name** as you would like it to appear in the address book. The full name will appear in the Display text box.

11. Type the **person's e-mail address** in the E-mail text box. The new address will be added to the list of e-mail addresses for this contact.

12. Click on the **other tabs** to enter additional information if desired.

13. Click on **Save and Close**. The Address Book will reappear.

NOTE

Chapter 16, "Creating New Contacts," covers building new Contact information in more depth.

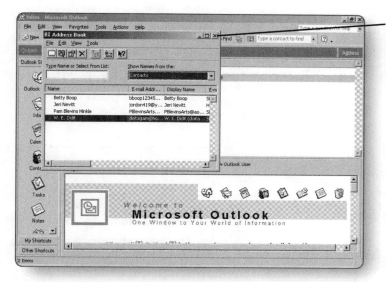

14. **Click** on the **Address Book Close button**. You will return to the Inbox.

Using Distribution Groups

You can send a message to multiple people by typing their names in the To box. If you send messages to the same group of people on a regular basis, creating a distribution group will save you time and will guarantee that you don't forget anyone.

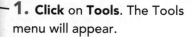

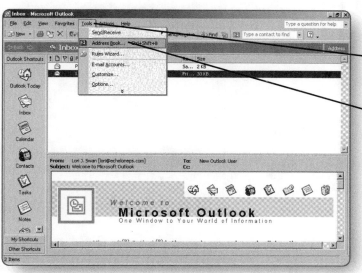

1. **Click** on **Tools**. The Tools menu will appear.

2. **Click** on **Address Book**. The Address Book will open.

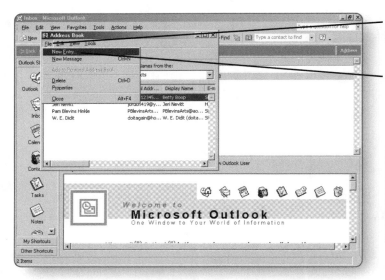

3. Click on **File**. The File menu will open.

4. Click on **New Entry**. The New Entry dialog box will appear.

TIP

Alternatively, you can click on the New Entry button on the Standard toolbar.

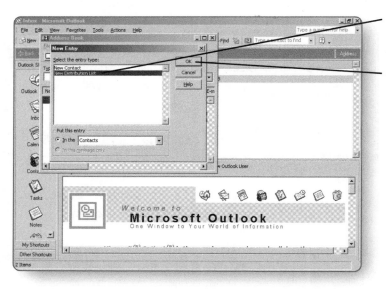

5. Click on **New Distribution List**. It will be highlighted.

6. Click on **OK**. A Distribution List will open.

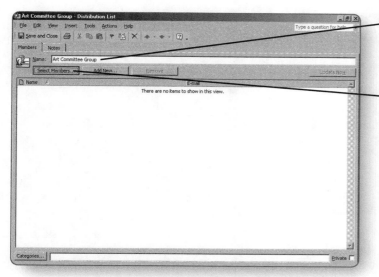

7. Type a **name** for the new group in the Name text box. The name will appear in the box.

8. Click on **Select Members** to add existing e-mail addresses to your new group. The Select Group Members dialog box will open.

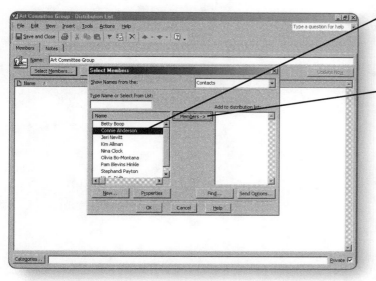

9. Click on a **name** in the list on the left. The name will be selected.

10. Click on the **Members button**. The name will appear in the distribution list on the **right.**

11. Repeat steps 9 and 10 until all appropriate names are included in the Members list.

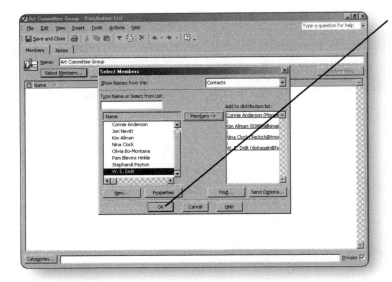

12. Click on **OK**. The Select Members dialog box will close.

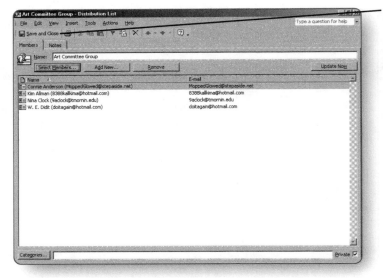

13. Click on **Save and Close**. The Distribution List will close and the Address Book will reappear.

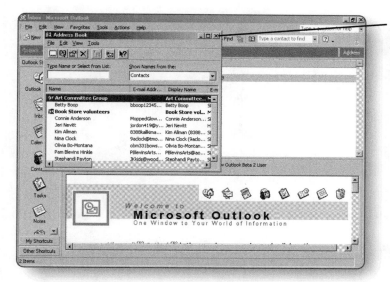

14. Click on **Close**. The Address Book will close.

Editing Distribution Groups

When you store your Group Lists in the Personal Address Book, it is your responsibility to keep them up to date. For example, if you have a list with members of a committee, you will need to edit the list as new members join and others leave the committee.

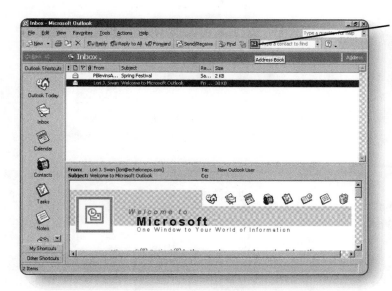

1. Click on the **Address Book button** on the Standard toolbar. The contents of your Personal Address Book will appear.

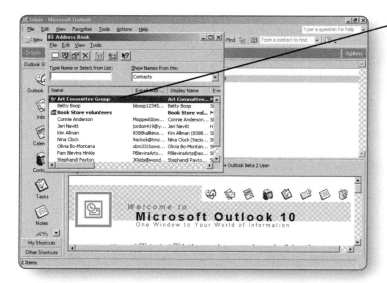

2. Double-click on the **group** you want to edit. The Distribution List dialog box will open.

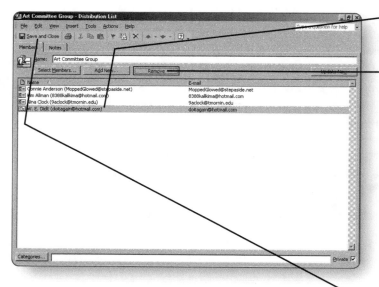

3. Click on a **name**. The name will be selected.

4. Click on the **Remove button**. The name will be removed from the Group list.

NOTE

Removing a name from this list does not remove it from the Address Book or other groups, just the current group.

TIP

Click on New Contact to create a new contact not already in your address book. When you create the new entry, it will be stored in the address book as well as in the Group list.

5. Click on **Save and Close**. The Address Book will reappear.

6. **Click** on **Close**. The Address Book will close.

Deleting Address Book Entries

You may create an e-mail group for a project and no longer need the group when the project is complete. It's easy to delete entries from the Personal Address Book.

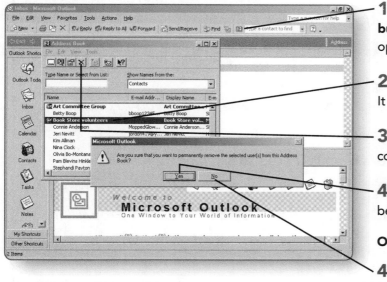

1. **Click** on the **Address Book button**. The Address Book will open.

2. **Click** on the **entry to delete**. It will be selected.

3. **Click** on the **Delete button**. A confirmation message will appear.

4a. **Click** on **Yes**. The entry will be permanently deleted.

OR

4b. **Click** on **No**. The deletion will be canceled.

Part I Review Questions

1. What application is Outlook a part of? *See "Installing Outlook 2002" in Chapter 1*

2. Which installation option allows you to chose which components to install or where to install them? *See "Choosing Components" in Chapter 1*

3. What should you do if an Office program begins behaving strangely or refuses to work? *See "Repairing or Reinstalling Office" in Chapter 1*

4. What screen stores your incoming e-mail messages? *See "Understanding the Outlook Environment" in Chapter 2*

5. Where is the Outlook Bar located? *See "Using the Outlook Bar" in Chapter 2*

6. What does a red exclamation point next to an item symbolize? *See "Understanding Outlook Symbols" in Chapter 2*

7. What is the Office Assistant? *See "Introducing the Office Assistant" in Chapter 3*

8. What are Internet directory services? *See "Setting up Accounts" in Chapter 4*

9. Which account type is probably used to get mail from an Internet Service Provider? *See "Creating a New E-mail Account" in Chapter 4*

10. What are distribution groups? *See "Using Distribution Groups" in Chapter 5*

PART II

Communicating Via E-mail and Faxes

6

Creating New Messages

Are you ready to let the world know that you're online? One of the first things you can do with Outlook is to communicate with others via e-mail. Using e-mail is a fast and effective way to send messages to people. In Outlook, you can completely customize your e-mail messages, automatically add a signature, and even send documents along with e-mail. In this chapter, you'll learn how to:

- Address and format an e-mail message
- Add an automatic signature and attach a file
- Check the spelling of a message
- Set message options
- Create draft messages

Addressing an E-mail Message

Every e-mail message must have an address so that Outlook knows how to deliver the message. An e-mail address can be a person's full name or some combination of their first and last name. Internet addresses have an @ symbol, such as president@whitehouse.gov.

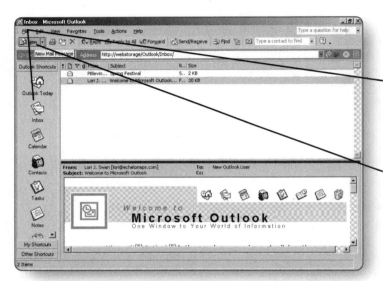

1. **Click** on the **Inbox icon** on the Outlook bar. The Inbox contents will appear in the Information viewer.

2. **Click** on the **New Mail Message button**. A new message will appear.

3. **Click** on the **To button** to access the Address Book. The Select Names dialog box will open.

NOTE

If you already know the e-mail address, you can type it directly in the text box.

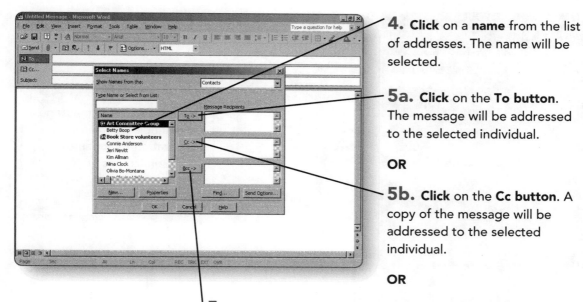

4. **Click** on a **name** from the list of addresses. The name will be selected.

5a. **Click** on the **To button**. The message will be addressed to the selected individual.

OR

5b. **Click** on the **Cc button**. A copy of the message will be addressed to the selected individual.

OR

5c. **Click** on the **Bcc button**. A "blind" copy of the message will be addressed to the selected individual.

NOTE

Cc and Bcc stand for "carbon copy" and "blind carbon copy." These terms are holdovers from the days when duplicate copies of memos were created using carbon paper. A blind carbon copy is one that is send to another recipient without the original recipient's knowledge.

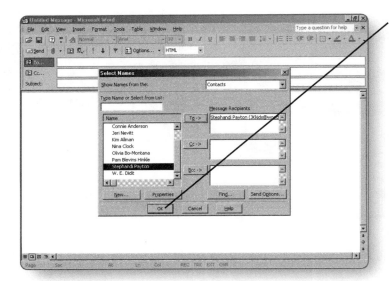

6. **Click** on **OK**. The Select Names dialog box will close.

TIP

You can send the message to multiple people by separating their names with semicolons or commas in the To text box.

Formatting a Message

You can type a message and send it immediately if you are pressed for time. However, if you have a few extra minutes, you can format your message so that the important points in the message stand out.

NOTE

By default, Outlook uses HTML format for all messages, enabling you to format your e-mail message like you would a Word document or Web page, using bold, italic, and other formatting options. However, some e-mail readers do not interpret HTML messages, and the reader's message may contain miscellaneous codes that make the message difficult to read. To send a plain-text message instead, click on the Message Format button and then click on Plain Text. After acknowledging the resulting dialog box, the message title bar will change to indicate the new format. Your formatting buttons will be dimmed.

Formatting Text

Outlook has a Formatting toolbar with numerous options to change the look of your message.

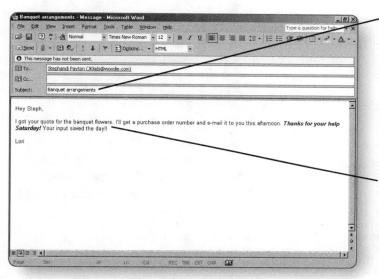

1. **Type** the **title** of the message in the Subject text box. The title will appear in the text box.

2. **Press** the **Tab key**. The insertion point will move to the message text box.

3. **Type** a **message**. The message will appear in the text box.

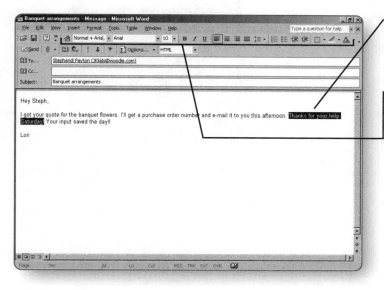

4. **Click** and **drag** the **mouse** over some text. The text will be selected.

5. **Click** on **any button or buttons** on the Formatting toolbar. The formatting will appear in the message.

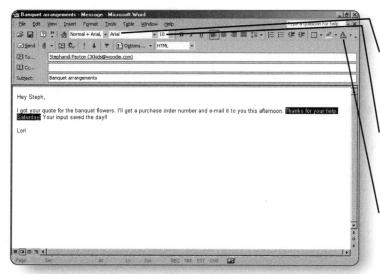

The options are:

- **Font**. Click on the down arrow to the right of the font name to select a different font.

- **Font Size**. Click on the down arrow to the right of the font size to select a larger or smaller font size.

- **Font Color**. Click on the button to select a different font color. A color palette will appear. Click the desired color to select it and close the palette.

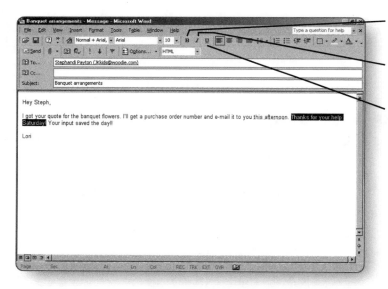

- **Bold**. Click on the button to make the text bold.

- **Italic**. Click on the button to make the text italic.

- **Underline**. Click on the button to make the text underlined.

Formatting Paragraphs

You can also format entire paragraphs by clicking buttons on the Formatting toolbar.

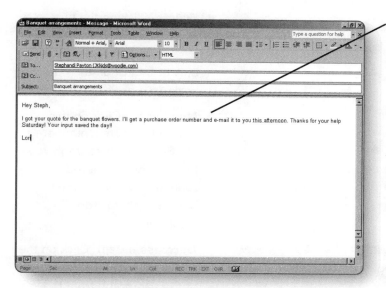

1a. **Click anywhere** in the paragraph you want to format. The insertion point will be in that paragraph.

OR

1b. **Click** and **drag** the **mouse** over several paragraphs to format more than one paragraph. The paragraphs will be highlighted.

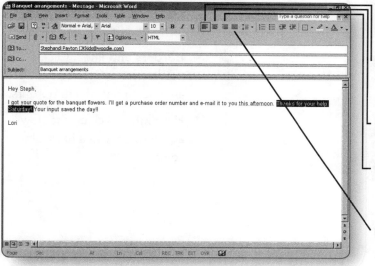

The paragraph formatting options are:

- **Align Left**. Click on the button to make the paragraph flush with the left margin.

- **Center**. Click on the button to center the paragraph.

- **Align Right**. Click on the button to make the paragraph flush with the right margin.

- **Justify**. Click on the button to align the paragraph on the left and right.

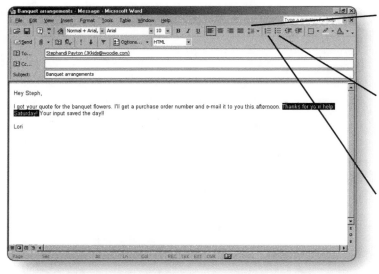

- **Line Spacing.** Click on the button to increase or decrease the line spacing of the document.

- **Bullets**. Click on the button to make a bulleted list. Each new paragraph you type will be bulleted. Click on the button again to turn off the bullets.

- **Numbering**. Click on this button to create a numbered list. Each new paragraph you type will be numbered sequentially. Click on the button again to stop numbering.

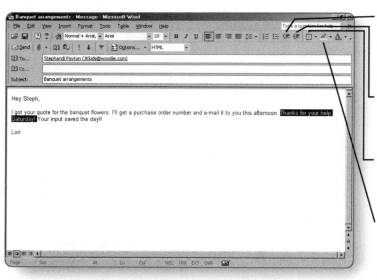

- **Decrease Indent**. Click on the button to decrease the indent of the paragraph from the left margin.

- **Increase Indent**. Click on the button to increase the indent from the left margin.

- **Borders and lines.** Click on the down arrow to select from an assortment of line borders.

- **Highlight**. Click on the down arrow to choose a highlight color.

TIP

Click on the down arrow next to the Style drop-down list to assign preset paragraph styles to the selected text.

Checking the Spelling of a Message

Just because e-mail is fast doesn't mean it needs to be sloppy! Before sending your message, it's a good idea to check the spelling of the message.

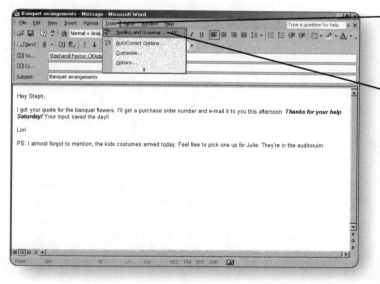

1. **Click** on **Tools** in the mail message. The Tools menu will appear.

2. **Click** on **Spelling and Grammar**. The Spelling and Grammar dialog box will open.

● **Click** on **Ignore Once** if you don't want to make the change in this particular instance. The Spell Check will continue.

OR

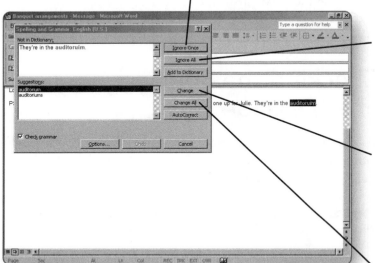

● **Click** on **Ignore All** if you want the search to ignore all identical errors. The search will continue.

OR

● **Click** on **Change** if you want to accept Outlook's proposed change. The change will be made in the message.

OR

● **Click** on **Change All** if you want to change each instance of the same error. Changes will be made.

TIP

Click on Options and view other choices for Spelling and Grammar. Click in the Check spelling as you type check box. When on, this feature will identify spelling and grammar errors with red edit markings in your document.

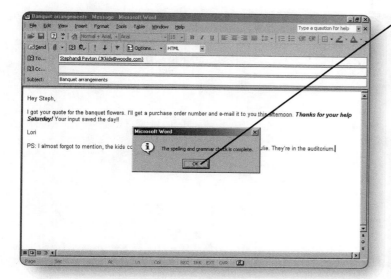

3. Click on **OK** when the message The spelling and grammar check is complete appears. The message box will close.

TIP

The AutoCorrect feature is a great help and when activated will assist you by automatically correcting misspellings as you type. By default, AutoCorrect is activated when you install Outlook. To toggle this switch off and on, click on Tools from the Message window, and then click AutoCorrect and select Replace text as you type.

Setting Message Options

Before you send the message, there are many options that you can set. Options can change the importance or sensitivity of a message.

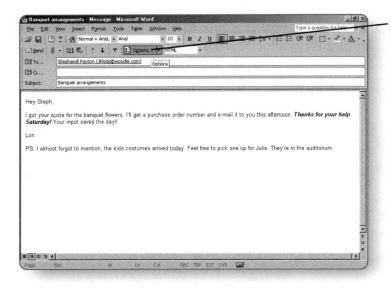

1. **Click** on the **Options button** in the mail message. The Message Options dialog box will open.

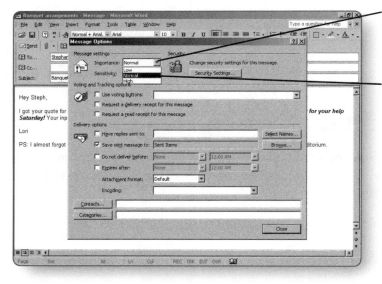

2. **Click** on the **down arrow** next to the Importance list box. A drop-down list will appear.

3. **Click** on **Low**, **Normal**, or **High**. The importance level will be selected.

NOTE

A low-importance message will have a blue, down-pointing arrow, and a high-importance message will have a red exclamation point when delivered.

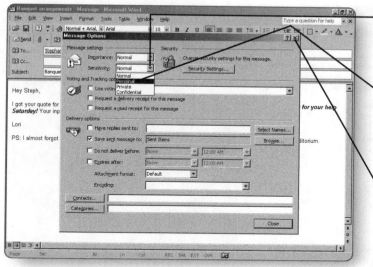

4. **Click** on the **down arrow** next to the Sensitivity list box. A drop-down list will appear.

5. **Click** on **Normal, Personal, Private**, or **Confidential**. The option you select will appear in the text box.

6. **Click** on the **Close button**. The Message Options dialog box will close and you will return to the message.

NOTE

Personal, Private, and Confidential messages will have a banner just below the To line at the top of the e-mail message with a note saying, "Please treat this message as Personal" (or Confidential or Private). Also, once you send a private message, the recipient will not be able to modify the contents.

Using Message Flags

You can add a message flag to an e-mail message. Message flags add notes to the message recipients, letting them know that a follow-up is due by a certain date, or that no follow-up is necessary.

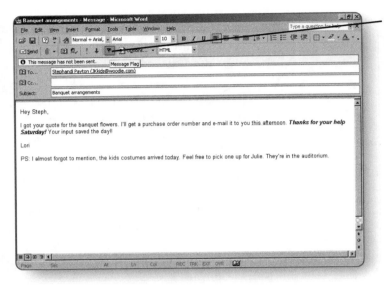

1. Click on the **Message Flag icon** on the toolbar. The Flag for Follow Up dialog box will open.

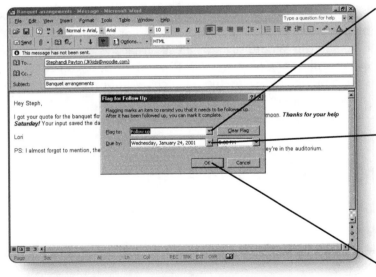

2. Click on the **down arrow** to the right of the Flag to list box. A drop-down list will appear.

3. Select a **message flag**. A message flag will be selected.

4. Click on the **down arrow** to the right of the Due by list box. A listing of dates will appear.

5. Select a **date**. A date will be selected.

6. Click on **OK**. The Flag for Follow Up dialog box will close and you will return to the message.

Creating a Draft Message

If you are composing a long e-mail and decide to finish it later, you can save the message as a draft.

1. Click on **File** on an unsent message. The File menu will appear.

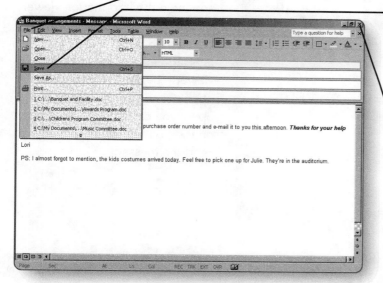

2. Click on **Save**. The message will be copied to the Drafts folder.

3. Click on **Close**. The message will close and be saved in the Drafts folder. You can finish it when you have more time.

Working with Draft Messages

1. **Click** on the **My Shortcuts group** on the Outlook bar. The My Shortcuts group will be revealed on the Outlook bar.

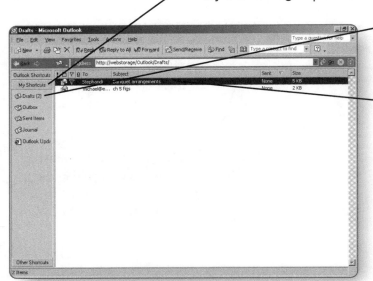

2. **Click** on the **Drafts icon**. The contents of the Drafts folder will appear in the Information viewer.

3. **Double-click** on the **draft message** in the Information viewer. The draft message will open. Once the message is open, you can continue working on the text until you are ready to send the message.

Attaching a File

Before you send a message, you may need to attach a file (document) to the e-mail message. Outlook gives you an easy way to attach files to e-mail messages.

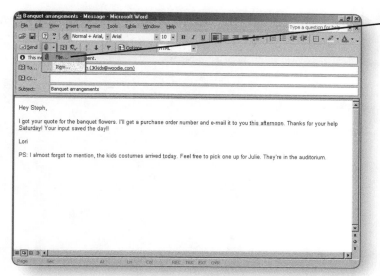

1. Click on the **Insert File button**. The Insert File dialog box will open.

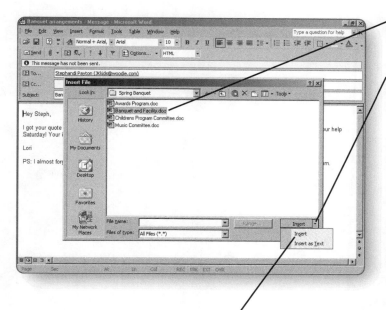

2. Click on the **file** you want to attach. The file will be selected.

3. Click on the **down arrow** next to the Insert button. A drop-down list will appear.

TIP

The file will be inserted as text in the body of the e-mail message. It's sometimes a good idea to use this option when sending files via the Internet.

4. Click on the **Insert option**. The file will be attached.

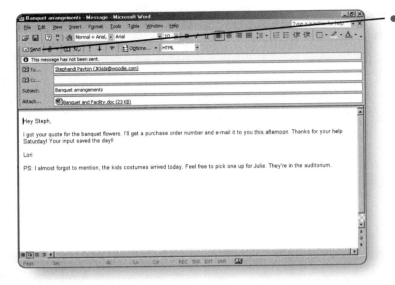

● The attachment is ready to send with the message. **Click Send.**

7

Sending and Tracking Messages

Once you have finished composing your e-mail message and setting options, it's a snap to send the message. Outlook will also allow you to view your sent messages, track the status of messages you've sent, and resend or forward them as many times as you like. In this chapter, you'll learn how to:

- Send a mail message
- View messages in the Sent Items folder
- Recall and resend a message
- Receive notification when a message is read
- Send replies to another individual
- Deliver a message at a specific time
- Expire a message

Sending a Mail Message

You've written the message, addressed it to the appropriate people, and set all the available options. You are now ready to send the message.

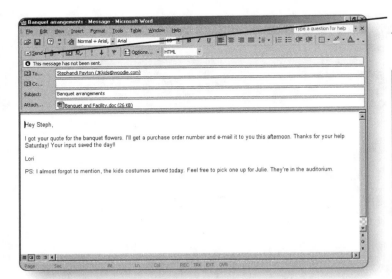

1. **Click** on the **Send button**. The message will be sent.

NOTE

When you send a message, it temporarily moves to the Outbox. Once the message has been sent, it moves to the Sent Items folder. If you are working offline, the message cannot be sent until you are connected and click Send/Receive.

Viewing and Sorting Sent Messages

Trying to remember if you sent a message to someone can be tricky. Luckily, Outlook allows you to view all the messages you have sent, and it helps keep your messages organized.

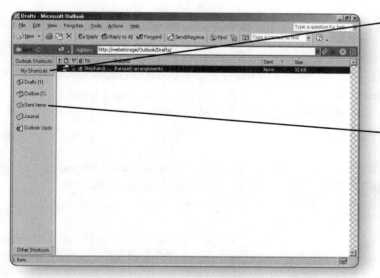

1. Click on the **My Shortcuts button** on the Outlook bar. The contents of the My Shortcuts folder will appear in the Information viewer.

2. Click on the **Sent Items icon** on the Outlook bar. The contents of the Sent Items folder will appear in the Information viewer.

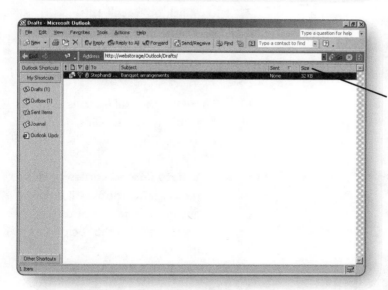

You can sort messages in the Sent Items folder to quickly locate them.

3. Click on **any column header**. The messages will be sorted by that field.

Recalling a Message

Ever had a sinking feeling as soon as you clicked the Send button? "I wish I hadn't sent that e-mail!" Outlook gives you a safety net with the Recall feature. Recall is also a good feature to use when you discover incorrect information in the message you just sent.

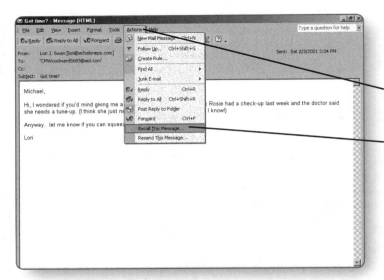

1. Click twice on a **message** in the Sent Items folder. The message will open.

2. Click on **Actions**. The Actions menu will appear.

3. Click on **Recall This Message**. The Recall This Message dialog box will open.

There are several options available when recalling a message. They are:

- **Delete unread copies of this message**. Outlook will delete any unread copies of the message from the recipient's Inbox.

- **Delete unread copies and replace with a new message**. A new message will open which will replace the message currently in the recipient's Inbox.

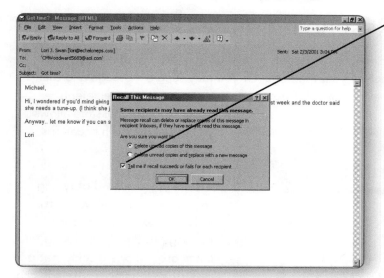

- **Tell me if recall succeeds or fails for each recipient.** Outlook sends you a new e-mail message informing you of success or failure of the attempt to recall the message.

NOTE

Recall failure occurs if the recipient has read the message before you attempt to recall it. If this occurs, the recipient receives a message warning that you are attempting to recall the original message. Also note that you can only recall messages sent to other users on your Exchange network. It doesn't work for Internet messages.

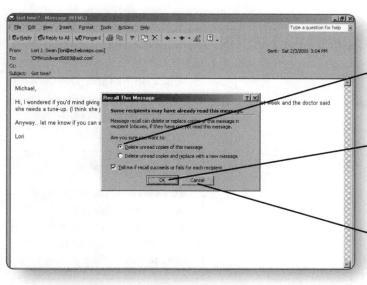

4. **Click** on the **options** you want to use. The options will be selected.

5a. **Click** on **OK**. The message will be recalled.

OR

5b. **Click** on **Cancel**. The message recall will be canceled.

Resending a Message

Sometimes message recipients may tell you that they didn't receive your message. Or you may send a message and then realize that you forgot to include an important recipient.

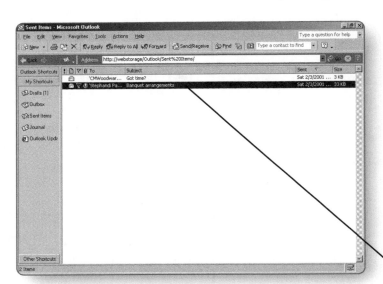

Resending the message allows you to handle both situations quickly.

Also, if you are tired of typing the same messages week after week (for example, an e-mail message to the office asking for lunch orders, or a weekly status report), resending a message can save you valuable time. Messages can be edited before they are resent.

1. Click twice on the **message** in the Sent Items folder. The message will open.

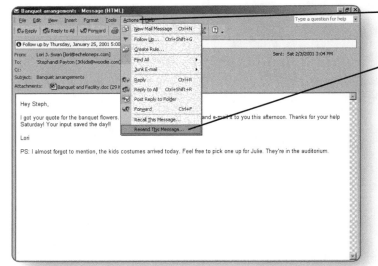

2. Click on **Actions**. The Actions menu will appear.

3. Click on **Resend This Message**. The message will open as a new e-mail message.

TIP

You can edit the message text, add or delete message recipients, and change message options before resending.

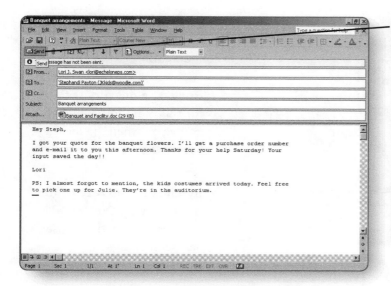

4. Click on the **Send button**. The message will be sent again.

Receiving Notification When a Message Is Read

Say you've sent an important e-mail message to someone and you want to follow up with a phone call. How do you know when the recipient has read the message? It's easy! You tell Outlook to notify you when the message has been read.

1. Create a new mail **message**.

2. Click on **Options**. The Message Options dialog box will open.

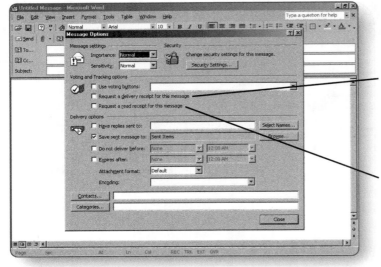

There are two notification options, depending on your configuration:

- **Request a delivery receipt for this message**. Outlook will notify you when the message has reached the recipient's Inbox.

- **Request a read receipt for this message**. Outlook will notify you when the message has been opened.

NOTE

If the message is sent to someone outside of your company via the Internet, Outlook will only be able to tell you when the message has been delivered, not when it has been read.

TIP

If you use tracking options frequently, you can set all of your new messages to be tracked automatically. In the Inbox, click on Tools, Options, and click on the E-mail Options button. When the E-mail Options dialog box opens, click on the Tracking Options button and select the tracking options you want to use.

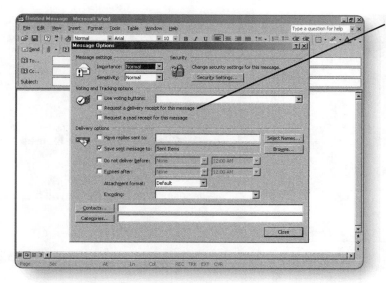

3. **Click** on a **tracking option**. The option will be selected.

Sending Replies to Another Individual

Normally, when people reply to an e-mail message, the reply is sent back to the message sender. However, you can have replies sent directly to another individual.

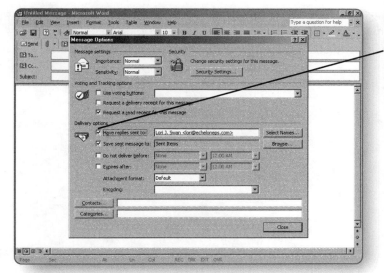

1. **Click** on the **Have Replies Sent to** check box. A check mark will be placed in the box.

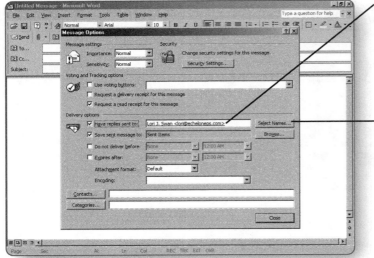

2a. **Type** the individual's **e-mail address** in the text box. The address will appear in the text box.

OR

2b. **Click** on the **Select Names button** and **select** the **individual's name** from the address book. The name will be selected.

Delivering a Message at a Specific Time

Messages are normally delivered as soon as you send them. However, you can delay the delivery of a message to a specific time. This feature works great if you are going to be out of the office and still want an e-mail delivered while you are gone.

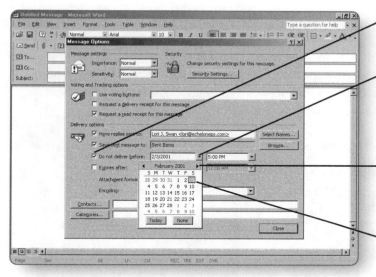

1. **Click** on the **Do not deliver before** check box.

2. **Click** on the **down arrow** to the right of the **Do Not Deliver Before** check box. The Date Navigator will open.

3. **Click** on the **left or right arrow** on either side of the month. The month will change.

4. **Click** on the **date** you want when the correct month is displayed. The date will be highlighted.

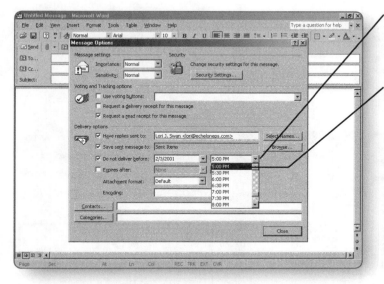

5. **Click** on the **down arrow** to the right of the time. A drop-down list will appear.

6. **Select** your **time preference**. The time will be selected.

TIP

You can type a different date or time directly into the Do Not Deliver Before text box.

NOTE

The message will remain in your Outbox until the specified delivery time. You can edit the message or delete the message from the Outbox.

Expiring a Message

Have you ever been out of the office and returned to find a ton of out-of-date e-mail messages in your Inbox? It's considered good e-mail manners to expire your messages if they contain time-sensitive material.

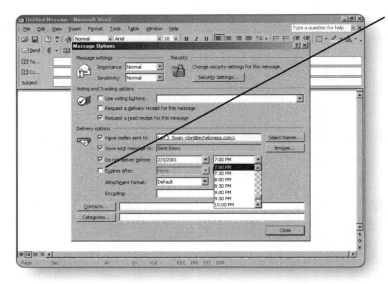

1. Click on the **Expires after** check box.

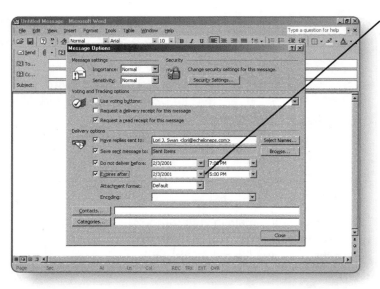

2. Click on the **down arrow** to the right of the **Expires after** check box. The Date Navigator will open.

NOTE

Expired messages remain in the recipient's Inbox, but they are highlighted with strikethrough formatting for easy identification.

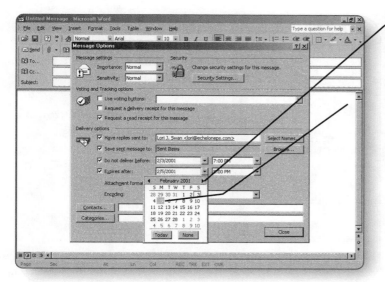

3. Click on the **left or right arrow** on either side of the month. The month will change.

4. Click on the **date** you want when the correct month is displayed. The date will be highlighted.

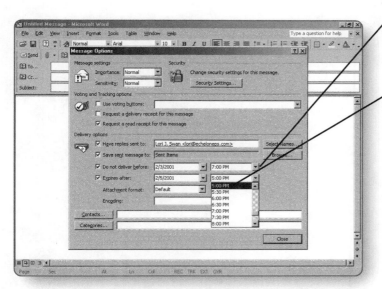

5. Click on the **down arrow** to the right of the time. A drop-down list will appear.

6. Select your **time preference**. The time will be selected.

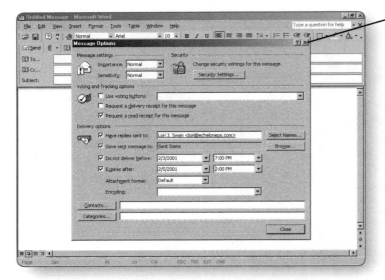

7. **Click** on the **Close button**. The Message Options dialog box will close and your unsent message will reappear.

8. **Click** on the **Close button** in the message window. The message will close.

8

Reading and Responding to Messages

You'll probably use e-mail more than any other feature in Outlook. Sending and receiving e-mail is now an integral part of doing business and communicating with others. Once you receive e-mail, you'll need to know what to do with it. In this chapter, you'll learn how to:

- Change how you view e-mail messages
- Use Auto Preview
- Read, reply, forward, delete, and print a message
- Navigate between e-mail messages

Changing How You View Your E-mail Messages

Views in Outlook provide you with different ways to look at information in a folder by putting it in different arrangements and formats. Use views to control how much detail appears in your e-mail messages.

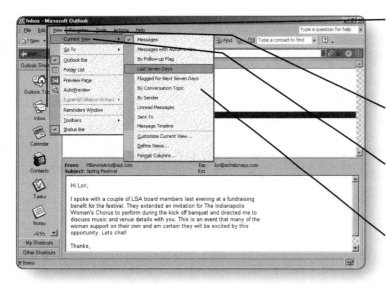

1. **Click** on the **Inbox icon** on the Outlook bar. The Inbox contents will appear in the Information viewer.

2. **Click** on **View**. The View menu will appear.

3. **Click** on **Current View**. The Current View submenu will appear.

4. **Click** on **any view**. Your e-mail messages will appear differently in the Information viewer.

TIP

If you find a view that is close to what you're looking for, you can click on View, Current View, and Customize Current View. From there, you can specify exactly how you want your e-mail messages to appear.

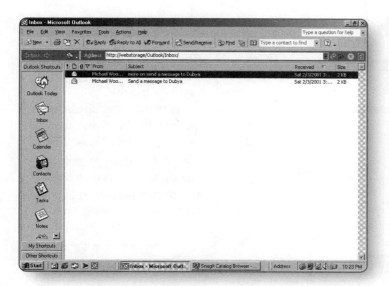

Using AutoPreview

AutoPreview is a way to quickly view the first three lines of an e-mail message without opening the message. Using AutoPreview saves you time and lets you open only the messages you want to read.

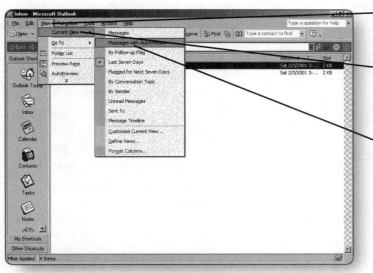

1. Click on **View.** The View menu will appear.

2. Click on **Current View.** The Current View submenu will appear.

3. Click on **Messages with AutoPreview.** Your Inbox will display up to the first three lines of e-mail messages you've received but have not yet read.

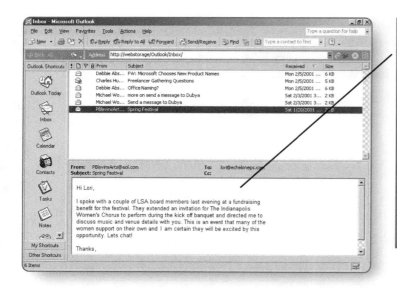

Responding to E-mail Messages

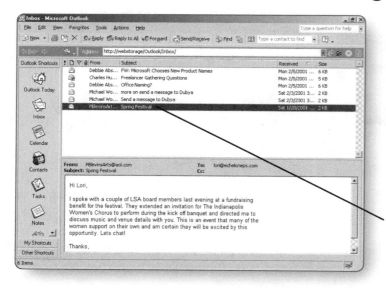

One great thing about e-mail is that there are so many options when you receive a message. You can reply to the sender of the message, or you can send your replies to everyone who received the message. You can forward the message on to someone else, and you can print the message for your files.

1. Click twice on **a message** in the Inbox. The message will open.

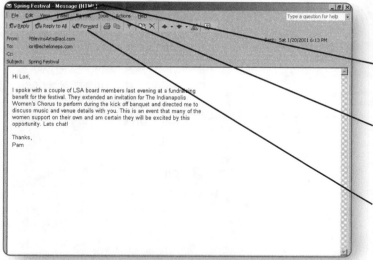

Choose one of the following options:

- **Reply**. Click on Reply to send a reply to the message sender.

- **Reply to All**. Click on Reply to All to send a reply to the message sender and all of the message recipients.

- **Forward**. Click on Forward to send the message to another person.

2. Type the **message text**. The message will appear in the text box.

3. Click on **Send**. Your message will be sent.

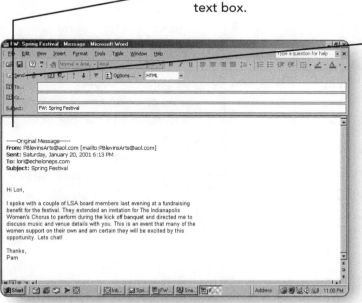

Printing a Message

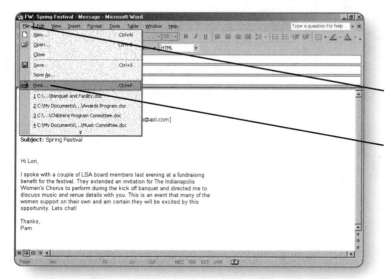

You can keep e-mail messages in your Inbox, or you can print messages for future reference.

1. **Click** on **File**. The File menu will appear.

2. **Click** on **Print**. The Print dialog box will open.

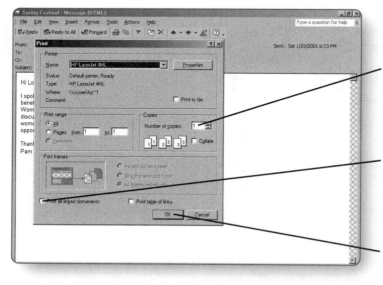

Choose from the following options:

● **Number of copies**. Click on the up or down arrow to increase or decrease the number of copies.

● **Print all linked documents**. Click on the check box to print the file attachment in addition to the e-mail message.

3. **Click** on **OK**. The Print dialog box will close.

Navigating Between E-mail Messages

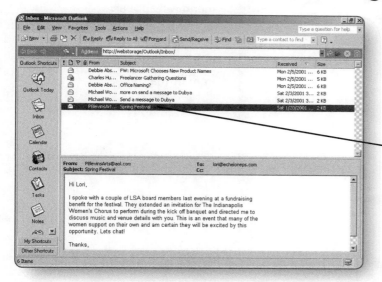

After a while, you will have numerous messages in your Inbox. Learning how to move around will help you locate the messages you want more quickly.

1. **Click twice** on **any message** in the Inbox. The message will open.

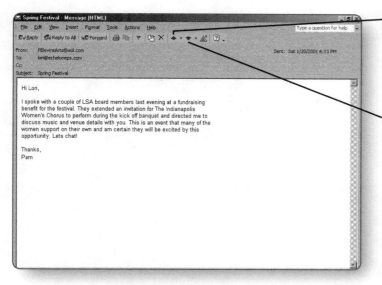

2a. **Click** on the **Previous Item button**. You will move to the previous e-mail message.

OR

2b. **Click** on the **Next Item button**. You will move to the next e-mail message.

There are down arrows to the right of the Next and Previous Item buttons. These give you more options so you can go to the next or previous item of a specific type.

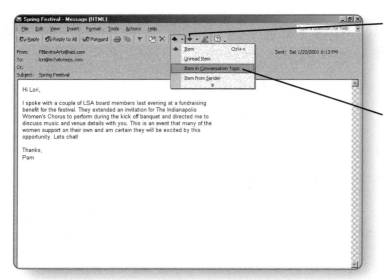

3. Click on the **down arrow** next to the Previous Item or Next Item button. A drop-down menu will appear.

4. Click on a **type**. You will move to the next or previous item of that type.

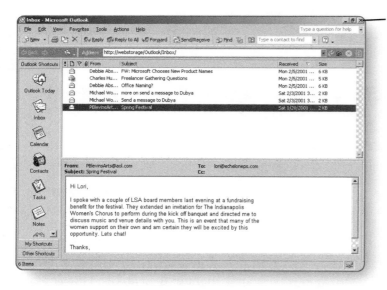

5. Click on the **Close button**. The message will close.

9

Managing Your Mail

You know how easy it is to let piles of papers stack up on your desk! Outlook gives you many tools to organize your messages so your Inbox remains uncluttered and you can easily locate the messages you need. In this chapter, you'll learn how to:

- Organize messages in folders
- Add and move folders using drag and drop
- Organizing files within folders
- Organize messages with color
- Control junk and adult-content mail
- Use the Rules Wizard
- Find, sort, and archive messages

Organizing Messages in Folders

Think of your Inbox as a drawer in a filing cabinet. Would you just toss all the messages into the drawer? No! You may read some mail immediately and throw it away, or you may need to store some messages while you wait for more information. Using electronic folders is an easy way to organize your messages, just as you would use file folders in a filing cabinet. Outlook lets you create new folders in your Inbox and moves messages into the folders manually or automatically.

1. **Click** on the **Inbox icon** on the Outlook Shortcuts bar. Outlook will display the contents of your Inbox in the Information viewer.

2. **Click** on the **Organize button**. The Ways to Organize Inbox pane will appear in the Information viewer.

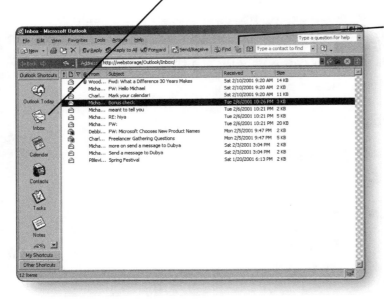

3. Click on **Using Folders**. The Using Folders pane will come to the front.

4. Click on the **message** that you want to place in a folder. The message will be highlighted.

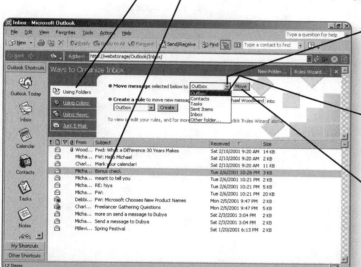

5. Click on the **down arrow** to the right of Move Message selected below to list box. A drop-down list will appear.

6. Click on the **folder** in which you want to store the message. It will be highlighted.

7. Click on **Move**. Your selection will move from the Inbox to the designated folder.

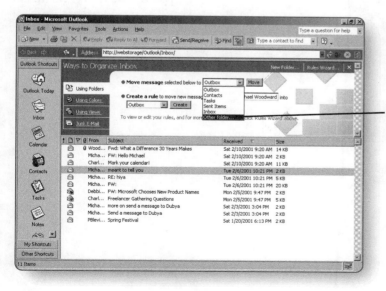

If the folder you wanted to select wasn't in the drop-down list, you can find it through the Other folder selection.

8. Click on **Other folder**. The Select Folder dialog box will open.

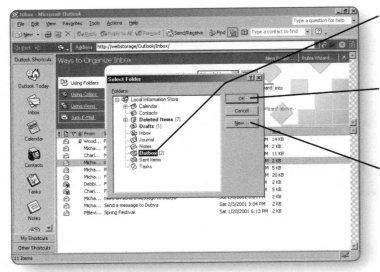

9. Click on the **folder** in which you want to store the message. It will be highlighted.

10a. Click on **OK**. The change will be accepted.

OR

10b. Click on **New** to set up a new folder. The Create New Folder dialog box will open.

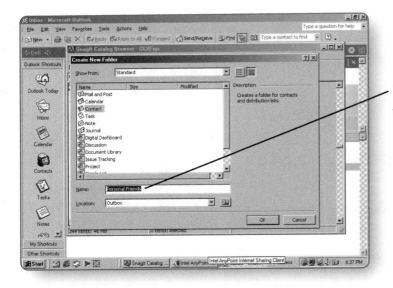

11. Type a **new folder name** in the Name box.

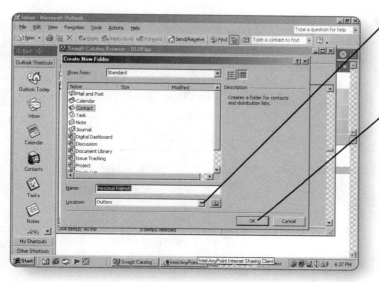

12. Click on the **location** under which you want the new folder to appear. The folder will be highlighted.

13. Click on **OK**. The choices will be accepted and the Add shortcut to Outlook Bar? message box will open.

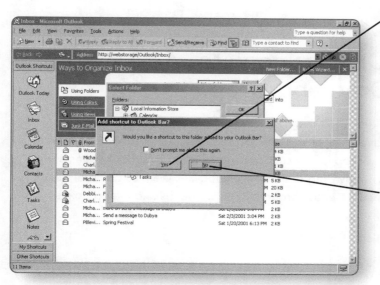

14a. Click on **Yes** to create a shortcut on your Outlook bar. The message box will close. Your new folder will appear in the Select Folder dialog box, and a new shortcut will appear on the Outlook bar.

OR

14b. Click on **No** to reject the offer. The message box will close. Your new folder will appear in the Select Folder dialog box.

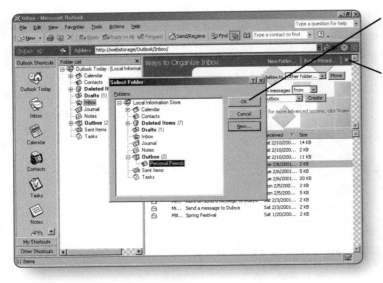

15. **Click** on **OK**. The Select Folder dialog box will close.

16. **Click** on **Close**. The Ways to Organize Inbox windows will close.

TIP

You can move multiple messages into a folder at once. When selecting the messages from the list of items in the Inbox, hold down the Ctrl key while you click on the messages.

Organizing with Drag and Drop

Like many other Windows programs, Outlook takes full advantage of the shortcut features built into Windows. Drag and drop is one such feature: Just grab Outlook items and instantly drag them where you want them to go. There's no need to wade through layers of menus and dialog boxes.

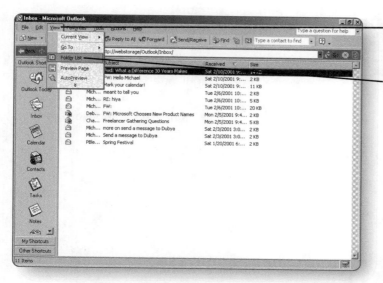

1. **Click** on **View**. A drop-down list will appear.

2. **Click** on **Folder List**. The Folder List will open.

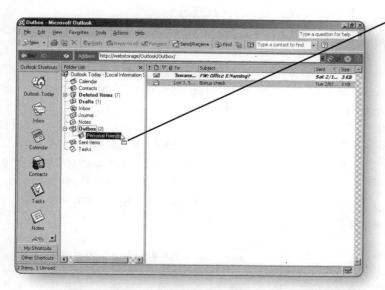

3. **Click and hold** on a **folder** you would like to move. The folder will be highlighted.

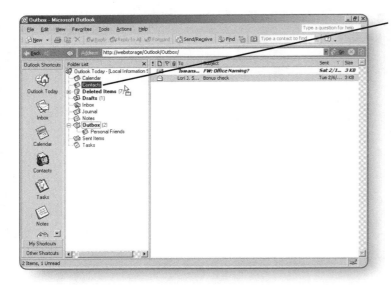

4. **Drag** the **folder** to the destination folder. The destination folder will be highlighted.

5. **Release** the **mouse**. The transfer will occur.

Dragging Objects Within Folders

Similarly, Outlook items can be moved or copied to different folders as well. Use the same drag-and-drop feature to organize your Outlook folders.

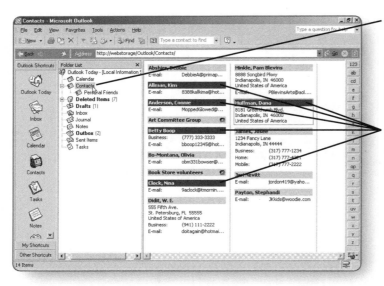

1. **Click** on the **folder** containing information to be moved. The folder will be highlighted and its contents will be displayed.

2. **Click and hold** on the **item or items** you wish to move. The items will be highlighted.

TIP

Remember that the Ctrl key is your friend! By holding the Ctrl key down you can select more than one item at a time. Try it!

3. Drag the **folder** where the items are to be placed. The folder will be highlighted.

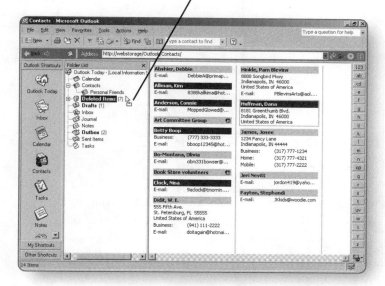

4. Release the **mouse**. The items will move. Leave the Ways to Organize Inbox window open for the next exercise.

NOTE

Outlook will prompt you for additional preferences when necessary, depending on the direction you move or copy your files and folders.

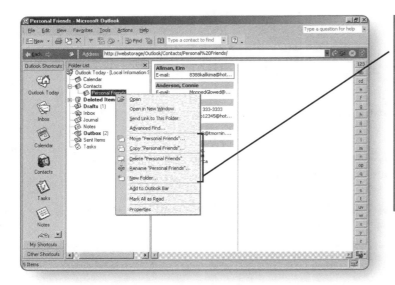

TIP

And yet another shortcut! Click the right mouse button to open a window of options, then walk through similar steps with move, copy, delete, rename, and new folder options. It's worth taking a minute to explore.

Organizing Messages with Color

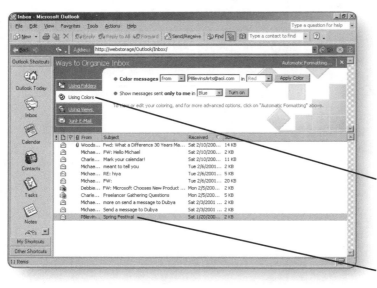

Another way to organize messages in the Inbox is by using color. If you are a visually oriented person, you'll appreciate this feature of Outlook. You can color messages sent to or received from a certain person.

1. **Click** on **Using Colors**. Your organizer pane will change to allow you to organize messages by color.

2. **Click** on a **message** you want to color. It will be highlighted.

3. Click on the **down arrow** to the right of Color messages. A drop-down list will appear.

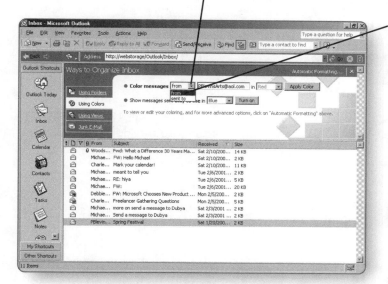

4a. Click on **from** to color messages from the sender of the selected message. The word will be highlighted.

NOTE

You can replace the selected sender by typing a new e-mail address in the edit box.

OR

4b. Click on **sent to** to color messages sent to the recipient of the selected message. The choice will be highlighted.

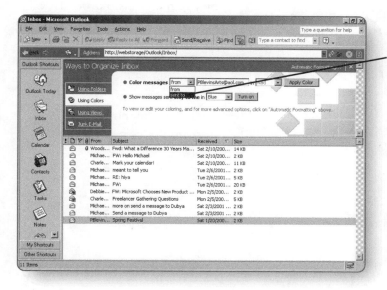

NOTE

You can replace the selected recipient by typing a new e-mail address in the edit box.

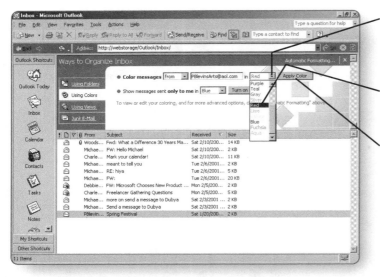

5. **Click** on the **down arrow** to the right of the color choices. A drop-down list will appear.

6. **Click** on a **color**. The color will be selected.

7. **Click** on the **Apply Color button**. Messages received from or sent to the individual you've selected will now be color-coded.

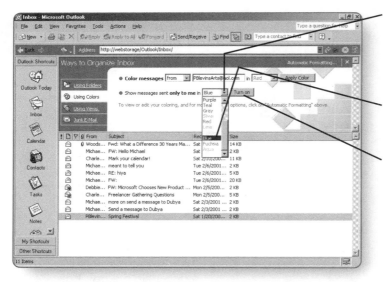

8. **Click** on the **down arrow** to the right of Show messages sent only to me. A drop-down list will appear.

9. **Click** on a **color**. The color will be selected.

10. **Click** on the **Turn on button**. The color will be applied.

Controlling Junk and Adult-Content Mail

Ever heard of *spamming*? This is a term often used to describe unsolicited e-mail that arrives in your Inbox. Unfortunately, once your e-mail address becomes public, you may frequently receive junk mail in your Inbox. Luckily, Outlook includes a special feature to control the junk and adult-content mail that you receive. You can automatically color, move, or delete any junk or adult-content e-mail.

1. **Click** on **Junk E-Mail**. Your organizer pane will change to allow you to control undesirable messages.

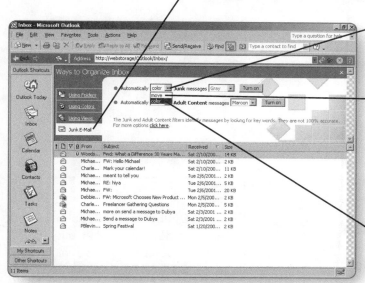

2. **Click** on the **down arrow** to the right of Automatically. A drop-down list will appear.

3a. **Click** on **move** to move junk messages automatically, and then **select** the **folder** in which it will be placed. The folder will be selected.

OR

3b. **Click** on **color** to automatically color junk messages, and then **select** a **color**. The color will be selected.

NOTE

If a junk e-mail folder does not exist, you may receive a message asking if you want to create one. Click on Yes to create the folder, or No to cancel.

TIP

Choosing to automatically move junk messages to the Deleted Items folder is the same as automatically deleting all junk e-mail.

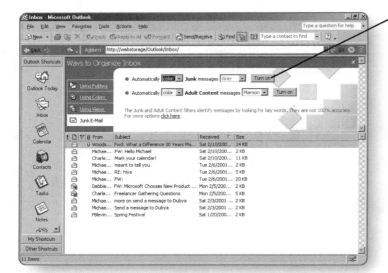

4. **Click** on the **Turn on button**. It will be activated.

When the junk e-mail rule is activated, the Turn on button changes to a Turn off button. To deactivate your rule, click on the Turn off button.

5. **Repeat steps 2 through 4** for Adult-Content e-mail.

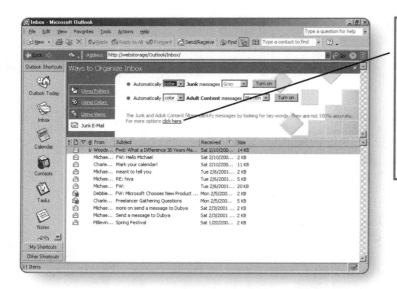

TIP

Outlook uses special rules to determine what is junk or adult-content e-mail. Click on For more options click here for more information about junk and adult-content mail.

Adding Names to the Junk E-mail List

Even after you have activated junk e-mail rules, certain junk messages may slip into your Inbox. You can quickly add the senders of these messages to your junk senders list.

1. Right-click on the **offending message** in the Inbox. A shortcut menu will appear.

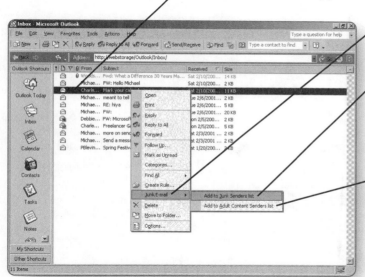

2. Click on **Junk E-mail**. The submenu will appear.

3a. Click on **Add to Junk Senders list**. The message will be added to the list.

OR

3b. Click on **Add to Adult Content Senders list**. The message will be added to the list.

Using the Rules Wizard

In the previous exercise, you created a rule to do something with junk or adult-content e-mail messages. Outlook has a Rules Wizard that walks you through the steps needed to create rules. Rules can be created to automatically move messages to a certain folder, automatically reply to messages, notify you when important messages arrive, and much more.

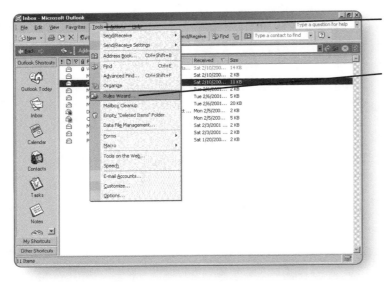

1. **Click** on **Tools**. The Tools menu will appear.

2. **Click** on **Rules Wizard**. The Rules Wizard dialog box will open.

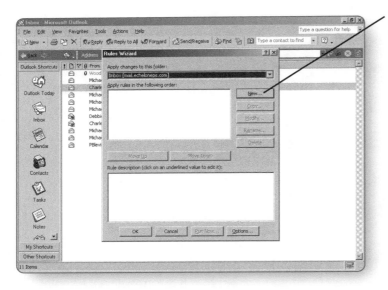

3. **Click** on the **New button**. The Rules Wizard will appear.

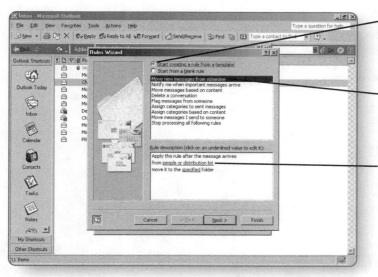

4. **Click** on **Start creating a rule from a template**. A list of rules will be listed.

5. **Click** on the **type of rule** that you want to create. It will be highlighted.

6. **Click** on an **underlined option**. The Rule Address dialog box will open.

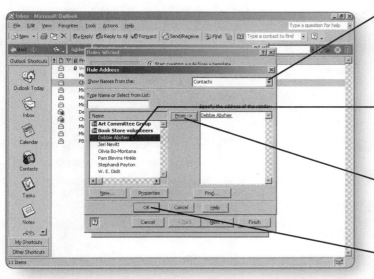

7. **Click** on the **drop-down list** of the Show Names from the window. Select your choice from the list.

8. **Select** the **contact** for the rule. The choice will be highlighted.

9. **Click** on **From**. The name will be copied to the Specify the address of the Sender window.

10. **Click** on **OK**. The dialog box will close.

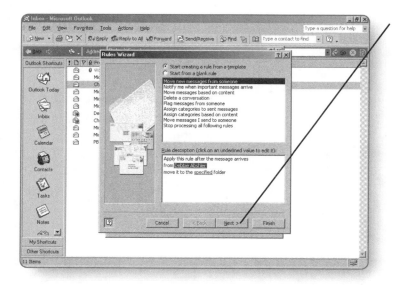

11. **Click** on **Next**. The wizard will present you with a list of conditions for the rule.

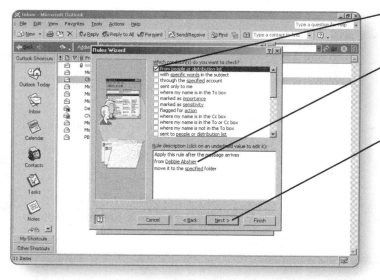

12. **Click** on a **check box** to select a condition.

13. **Click** on the **underlined options** to edit the rules description.

14. **Click** on **Next**. The wizard will present a list of options on how to handle the message.

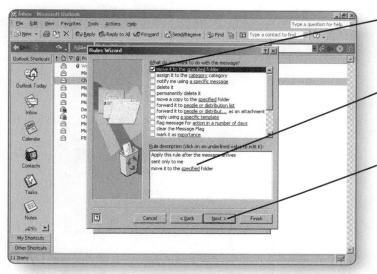

15. **Click** on a **check box** to select what Outlook should do with the message.

16. **Click** on the **underlined options** to edit the rules description.

17. **Click** on **Next**.

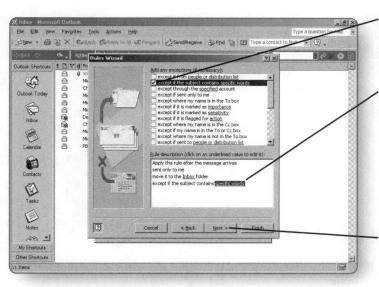

18. **Click** on a **check box** to select any exceptions. It will be highlighted.

19. **Click** on the **underlined options** to edit the rules description. The option will open dialog boxes in which to specify your rules. When you've completed the rule setup, you will be returned to this window.

20. **Click** on **Next**.

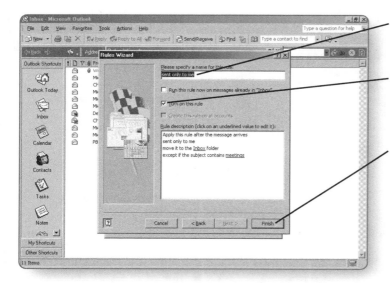

21. Type a **name** for the rule. It will be inserted.

22. Click on the **Turn on this rule check box** to turn the rule on or off.

23. Click on **Finish**.

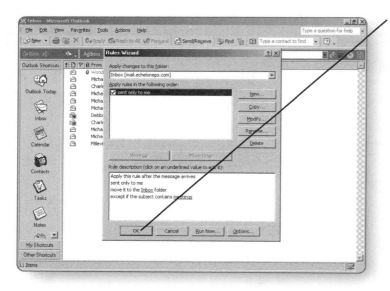

24. Click on **OK**. The Rules Wizard will close.

Finding Messages

After you have used Outlook for a while, you may have many messages stored in the Inbox or other folders. Outlook has extensive searching capabilities so you can always locate your messages.

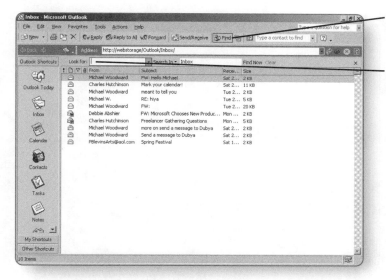

1. **Click** on the **Find button**. The Find pane will appear.

2. **Type text** in the Look for: text box. The text will appear.

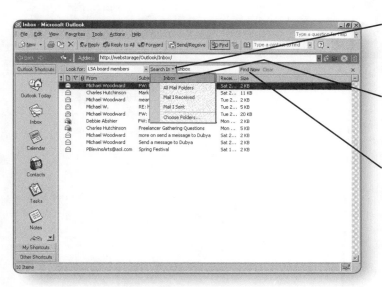

3. **Click** on the **down arrow** next to the Search In box. A drop-down list will appear.

4. **Click** on your **search location**. The selection will appear.

5. **Click** on the **Find Now button**. All messages matching the typed text will be displayed in the Information viewer at the bottom section of the screen.

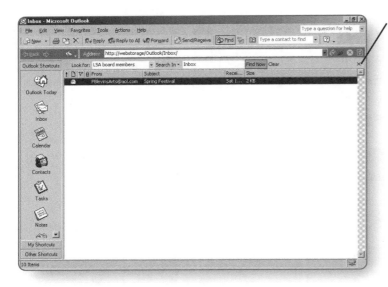

6. Click on the **Close button**. The Find window will close.

Sorting Messages

Another way to organize your e-mail is by sorting the messages in your Inbox. Incoming messages can be sorted by several criteria. You can view your messages in the order in which they were sent, by sender, or by several other options.

1. Click on the **Received column header** to sort all messages based on order received.

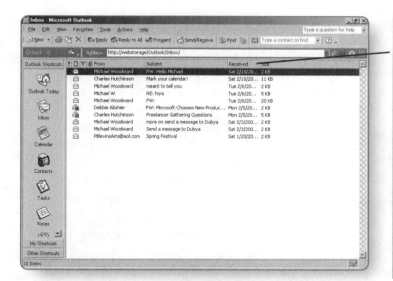

NOTE

The column headers are toggle buttons that let you sort in ascending or descending order. Click once on a column header to sort in ascending order; click again on the column header to sort in descending order. The small gray triangle to the right of the column header indicates ascending or descending order.

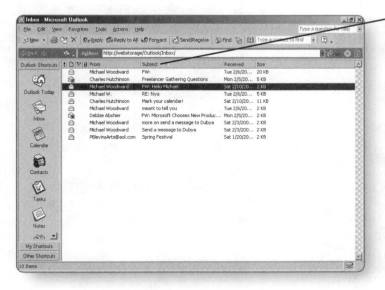

2. Click on the **Subject column header** to sort all messages based on subject.

TIP

You can use many fields to sort; however, not all of them appear in the Information viewer. Click on View, Current View, Customize Current View, and Fields to change which fields are displayed.

Archiving Messages Automatically

Outlook will occasionally poll your mailbox to determine whether it is time to archive. Archiving is the process of moving messages from the Inbox to another file. These messages are still available to you after they have been archived. Archiving helps to prevent cluttered or outdated materials from being stored in your everyday mailbox.

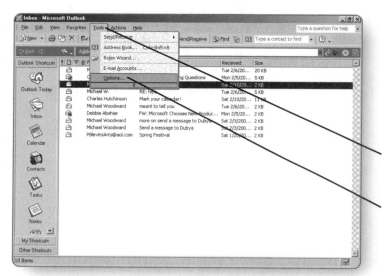

1. Click on **Tools**. The Tools menu will appear.

2. Click on **Options**. The Options dialog box will open.

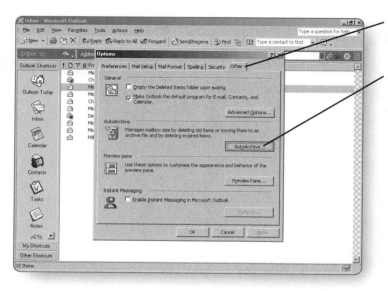

3. Click on the **Other tab**. The tab will come to the front.

4. Click on the **AutoArchive button**. The AutoArchive dialog box will open.

Choose from the following options:

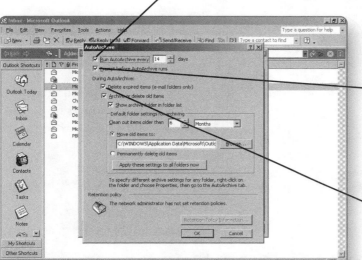

- **Run AutoArchive every 14 days**. Outlook will automatically archive according to the number of days set here. Click on the up or down arrows next to the number of days to increase or decrease the number of days.

- **Prompt before AutoArchive runs**. Before archiving, Outlook will display a message with an option to cancel that particular day's scheduled archiving.

- **Delete expired items (e-mail folders only)**. Outlook will delete any expired e-mail messages instead of archiving the messages.

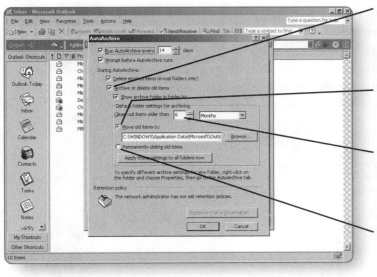

- **Archive or delete old items**. Define time frames for the age of your archives before deleting.

- **Move old items to**. The storage location for archived messages.

- **Clean out items older than**. Specify by days, weeks, or months how long to archive files.

- **Permanently delete old items**. Select for deletion preferences.

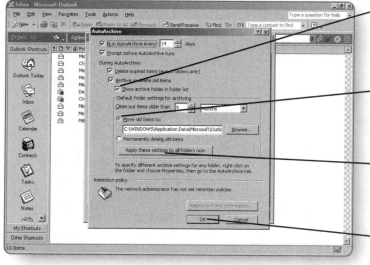

- **Show archive folder in folder list**. Select to have your archive folder appear in the list.

5. **Click** on the **options** that you want to use. They will be checked.

6. **Click** on **Apply these settings to all folders now**. Your settings will be applied.

7. **Click** on **OK**. Your AutoArchive settings will update any changes.

Importing and Exporting Items from Archives and Other Programs

You may have messages or other items stored in archives or in mail folders from other applications, such as Outlook Express, that you want to bring into Outlook. You also can export Outlook items to these programs so you can work with them there. In this example, you will import any mail messages from your Outlook Express Inbox into Outlook.

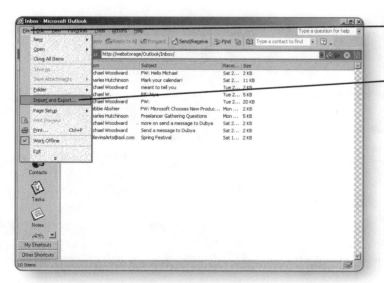

1. Click on **File**. The File menu will appear.

2. Click on **Import and Export**. The Import and Export Wizard will appear.

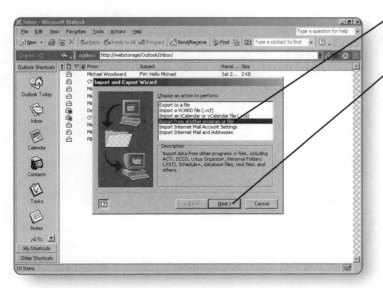

3. Click on the **action** you want to perform. It will be highlighted.

4. Click on **Next**. The Outlook Import and Export Wizard dialog box will appear.

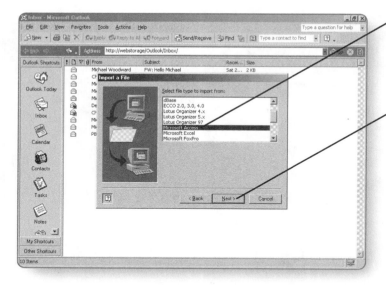

5. Click on the **program** from which you want to import the messages. The program will be highlighted.

6. Click on **Next** and continue the import instructions as applicable for your selections.

7. Click on **Finish** when you reach the end of the Wizard. The Import and Export wizard will close and the items you selected will be imported.

10

Working with Newsgroups

It's difficult to believe that the Internet is still in its infancy, relatively speaking. As the world becomes more and more online-oriented both at home and at the office, Outlook's advanced communication features are no longer a luxury—they are a vital necessity. To help extend you to the world beyond your own computer, Outlook 2002 includes more fully integrated news-reading capabilities than previous versions. Although this feature relies on an application separate from Outlook, it is easily accessible directly from "Outlook proper." In this chapter, you'll learn how to:

- Use the Microsoft Outlook Newsreader
- Subscribe to newsgroups of interest
- Read, reply to, and create new newsgroup messages

Welcome to Newsgroups

If you have never dealt with newsgroups before, you are in for quite a treat! In a nutshell, newsgroups are online, e-mail based communities in which members share thoughts, ideas, and discussions on whatever the topic of the newsgroup might be. Usenet.org, which has dominated the newsgroup "market" almost since its inception, calls them "distributed discussions." Some newsgroups are public, open to literally anyone with news server access; others are privately owned and operated, such as a corporate newsgroup whose subscribers are limited to company employees. Newsgroups can be an excellent way to

- Distribute news and announcements
- Research information
- Find support or help with a particular question or topic
- Meet people who share the same interests as you

You'll find newsgroups on just about any topic you can imagine, from "Barney.Dinosaur," to computer and software help, to political debates, to home beer brewing, to . . . well, let's just say some topics are only suitable for adult audiences.

Opening the Outlook Newsreader

Whatever your topic of interest, you can use the Outlook Newsreader (new to Outlook 2002) to search for and subscribe to groups. To access the newsreader, follow these steps.

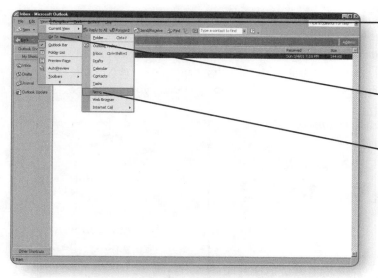

1. **Click** on **View** from the main Outlook menu bar. A submenu will appear.

2. **Click** on **Go To**. Another submenu will appear.

3. **Click** on **News**. The Outlook Newsreader will open and, assuming this is your first time in the Newsreader, the Internet Connection Wizard will open.

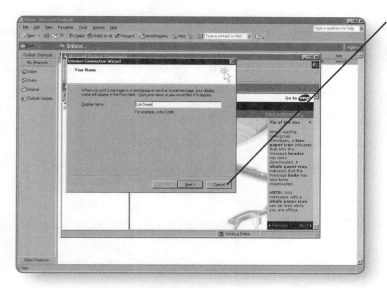

4. **Click** on **Cancel** for now, and **click** on **Yes** when asked to confirm the cancel. (You will learn how to set up an account in the next section.) The wizard will close and the Outlook Newsreader interface will be revealed.

As you can see, the Outlook Newsreader looks very much like Outlook itself, and you'll be happy to know that it works very much the same way too. You can customize your newsreader by displaying the folder list, for example, which in this case displays the list of newsgroups to which you subscribe.

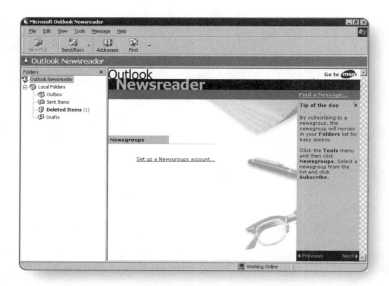

NOTE

If you already have another newsreader configured on your computer, Outlook will ask which newsreader you want to use now—the one you already have installed or the Outlook Newsreader. If you change your mind later, you can change the default newsreader that Outlook opens in step 3 by going to the Windows Control Panel, clicking on Internet Options, clicking on the Programs tab, and choosing the desired newsreader from the Default Newsreader drop-down list.

Creating a News Account

Just like sending and receiving e-mail, you need to have an account from which to post and read newsgroup messages. Most public newsgroups are hosted by Usenet, but you have to go through a special server (sometimes called an NNTP server) to access them. Many ISPs (Internet Service Providers) include news server access at no additional cost to you.

NOTE

The examples in this book use the services provided by Earthlink, a popular national ISP. Your information may vary slightly depending on which service you use.

Before you begin, you'll need to know the name of the newsgroup server you're accessing. You also need to know whether the server requires you to log in (meaning you'll need an account name and password, which is likely), and whether it requires you to log in using SPA (Secure Password Authentication, a security feature). Check with your service provider or visit its Web site to find the answers.

NOTE

If you don't have any free access, you may want to consider subscribing to a commercial news service. A paid subscription can range between $5 to $20 per month. Alternatively, you can always access newsgroups for free via your Web browser at sites like http://www .usenet.com, but you must work directly in your Web browser, which is not very conducive to newsgroup usage.

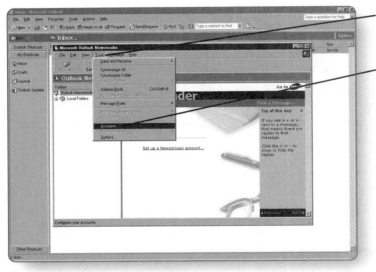

1. Click on **Tools**. The Tools menu will appear.

2. Click on **Accounts**. The Internet Accounts dialog box will open, and a list of any current accounts or directory services will appear.

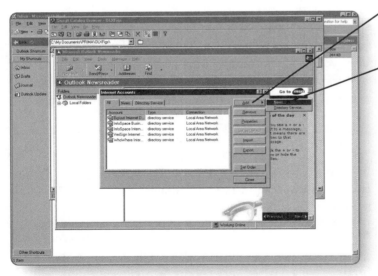

3. Click on **Add**. A small shortcut menu will appear.

4. Click on **News**. The Internet Connection Wizard will open.

NOTE

The next several steps closely resemble those for setting up an e-mail account in Outlook, as you did in Chapter 6, "Creating New Messages." Just remember that you are now working in a separate application, setting up a different type of account, and accessing a different type of server.

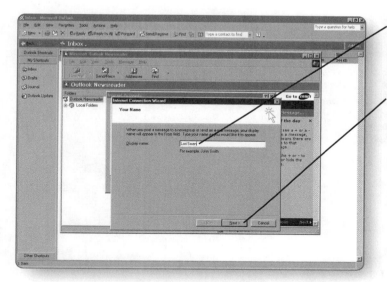

5. Type your **name**. Whatever you enter here is what will appear on your postings.

6. Click on **Next**. The wizard will progress to the next step.

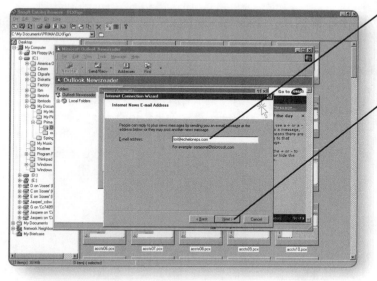

7. Type your **e-mail address**. This is the address to which people can send replies to your postings.

8. Click on **Next**. The wizard will progress to the next step.

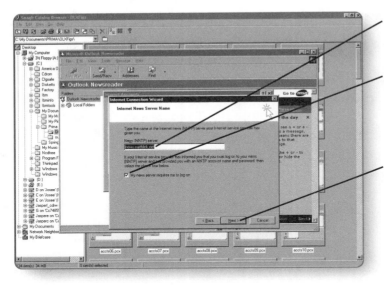

9. **Type** the **newsgroup server name** to which you have access.

10. **Click** on **My news server requires me to log on**, if applicable. The option will be selected.

11. **Click** on **Next**. The wizard will progress to the next step.

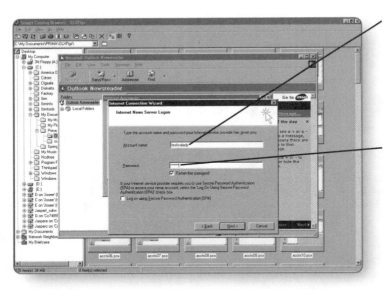

12. **Type** your **account name** as provided by your news service.

13. **Press Tab**. The cursor will move to the Password field.

14. **Type** your **password** carefully. Asterisks (*) will appear in place of your actual password, so others can't see what you type.

15. Click on **Remember password.** You will not be prompted for your password when downloading new postings.

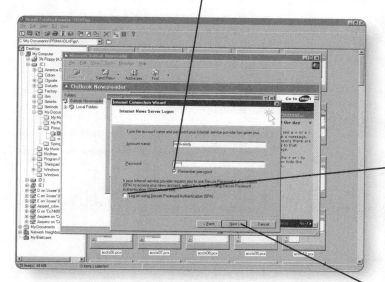

CAUTION

You should only do this if you are positive that you are the only one who accesses your computer.

16. Click on **Log on using Secure Password Authentication (SPA),** if required by your service provider. The option will be selected.

17. Click on **Next.** The wizard will progress to the next step.

18. Click on **Finish.** The wizard will close and your new account will appear in the Internet Accounts dialog box.

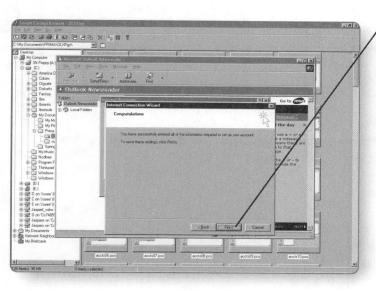

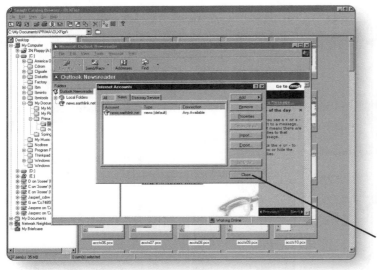

TIP

Any time you want to edit your account settings, such as changing your e-mail address or disabling the Remember Password feature, return to this dialog box, click on the account you want to edit, and click on Properties.

19. **Click** on **Close**. The Internet Accounts dialog box will close.

NOTE

After clicking Close, you might see a window inviting you to download newsgroups now. Click Yes to download newsgroups or click No and follow the next section to subscribe to newsgroups.

Subscribing to Newsgroups

Now that you have the account established, you can finally get up there and see what all the fuss is about. Without further ado, let's jump right in.

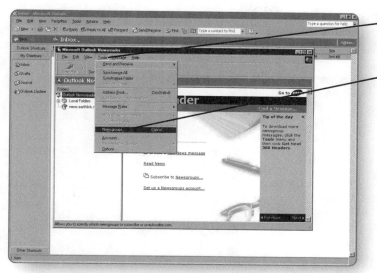

1. **Click** on **Tools**. The Tools menu will appear.

2. **Click** on **Newsgroups**. The Newsgroups Subscriptions dialog box will open.

TIP

Alternatively, just click on the Newsgroups button on the toolbar.

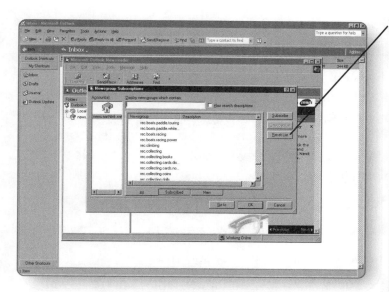

3. **Click** on **Reset List**. Outlook will download the most current list of available newsgroups.

NOTE

Not every ISP carries every available newsgroup. Some, for example, do not allow access to adults-only newsgroups. Regardless of the source, there will still be literally thousands and thousands of lists from which you can choose. Thus, downloading the list of groups may take several minutes, especially the first time.

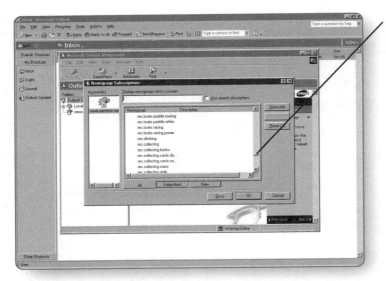

4. **Click** on the **scroll box** and **drag downward**. You will notice all the different types of newsgroups available.

What are all these abbreviations?

It's not always possible to tell much about a newsgroup by its name, but sometimes it may be blatantly obvious. You can, however, get a clue by the way in which the newsgroup is categorized. A newsgroup that begins with the prefix sci, for example, is likely to be about a science topic; comp is about computers. Following are the most common newsgroup categories. Note that not all newsgroups follow this structure, but most do.

- **alt. (alternative).** Just about anything, from UFOs to sex.
- **news. (news).** Discussions about the Usenet news network and software.
- **rec. (recreation).** Games, hobbies, music, sports, and the like.
- **biz. (business).** Business products, services, enhancements, and reviews.

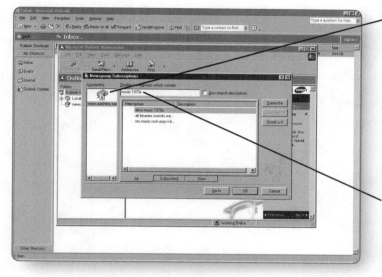

1. **Click** on the **server name** to which you want to subscribe. The name will be highlighted.

2. **Click** in the **edit box** below Display newsgroups which contain. The cursor will appear in the edit box.

3. **Type** a **keyword** that describes a subject of interest. The word you type will appear in the edit box, and the list of newsgroups will change to include only groups that include that word in the name.

- **comp. (computers).** Hardware, software, languages, and consumer advice.
- **k12. (k through 12).** Topics related to education.
- **soc. (society).** Social and cultural issues and people.
- **humanities. (humanities).** Literature, fine arts, and similar topics.
- **misc. (miscellaneous).** Miscellaneous discussions covering such diverse topics as employment, children, health, and consumer issues.
- **talk. (talk).** Discussions and debates about current issues and more.
- **sci. (science).** Pure- and applied-sciences discussions.
- **Regional.** Some prefixes represent newsgroups that relate to particular countries or regions of the world, such as de. for Germany or uk. for the United Kingdom.

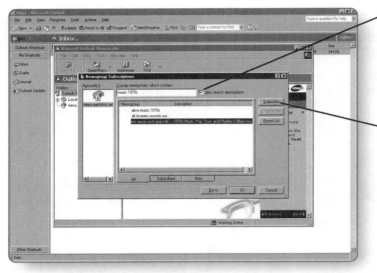

4. Click on **Also search descriptions** (optional). Outlook will display all newsgroups whose names or descriptions contain the keyword.

5. Click on **Subscribe**. An icon will appear next to the newsgroup name, indicating you have subscribed to it.

NOTE

You can only use step 4 if you downloaded the descriptions with the newsgroups list, which is not the default action. To tell Outlook to always download both newsgroup names and descriptions, click on Tools, Accounts, and then double-click on the appropriate account name. Click on the Advanced tab in the Properties dialog box that opens, and click on the check box to enable the Use newsgroup descriptions option. Click on OK to close the dialog box, and then click on Close. Then open the Newsgroups Subscriptions dialog box again and click on Reset List.

This procedure will take even longer than the first download, but when complete, you'll have a better feel for what some of the newsgroups are all about.

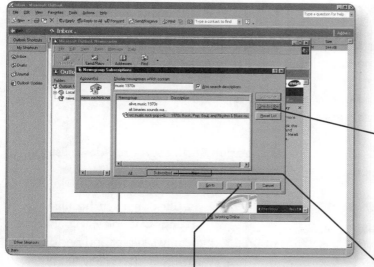

6. Click on **Unsubscribe**. The icon will disappear, and you will no longer be subscribed.

7. Repeat step 5 for whatever newsgroups you want to try.

8. Click on the **Subscribed tab**. Outlook will display only the newsgroups to which you are currently subscribed.

9. Click on **OK**. The Newsgroup Subscriptions dialog box will close and your list of newsgroups will appear in the Information viewer.

Downloading Newsgroup Messages

Now that you have established some groups of interest, it's time to see what they're talking about in these forums.

1. **Right-click** on a **newsgroup**. The group name will be highlighted.

2. **Click** on **Synchronization Settings**. A drop-down list will appear.

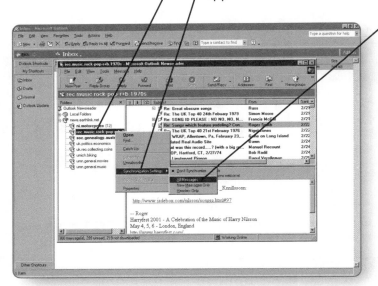

3. **Click** on a **synchronization setting**. Outlook will connect to the news server and perform the download according to your settings:

- **Don't Synchronize**. Choose this option if you don't want to download any messages for this group at this time.

- **All Messages**. Download all messages currently posted to the group.

- **New Messages Only**. Download only the messages that have been posted since your last download.

- **Headers Only**. Use this option to download the subject lines of the newsgroup messages. The full text of the message will not be downloaded until you actually view the message (a big time-saver if you subscribe to a lot of lists).

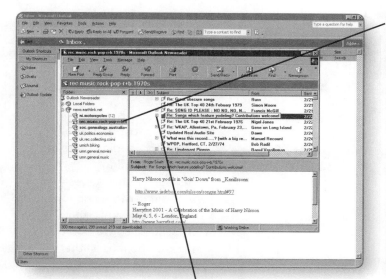

4. **Double-click** on a **newsgroup folder name**. The contents of the folder will appear in the Information viewer.

NOTE

On your first viewing, there will likely be dozens if not hundreds of new messages. Like the main Outlook interface, new and unread messages will be shown in bold.

5. **Click** on a **+ button** next to a message to see all the replies in a thread.

NOTE

A *thread* is another name for a group of messages on the same topic. The Outlook Newsreader groups threads together by default so you can easily follow one conversation at a time without having to pick through unrelated replies.

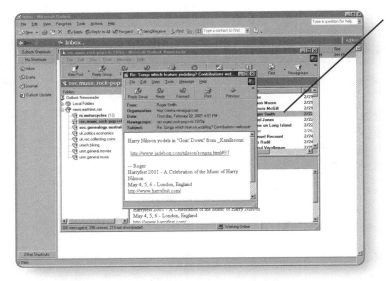

6. Double-click on a **message** you want to read. The message will open in a new window.

NOTE

For the most part, the steps for reading, replying to, and creating newsgroup messages are very similar to those for regular Outlook e-mail messages, so we don't need to go into all that again! If you need help with those procedures, see Chapters 4, 5, and 6.

TIP

If you send the URL of a newsgroup to someone in an e-mail message, Outlook will open the default newsreader automatically when the reader clicks on the link.

Part II Review Questions

1. When sending an e-mail to multiple recipients, what character must you type in between the addresses? *See "Addressing an E-mail Message" in Chapter 6*

2. What are message flags and why are they used? *See "Using Message Flags" in Chapter 6*

3. Does resending a message remove the original message from the recipient's Inbox? *See "Resending a Message" in Chapter 7*

4. Can a message reply be sent to someone other than the sender? *See "Sending Replies to Another Individual" in Chapter 7*

5. Name three ways you can respond to an e-mail message. *See "Responding to E-mail Messages" in Chapter 8*

6. What key must be pressed in order to move multiple messages at the same time? *See "Organizing Messages in Folders" in Chapter 9*

7. What is spamming? *See "Controlling Junk and Adult-Content Mail" in Chapter 9*

8. What feature does Outlook provide to assist you in locating certain messages? *See "Finding Messages" in Chapter 9*

9. What are Newsgroups? *See "Welcome to Newsgroups" in Chapter 10*

10. When referring to newsgroups, what is a thread? *See "Downloading Newsgroup Messages" in Chapter 10*

PART III

Scheduling with the Calendar

11

Viewing Your Calendar

When scheduling appointments, it's sometimes necessary to see what is going on around the same time period in a different calendar format. Outlook keeps your calendar of appointments and provides you with the flexibility to view your calendar in many different ways. In this chapter, you'll learn how to:

- Show different calendar views
- Use Organize to select different calendar views
- Create your own views
- Use the Date Navigator
- Move to dates in the past or future

Showing Different Calendar Views

There are three primary calendar views in Outlook: daily, weekly, and monthly. To choose any of these views, click on the corresponding toolbar button or menu command. Use views to control what appears on your screen.

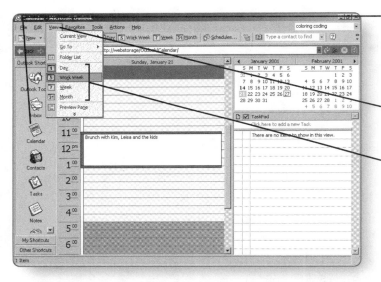

1. **Click** on the **Calendar icon** on the Outlook bar. The Outlook calendar view will show in the Information viewer.

2. **Click** on **View**. The View menu will appear.

3. **Click** on **Day, Work Week, Week, or Month**. Your calendar will change accordingly.

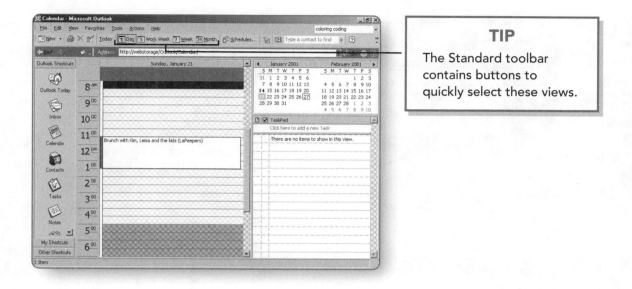

TIP

The Standard toolbar contains buttons to quickly select these views.

Using Organize to Change Views

Outlook has a feature called Organize that lets you arrange your calendar. There are two ways to organize the calendar: by categories or by views. Categories are words or phrases (such as Business or Personal) that are used to keep track of items in Outlook. Use categories to organize your Christmas card mailing list, expense-related contacts, suppliers and vendors, or other details.

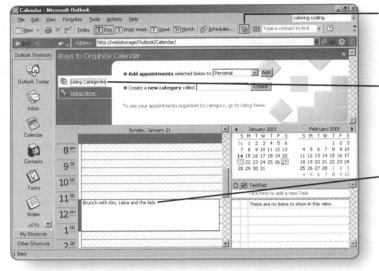

1. Click on **Organize**. The Ways to Organize Calendar pane will appear.

2. Click on **Using Categories**. The Organize pane will change, allowing you to organize your appointments by category.

3. Click on **any item(s)** in the calendar. The item(s) will appear selected.

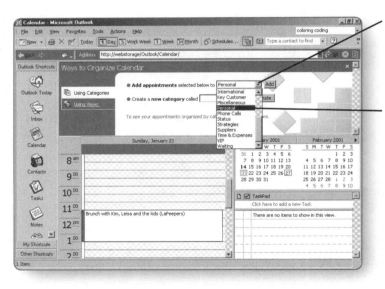

4. Click on the **down arrow** next to Add appointments selected below to. A drop-down list will appear.

5. Click on **any category** in the drop-down list. It will be highlighted.

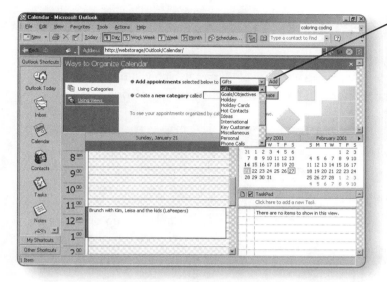

6. Click on the **Add button**. A message saying "Done!" will appear to the right of the Add button and the appointment(s) you've selected will be added to the category you chose.

Adding Categories

Outlook comes with numerous categories, but you can always add more.

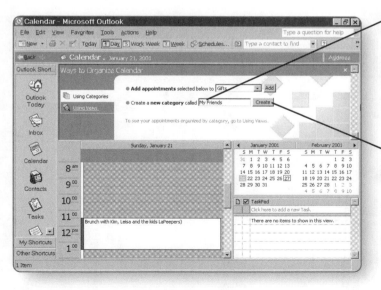

1. Click in the **text box** next to Create a new category called.

2. Type the **name** of the new category. The name will appear in the text box.

3. Click on **Create**. A message saying "Done!" will appear to the right of the Create button and your category will be created. Once this is done, you can add calendar items to the new category.

Changing Your Calendar View

By changing your calendar view, you can control the look of the calendar. Some views apply filters, which will display only certain items in the calendar, such as active appointments.

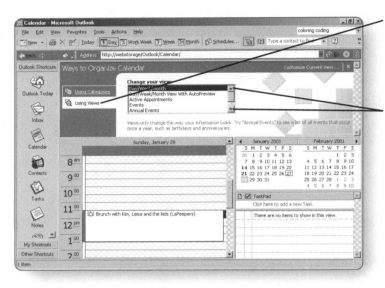

1. **Click** on **Using Views**. Your Organize pane will change, allowing you to organize your appointments visually.

2. **Click** on the **up or down arrow** to scroll through the list of views. Scroll until you find your selection.

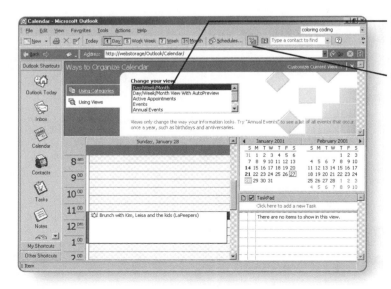

3. **Click** on **any view**. The view will change accordingly.

4. **Click** on **Organize**. The Organize pane will close.

Creating Your Own Views

If the Outlook views do not provide the options you want, you can create your own views.

1. **Click** on **View**. The View menu will appear.

2. **Click** on **Current View**. The Current View submenu will appear.

3. **Click** on **Define Views**. The Define Views for "Calendar" dialog box will open.

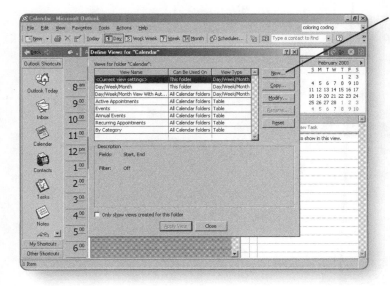

4. **Click** on **New**. The Create a New View dialog box will open.

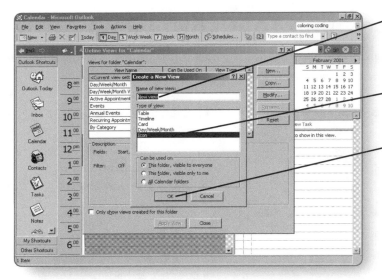

5. **Type** the **name** of the new view. The name will appear in the Name of new view: text box.

6. **Click** on a **type of view**. The view will be selected.

7. **Click** on **OK**. The View Summary dialog box will open.

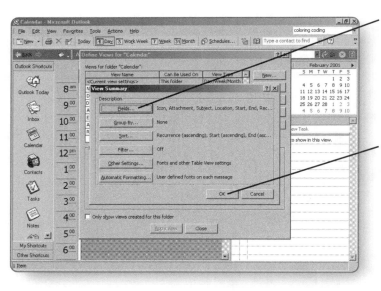

8. **Click** on the **description buttons** to choose the view settings. Adjust as many of these settings as you like. The dialog box will change to reflect your settings.

9. **Click** on **OK**. The View Summary dialog box will close.

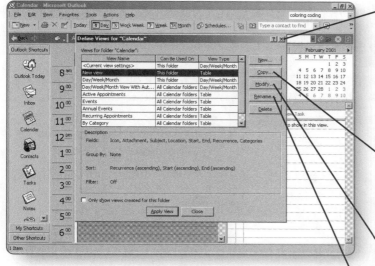

10. **Click** on the **Close button**. The Define Views for "Calendar" dialog box will close and the calendar will reappear in the Information viewer.

TIP

To copy an existing view and make changes to the copy, click on Copy and then follow the previous steps 5–10.

To change the settings for an existing view, click on Modify, and then follow the previous steps 8–10 to modify the entry.

To change the name of an existing view, click on Rename, enter the new name for the view, click on OK, and then follow the previous steps 9 and 10.

Using the Date Navigator

The Date Navigator appears in the right corner of the calendar. A red box appears around today's date, and any day with items scheduled appear in bold. You can use the Date Navigator to jump to any date in the calendar to schedule an appointment or an event.

Viewing Different Months

1. **Click** on **any date**. You will jump to the date.

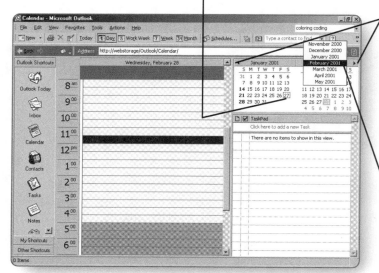

2a. **Click** on the **left or right arrow** next to the month to move backward or forward one month. The calendar will change to show the previous or following month.

OR

2b. **Click** on the **current month button** and select a new month from the pop-up list. The calendar will change to show the selected month.

Using the Date Navigator to Select a Series of Days

The Date Navigator can also be used to change the days that display on the calendar. If one of the predefined day, week, or month views doesn't fit your needs, you can use the Date Navigator to customize the days that display in the calendar.

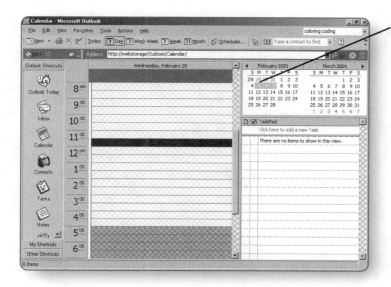

1. Click on the **beginning date** in the Date Navigator. The date will be selected.

2. Press and hold the **Shift key** and **click** on the **ending date** in the Date Navigator. All dates from the initial date to the ending date will be selected, and you will see those days in the Information viewer.

TIP

You can also drag your mouse across the consecutive dates you wish to view. Your viewing window will display up to 14 days.

Using the Date Navigator to Select Non-Contiguous Days

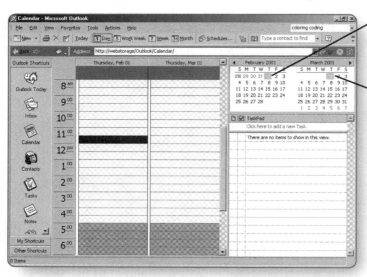

1. **Click** on the **beginning date** in the Date Navigator. It will be selected.

2. **Press and hold** the **Ctrl key** and **click** on **non-contiguous** days in the calendar. Only those days will be selected.

Going to a Specific Date

If the date you want doesn't appear in the Date Navigator, you can use the Go to Date feature to display it. Go to Date can also be used when you do not know the exact calendar date, but you know that it occurs three weeks from today or on a certain holiday.

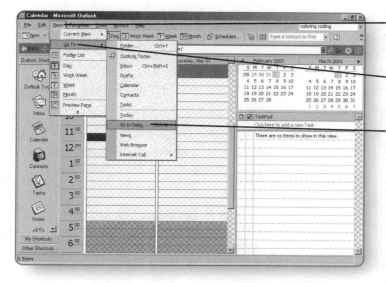

1. **Click** on **View**. The View menu will appear.

2. **Click** on **Go To**. The Go To submenu will appear.

3. **Click** on **Go to Date**. The Go To Date dialog box will open.

NOTE

You may need to expand the menu to see the Go to Date command.

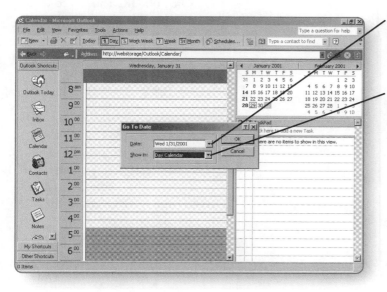

4. **Click** on the **down arrow** to the right of the Date: list box and select a particular date.

5. **Click** on the **down arrow** to the right of the Show in: list box and select a view.

If you don't know the particular date, there are numerous phrases you can type in the Date: list box on the Go to Date dialog box. Here are a few you might find helpful:

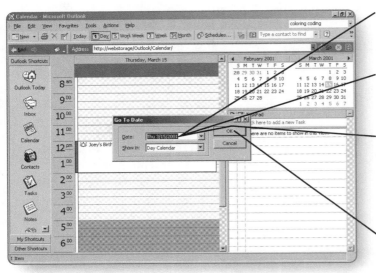

- **Dates**. You can type "5 weeks from today," "1st week in September," or "3 wks ago."

- **Description of Dates**. You can type "now," "today," "yesterday," or "last week."

- **Holidays**. You can type the name of any holiday recorded in Outlook, such as President's Day, Boxing Day, or Cinco de Mayo.

6. **Click** on **OK**. The Go to Date dialog box will close and you will return to the Calendar.

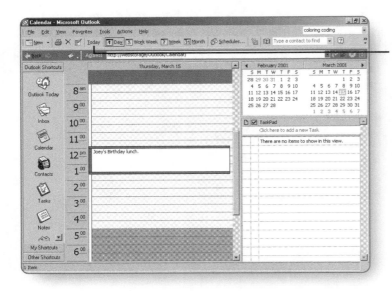

TIP

After using the Date Navigator, you may need to return to today's date. Click on the Today button to return the calendar to the current date.

12

Scheduling Appointments

It's difficult to remember and keep track of all the appointments and obligations on your calendar. When you use Outlook to manage your appointments, you can keep them all in one location and quickly edit or delete them, should the appointment be changed or canceled. In this chapter, you'll learn how to:

- Create an appointment
- Set up a reminder
- Move an appointment to a different date or time
- Schedule a recurring appointment
- Delete an appointment

Creating an Appointment

Scheduling an appointment in Outlook is simple. Just follow these easy steps.

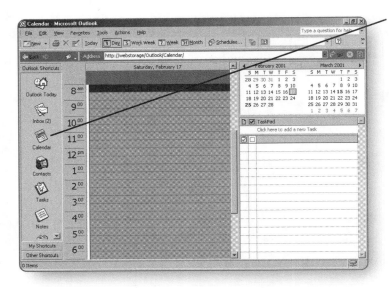

1. **Click** on the **Calendar icon** on the Outlook bar. The Calendar will appear in the Information viewer.

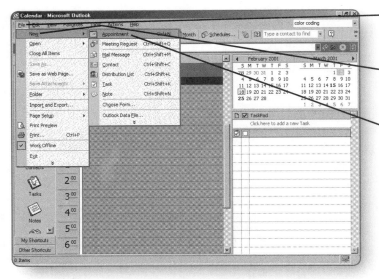

2. **Click** on **File**. The File menu will appear.

3. **Click** on **New**. The New submenu will appear.

4. **Click** on **Appointment**. The Appointment dialog box will open.

5. **Click** in the **Subject: text box**.

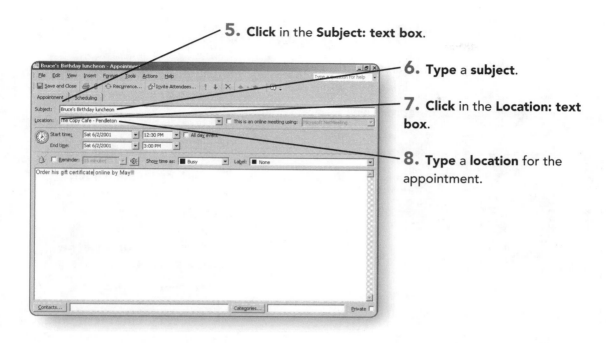

6. **Type** a **subject**.

7. **Click** in the **Location: text box**.

8. **Type** a **location** for the appointment.

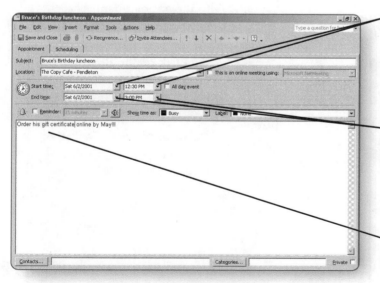

9. **Click** on the **down arrows** next to the Start time: list boxes and click on a starting date and time. A date and time will be selected.

10. **Click** on the **down arrows** next to the End time: list boxes and click on an ending date and time. An end time will be selected.

11. **Click** on the **notes section** and **begin typing** to add any notes or comments related to the appointment. The notes will appear in the window.

Setting a Reminder

A reminder is a great way to guarantee that you won't miss any important appointments. Once a reminder is activated, you can dismiss the reminder or click on the Snooze button and have the reminder pop up again later.

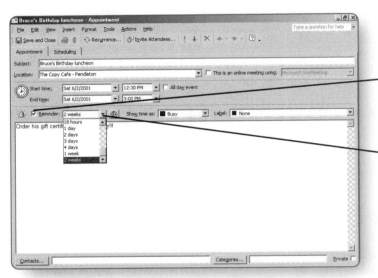

1. **Click** on the **Reminder: check box**. A check mark will be placed in the box.

2. **Click** on the **down arrow** next to Reminder. A list of times will appear.

3. **Select** the **amount of time** the reminder should appear prior to the appointment. The reminder will be selected.

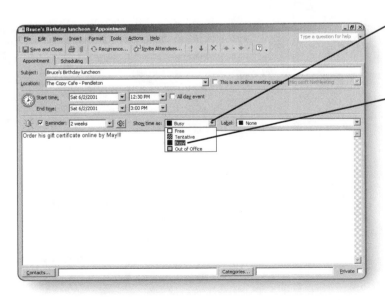

4. **Click** on the **down arrow** next to the Show time as: list box. A list of options will appear.

5. **Click** on **Free**, **Tentative**, **Busy**, or **Out of Office**. The choice will be selected.

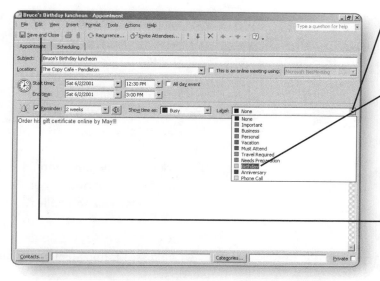

6. Click on the **down arrow** next to the Label: list box. A list of options will appear.

7. Click on a **color-coded category**. Your selection will attach the category to your appointment. The color choice assigned to that category will appear in your calendar.

8. Click on **Save and Close**. The appointment will be saved and closed.

Optimizing Your Calendar Options

Other calendar options are easily modified to suit your needs. Changes to the appearance and settings of your calendar can be done with these simple steps.

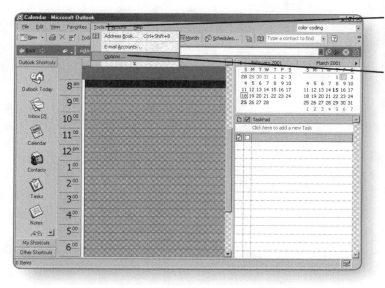

1. Click on **Tools**. The Tools dialog box will appear.

2. Click on **Options**. The Options dialog box will open.

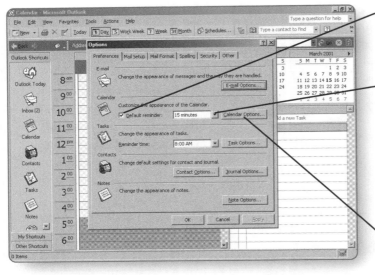

3. **Click** on **Default Reminder**. A check mark will appear in the option box.

4. **Click** on the **down arrow** next to the Default reminder. A drop-down list will appear.

5. **Click** on a **time selection**. The selection will appear. Your default settings will be applied.

6. **Click** on **Calendar Options**. The Calendar Options dialog box will open.

7. **Click** on the **days** you want to appear in your Work Week view. A check mark will appear.

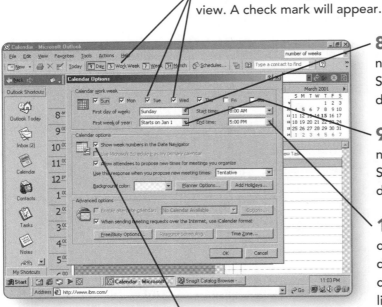

8. **Click** on the **down arrow** next to the First day of week. Select your choice from the drop-down list.

9. **Click** on the **down arrow** next to the First week of year. Select your preference from the drop-down list.

10. **Click** on the **down arrows** of the Start time and End time drop-down list. Select your choices from the drop-down lists.

11. **Click** on the **check box** next to Show week numbers in the Date Navigator. Week numbers will appear in the Date Navigator.

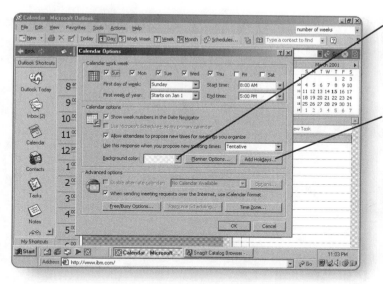

12. **Click** on the **down-arrow** next to Background color. Select your preferred color; the color will appear.

13. **Click** on **Add Holidays** if you would like for specified Holidays to be posted automatically to your calendar view. The Add Holidays to Calendar dialog box will open.

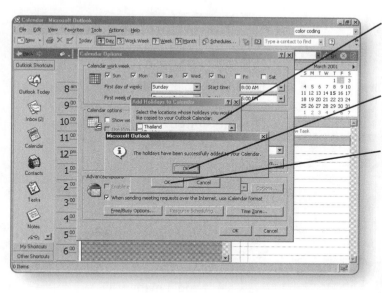

14. **Click** on **your selection** in the Add Holidays to Calendar dialog box.

15. **Click** on **OK**. Your changes will be accepted.

16. **Click** on **OK**. The Calendar Options dialog box will close.

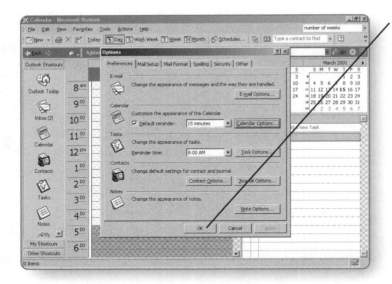

17. **Click** on **OK**. The Options dialog box will close.

Moving the Appointment to a Different Date

Once you have scheduled an appointment, it's easy to change the day of the appointment. Appointments can be dragged to any day on the Date Navigator to reschedule the appointment.

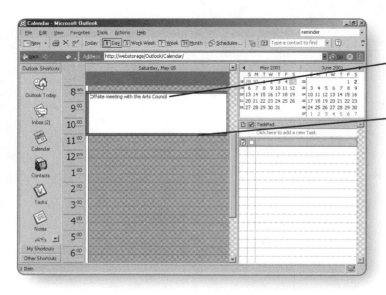

1. **Click** on the **appointment** in the calendar. It will be selected.

2. **Drag** the **appointment** by its border to another day in the Date Navigator. The appointment will be rescheduled.

Changing Appointment Times

You can change the appointment time by dragging the appointment boundaries on the calendar.

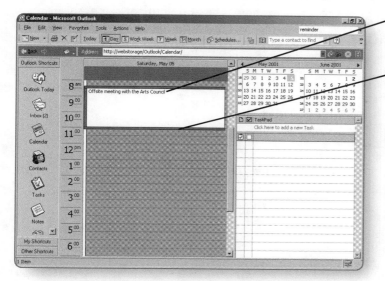

1. **Click** on the **appointment** in the calendar. It will be selected.

2. **Move** the **mouse pointer** over the top or bottom border of the appointment. The mouse pointer will change to a double-headed arrow.

3. **Click** and **drag** either **border** to increase or decrease the length of the appointment. The appointment will be changed.

TIP

You can change the starting and ending times of the appointment by placing the mouse pointer over the left border of the appointment. The pointer changes to a four-sided arrow, and you can click and drag the appointment to a different time.

NOTE

Another way to change the date, time, or duration of an appointment is to double-click on the appointment. When the appointment window opens, make the necessary changes, and then save and close the appointment.

Scheduling a Recurring Appointment

A recurring appointment is an appointment that occurs more than once at a regular time. The appointment can occur every day, week, month, or year. Outlook even lets you designate how the appointment occurs (for example, the first Thursday of every month or the 15th of every month).

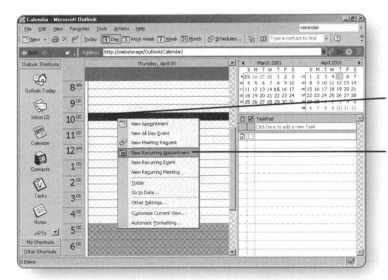

1. **Right-click** on the **calendar**. A shortcut menu will appear.

2. **Click** on **New Recurring Appointment**. The Appointment Recurrence dialog box will open.

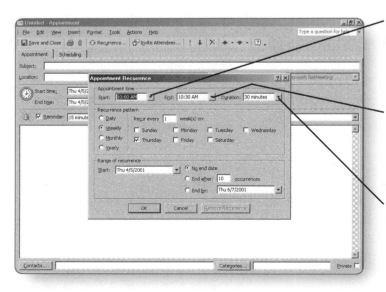

3. **Click** on the **down arrow** to the right of the Start: list box and click on a start time. The starting time will be selected.

4. **Click** on the **down arrow** to the right of the End: list box and click on an ending time. The ending time will be selected.

5. **Click** on the **down arrow** to the right of the Duration: list box and click on a duration. The duration will be indicated.

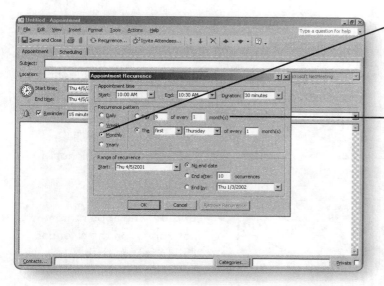

6. Click on one of the four **Recurrence pattern option buttons**. The option will be selected.

7. Click on the **options** to the right of the recurrence pattern to establish the pattern. The pattern will be selected.

NOTE

The options next to the recurrence pattern changes depending on the recurrence pattern that you select. Your screen may not look like the figure if you have selected a different recurrence pattern.

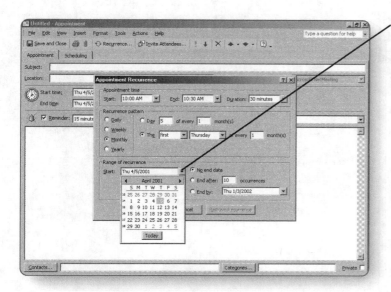

8. Click on the **down arrow** to the right of the Start: list box to establish the beginning range of recurrence.

There are several options for ending the appointment. They are:

- **No end date**. The appointment will be repeated indefinitely on the calendar.

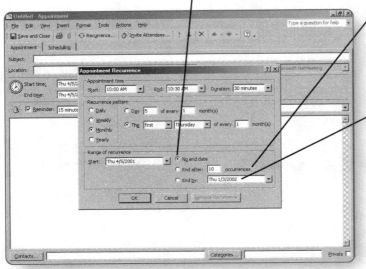

- **End after "x" occurrences**. The appointment will be repeated on the calendar for a specific number of occurrences.

- **End by**. The appointment will not appear on the calendar after a certain date.

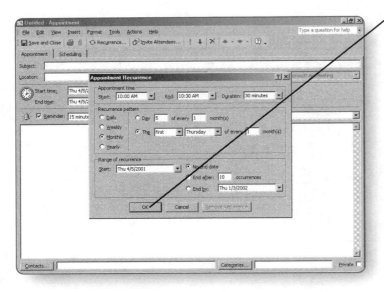

9. Click on **OK**. The Appointment Recurrence dialog box will close.

You can now follow the same steps that you followed earlier to fill in the Appointment window. Remember to save and close the appointment when you are finished.

Deleting an Appointment

If an appointment is canceled, it's important to delete the appointment from your calendar. If you work with others who may be viewing your calendar to schedule a meeting, it's best to delete appointments as soon as possible.

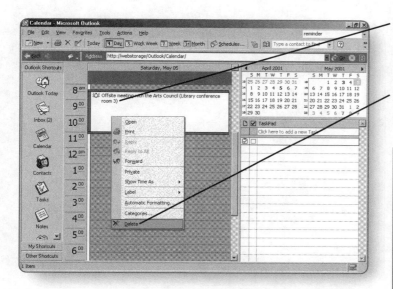

1. **Right-click** on the **appointment** in the calendar. A shortcut menu will appear.

2. **Click** on **Delete**. The appointment will be deleted.

NOTE

If you are deleting a recurring appointment, a message will ask if you want to delete all occurrences of the appointment or just the one occurrence.

13

Planning an Event

You have already learned how to schedule appointments. *Events* are special types of appointments that last 24 hours or more. Events are a great way to record such calendar items as birthdays, anniversaries, trade shows, or vacations. In this chapter, you'll learn how to:

- Create an event
- View and modify an event
- Schedule a recurring event
- Edit a recurring event
- Delete a recurring event

Creating an Event

Events can be split into two categories: an annual event or a standard event. An anniversary is a perfect example of an annual event. It occurs on a particular day and it lasts all day. An example of a standard event is a seminar. A seminar can last one or several days. Events can be added to the calendar as easily as appointments.

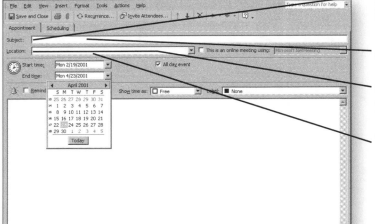

1. **Click** on the **Calendar icon** on the Outlook bar. The contents of your Calendar will appear in the Information viewer.

2. **Right-click** on the **daily appointment area** of the calendar. A shortcut menu will appear.

3. **Click** on **New All Day Event**. The Event window will appear.

4. **Click** in the **Subject: text box**.

5. **Type** a **subject**.

6. **Click** in the **Location: text box**.

7. **Type** a **location**.

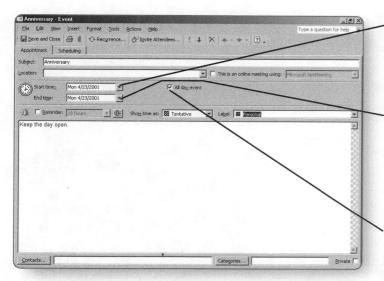

8. Click on the **down arrow** to the right of the Start time list box and select a starting date. The start date will be selected.

9. Click on the **down arrow** to the right of the End time list box and select an ending date. An ending date will be selected.

NOTE

The All day event check box is automatically selected for events. If you remove the check mark from the All day event check box, the event will automatically be changed to an appointment.

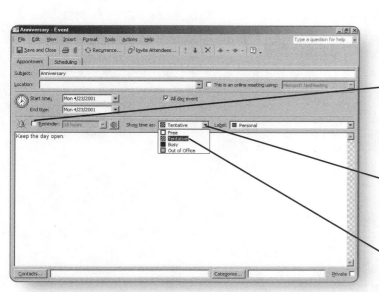

10. Click on the **Reminder check box** to set a reminder. A check mark will be placed in the box.

11. Click on the **down arrow** to the right of the Show time as: list box. A list of options will appear.

12. Click on **Free**, **Tentative**, **Busy**, or **Out of Office**. The choice will be selected.

NOTE

By default, events appear as free time on your calendar, while appointments appear as busy time.

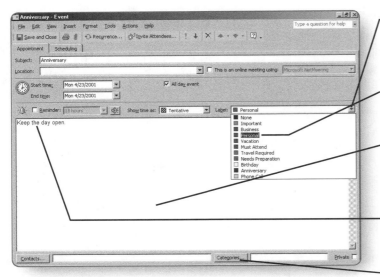

13. Click on the **down arrow** to the right of the Label: list box. A list of options will appear.

14. Click on a **label**. Your choice will be selected.

15. Click in the **text area**. An insertion point will be in the text area.

16. Type any **notes** regarding the event.

17. Click on the **Categories button** and add categories to the event, if desired. The categories will be selected.

18. Click on the **Save and Close button**. The event will be scheduled.

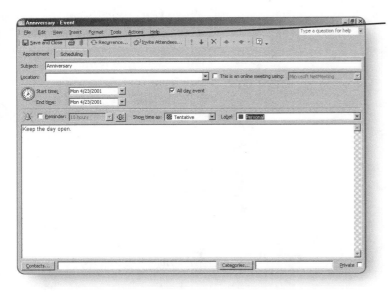

Viewing and Modifying Events

Events do not always appear in the same area as appointments. In Day view, they appear in the banner area, underneath the date. If you are in a monthly view, a shaded box surrounds events.

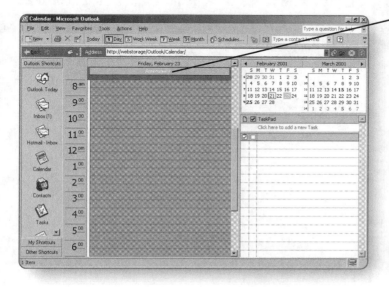

1. Click twice on the **event**. The Event window will appear.

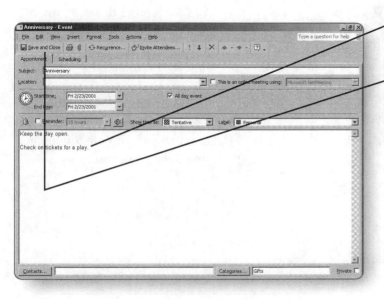

2. Type any **changes** to modify the event. The text will appear.

3. Click on the **Save and Close button**. Your changes will be saved and the Event window will close.

Scheduling a Recurring Event

An annual event, such as a birthday, is an example of a recurring event. Events can recur daily, weekly, monthly, or yearly.

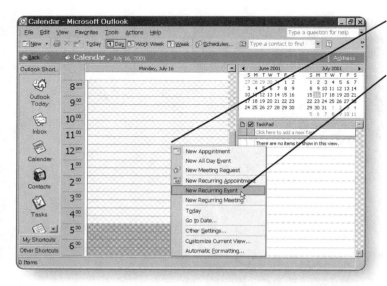

1. **Right-click** on the **calendar**. A shortcut menu will appear.

2. **Click** on **New Recurring Event**. The Appointment Recurrence dialog box will open.

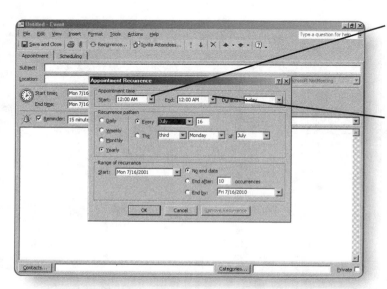

3. **Click** on the **down arrow** to the right of the Start: list box and select a start time. A start time will be selected.

4. **Click** on the **down arrow** to the right of the End: list box and select an ending time. An ending time will be selected.

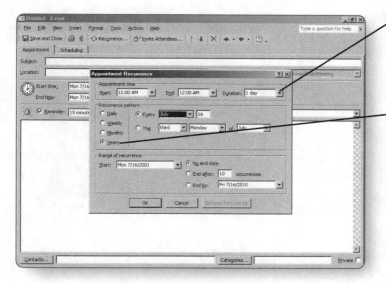

5. Click on the **down arrow** to the right of the Duration: list box and select a duration. A duration will be selected.

6. Click on **one of the four recurrence patterns**. A recurrence pattern will be chosen.

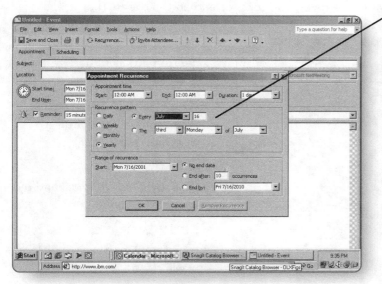

7. Click on the **options** to the right of the recurrence pattern to establish the pattern. An option will be selected.

NOTE

The windows next to the recurrence pattern change depending on the recurrence pattern selected. Your screen may not look like the figure if you have selected a different recurrence pattern.

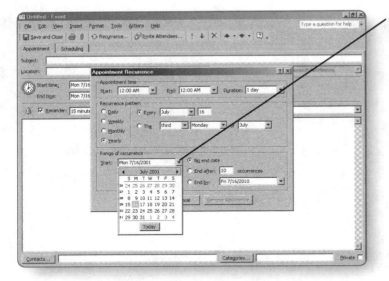

8. Click on the **down arrow** to the right of the Start: list box to establish the beginning range of recurrence.

There are several options for ending the event. They are:

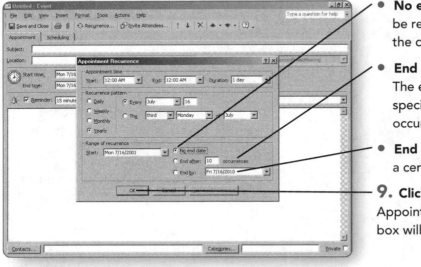

- **No end date**. The event will be repeated indefinitely on the calendar.

- **End after "x" occurrences**. The event will end after a specified number of occurrences.

- **End by**. The event will end by a certain date.

9. Click on **OK**. The Appointment Recurrence dialog box will close.

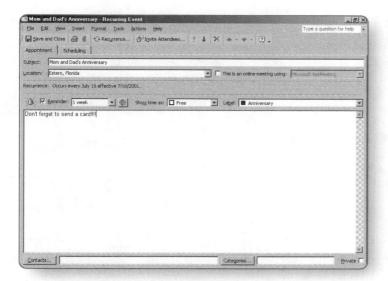

You can follow the same steps you followed earlier to fill in the Event window. Remember to save and close the event when you are finished.

NOTE
Recurring events are indicated on the calendar with a circular arrow icon.

Editing a Recurring Event

After an event has been scheduled, you may find that you need to make changes to a single instance of the event, or to the entire series. Outlook allows you to edit the event and to change the recurrence pattern.

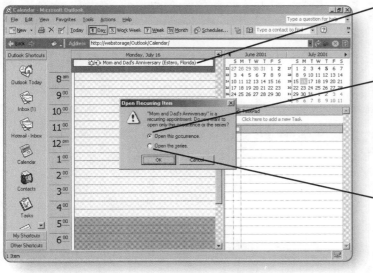

1. **Click twice** on the **event**. The Open Recurring Item dialog box will open.

2a. **Click** on the **Open this occurrence option button** to edit a single occurrence of the event. The option will be selected.

OR

2b. **Click** on the **Open the series option button** to edit the series of recurring events. The option will be selected.

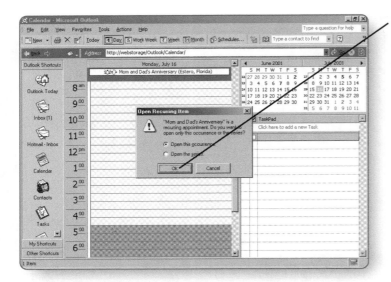

3. Click on **OK**. Either that occurrence of the event or the entire series will open, depending on your choice in step 2.

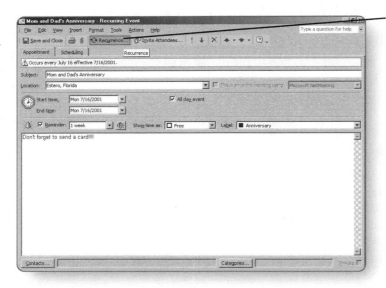

4. Click on the **Recurrence button** to change the recurrence pattern of the series. The Appointment Recurrence dialog box will open.

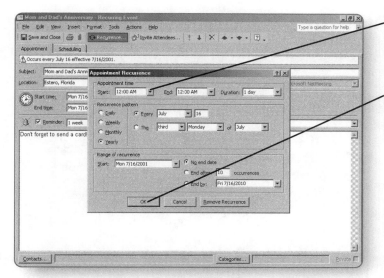

5. Type any **changes** to the recurrence pattern. The changes will be made.

6. Click on **OK**. The Appointment Recurrence dialog box will close.

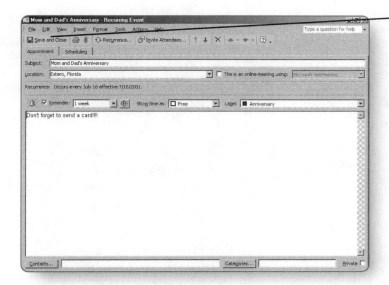

7. Click on the **Save and Close button**. Your changes will be saved and the window will close.

Deleting Recurring Events

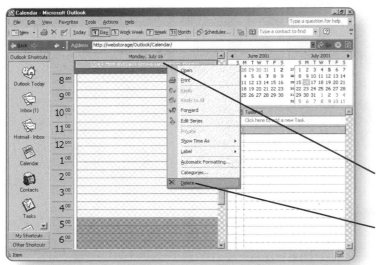

Once an event has been scheduled, you may have reason to delete the event. Do you have to search through the entire calendar, deleting each event? Of course not! Outlook can easily handle the situation for you.

1. Right-click on the **event**. A shortcut menu will appear.

2. Click on **Delete**. The Confirm Delete dialog box will open.

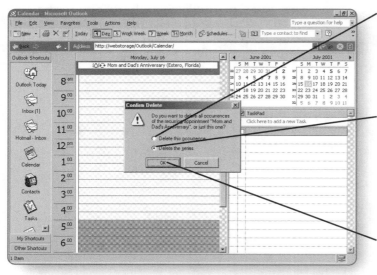

3b. Click on the **Delete this occurrence option button** to delete the one selected instance of the event. The option will be selected.

3a. Click on the **Delete the series option button** to delete all instances of the event. The option will be selected.

OR

4. Click on **OK**. Either this single event or every recurrence of it will be deleted, depending on the option you chose in step 3. The Confirm Delete dialog box will close.

14

Requesting a Meeting

Have you ever tried to coordinate a meeting with several people? Normally, several calls or e-mails fly back and forth before you can find a time that is convenient for everyone. If you are using Outlook on a network, you can use some powerful tools that are included in the program to take all of the hassle out of scheduling a meeting. In this chapter, you'll learn how to:

- Plan, reschedule, or cancel a meeting
- Create or respond to a new meeting request
- Include resources in the meeting request
- Schedule a recurring meeting
- Turn an appointment into a meeting

Planning a Meeting

The most difficult part of scheduling a meeting is finding a time when everyone can attend. You can use the Plan a Meeting feature to quickly determine the best time for the meeting.

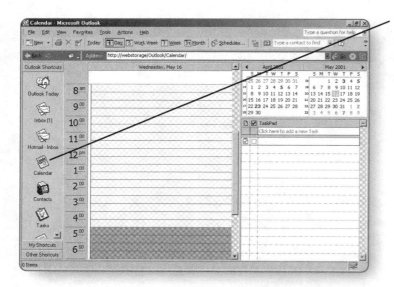

1. **Click** on the **Calendar icon** on the Outlook bar. The contents of your calendar will appear in the Information viewer.

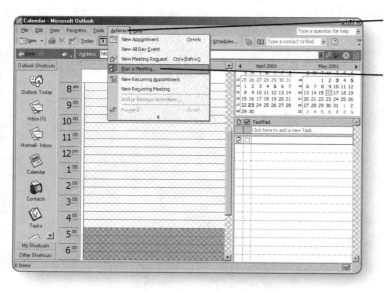

2. **Click** on **Actions**. The Actions menu will appear.

3. **Click** on **Plan a Meeting**. The Plan a Meeting dialog box will open.

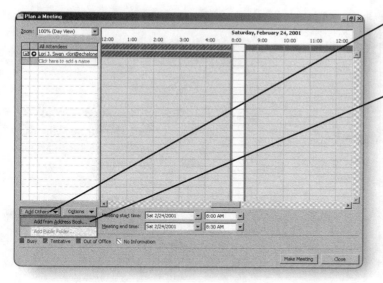

4. **Click** on the **Add Others button**. A pop-up menu will appear.

5. **Click** on **Add from Address Book**. The Select Attendees and Resources dialog box will open.

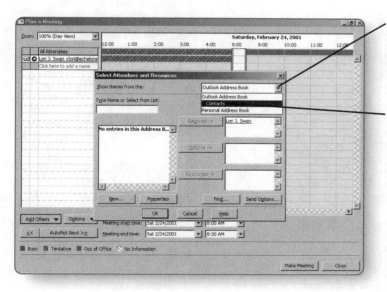

6. **Click** on the **down arrow** to the right of the Show Names from the: list box. A drop-down window will appear.

7. **Select** the **folder** that contains the names of your attendees. The names will appear.

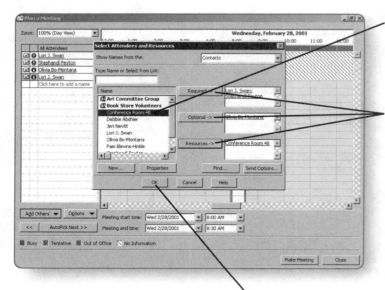

8. Click on a **name** in the address list to select the individual. The individual will be selected.

9. Click on **Required**, **Optional**, or **Resources**. The name will appear in the appropriate list.

NOTE

A resource can be a conference room or a piece of audiovisual equipment. If selected, resources will appear in the Location text box in the Meeting Request. The people who are required or optional will appear in the To line of the meeting request.

---

10. Click on **OK**. The dialog box will close.

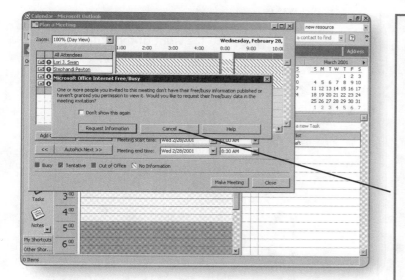

NOTE

If you have not previously used the Microsoft Office Internet Free/Busy Service, Outlook will prompt you to sign up. This feature is particularly useful when you need to compare your busy schedule with others who are not on your Microsoft Exchange network. For now, **click on Cancel**. A later section in this chapter will walk you through setting up and using Free/Busy.

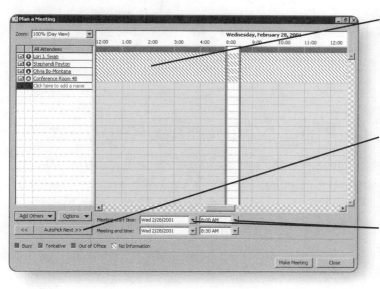

11a. **View** the **free and busy times** for each attendee. This is done manually for each attendee.

OR

11b. **Click** on the **AutoPick button**. Outlook will search for the next available free time for all attendees.

12. **Click** on the **down arrows** to the right of the Meeting start time: list box and select a starting date and time.

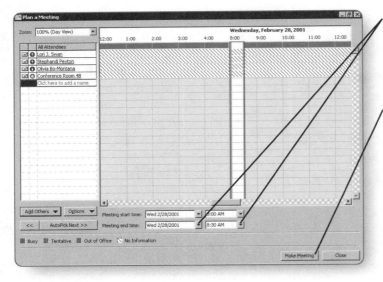

13. **Click** on the **down arrows** to the right of the Meeting end time: list box and select an ending date and time.

14. **Click** on the **Make Meeting button** when you have found a suitable meeting time. A new meeting request will appear.

TIP

If you don't want to use the Plan a Meeting feature, you can send a meeting request by clicking on the Calendar icon and then clicking on Actions, New Meeting Request.

Creating a Meeting Request

Now that you've planned your meeting, it's time to invite everyone. A meeting request is a lot like an e-mail message, but it has the added advantage of coordinating with the calendar.

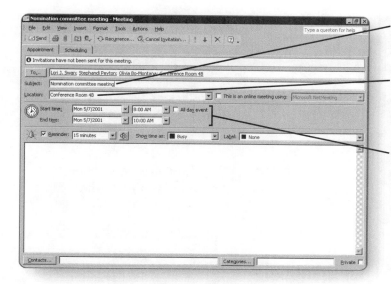

1. **Type** a **subject** for the meeting in the Subject: text box.

2. **Type** a **location** for the meeting in the Location: text box.

3. **Click** on **Start time:** and **End time:** to modify your date and time selections. The changes will appear.

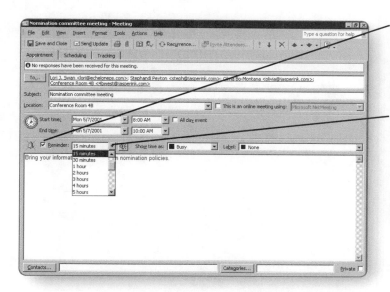

4. **Click** on the **Reminder: check box** to activate a meeting reminder. A check mark will be placed in the box.

5. **Click** on the **down arrow** next to Reminder and **select** the **amount of time** the Reminder should appear prior to the appointment. The reminder will be selected.

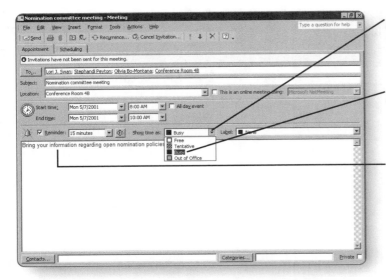

6. Click on the **down arrow** to the right of the Show time as: list box. A list of options will appear.

7. Click on **Free**, **Tentative**, **Busy**, or **Out of Office**. The choice will be selected.

8. Type any notes in the message text area. The text will appear in the text area.

TIP

Click on the Categories button if you want to add categories to the meeting request.

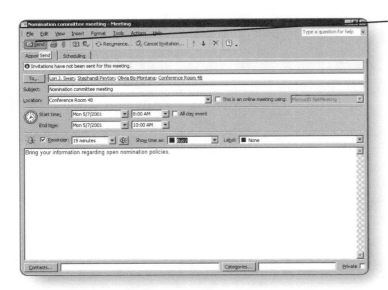

9. Click on the **Send button**. The meeting request will be sent.

Publishing Your Free/Busy Information

Calendars are automatically published to the Microsoft Exchange server but if you are not running on the Exchange server, Microsoft Outlook's Free/Busy is a server that stores a collection of calendars as well.

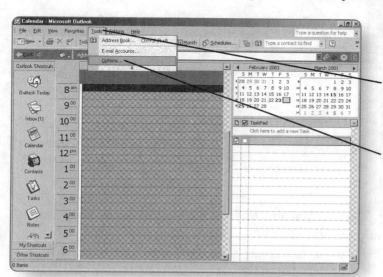

1. Click on **Tools**. A drop-down list will appear.

2. Click on **Options**. The Calendar Options dialog box will appear.

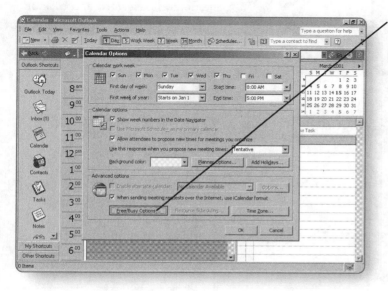

3. Click on **Free/Busy Options**. The Free/Busy dialog box will appear.

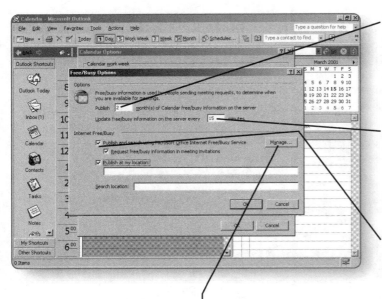

4. **Click** in the **Publish box** and **type** the **number of months** of free/busy information you wish to display. The number will appear.

5. **Click** in the **Minutes box** and **type** the **number of minutes** you would like Outlook to update your information. Your selection between 1 and 99 will appear.

6. **Click** on **Publish and search using Microsoft Office Internet Free/Busy Service**. A check mark will appear.

7. **Click** on **Manage**. Internet Explorer will launch and your Internet connection will be established (if needed). The Microsoft Passport Sign In page will appear in the browser.

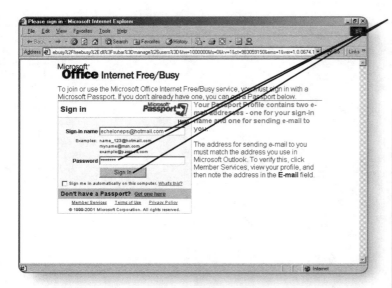

8. **Enter** your **Passport Sign-in name** and password and click on Sign In. The Terms of Use page will appear.

NOTE

If you don't already have a Microsoft Passport (required to access many of the free services Microsoft offers on its site), click on the Passport logo and follow the onscreen instructions to establish a new Passport account.

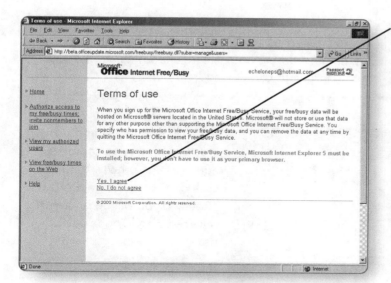

9. **Read** the **Terms of Use** agreement, and then **click** on **Yes, I agree**. The Authorize Access and Invite Nonmembers to Join page will appear.

NOTE

If you choose No, I do not agree, you won't be able to use this service.

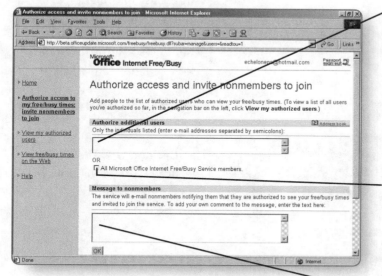

10a. **Click** in the **Authorize additional users** edit box and **type** the **e-mail addresses** of those to whom you want to grant viewing rights for your schedule. Your entries will appear in the edit box.

OR

10b. **Click** on the **check box** next to All Microsoft Office Internet Free/Busy Service members. The option will be enabled.

11. **Click** in the **Message to nonmembers** edit box and **type** your **message**, then enter the e-mail addresses of those to whom you want to send the invitation. Your entries will appear in the edit box, and the addresses you indicated will appear.

TIP

Click on the Address book link to choose names already entered into your Outlook address book.

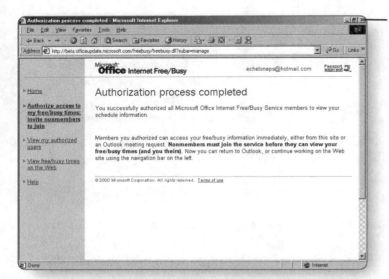

12. Complete any **additional steps necessary** to complete the authorization process, and then **click** on **Close**. The browser will close and you will be returned to the Free/Busy Options dialog box.

NOTE

If you want to publish your free/busy information to somewhere other than the Microsoft service, click on the Publish at my location: box and enter the desired pathname.

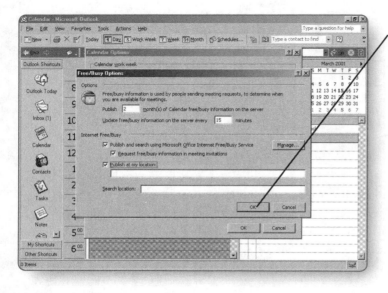

13. Click on **OK**. The Free/Busy Options window will close.

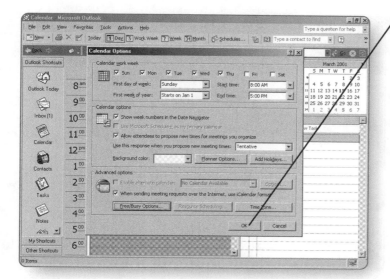

14. Click on **OK**. The Calendar Options window will close.

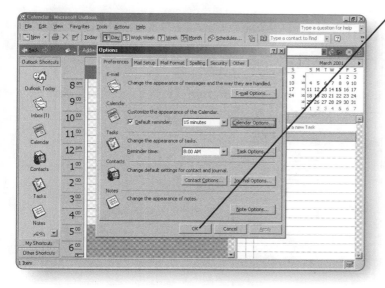

15. Click on **OK**. The Options window will close.

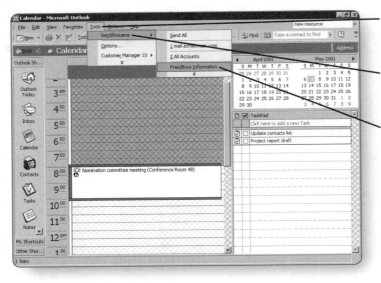

16. **Click** on **Tools**. The Tools menu will appear.

17. **Click** on **Send/Receive**. A submenu will appear.

18. **Click** on **Free/Busy Information**. Outlook will connect to the Internet and send your information.

Scheduling a Recurring Meeting

You can take any meeting and turn it into a recurring meeting. A recurring meeting can occur on any series of days, weeks, months, or years.

1. **Click** on **Actions**. The Actions menu will appear.

2. **Click** on **New Recurring Meeting**. The Appointment Recurrence dialog box will open.

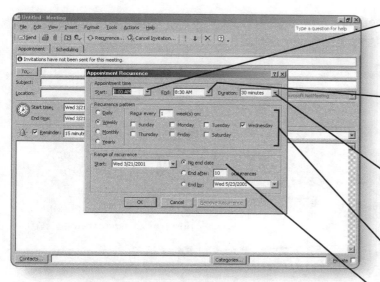

3. Click on the **down arrow** to the right of the Start: list box and select a start time.

4. Click on the **down arrow** to the right of the End: list box and select an end time.

5. Click on the **down arrow** to the right of Duration: and select a duration.

6. Click on **one of the four recurrence patterns**.

7. Click on the **options** to the right of the recurrence pattern to establish the pattern.

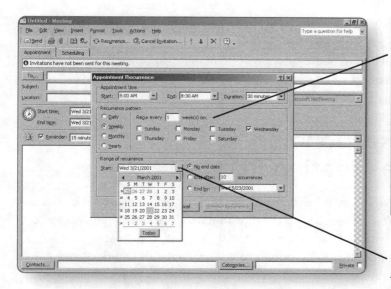

NOTE

The windows next to Recurrence pattern change depending on the recurrence pattern selected. Your screen may not look like the figure if you have selected a different recurrence pattern.

8. Click on the **down arrow** to the right of the Start: list box to establish the beginning range of recurrence.

There are several options for how the recurring meeting will appear on the calendar. They are:

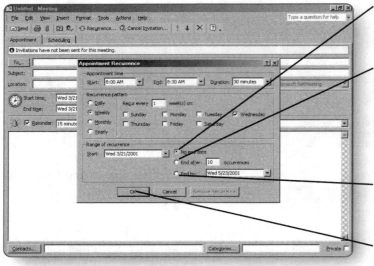

- **No end date**. The meeting will be repeated indefinitely on the calendar.

- **End after "x" occurrences**. The meeting will not appear on the calendar after a specified number of occurrences. The default number of occurrences is 10.

- **End by**. The meeting will not appear on the calendar after a certain date.

9. **Click** on **OK**. The Appointment Recurrence dialog box will close.

You can follow the same steps that you followed previously to fill in the meeting request. Remember to send the meeting request when you are finished.

Responding to a Meeting Request

When you receive a meeting request, you have three choices. You can accept, decline, or tentatively accept. If you accept or tentatively accept the meeting request, the meeting will automatically be added to your calendar. If you decline the request, the meeting will not be added to your calendar.

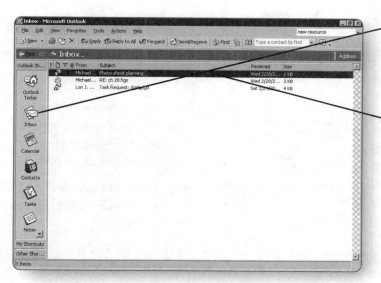

1. Click on the **Inbox icon** on the Outlook bar. The contents of your Inbox will appear in the Information viewer.

2. Double-click on the **meeting request**. The request will appear.

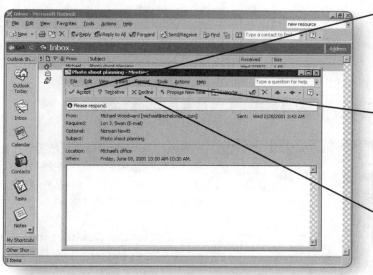

3a. Click on **Accept**. A message will open with three options.

OR

3b. Click on **Tentative**. A message will open with three options.

OR

3c. Click on **Decline**. A message will open with three options.

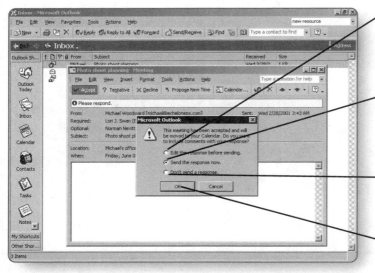

- **Edit the response before sending**. Outlook will open a new message window so that you can edit your response.

- **Send the response now**. The meeting organizer will receive an automatic response that you will not be able to edit.

- **Don't send a response**. The meeting organizer will receive no response.

4. Click on **OK**. The message window will close, and your choice will be registered. Also, your response will be sent to the sender unless you chose Don't send a response from the previous list.

Rescheduling a Meeting

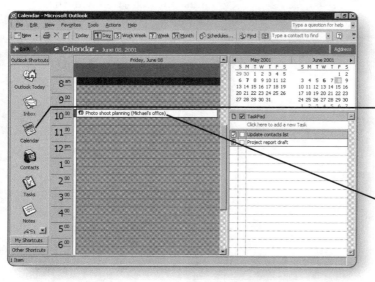

Sometimes a meeting may need to be rescheduled. Outlook gives you a fast and easy way to inform everyone of the change.

1. Click on the **Calendar icon** on the Outlook bar. The Calendar will appear in the Information viewer.

2. Double-click on the **meeting** in the calendar you want to edit. The Meeting window will appear.

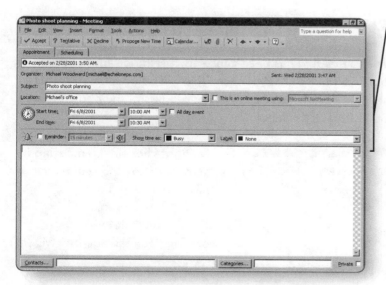

3. Enter any **changes**, such as start time, end time, or location. The changes will be indicated.

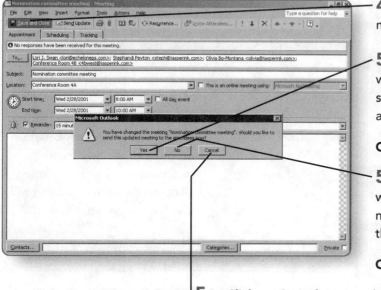

4. Click on **Save and Close**. A message box will open.

5a. Click on **Yes**. The change will be made and Outlook will send a message to update attendees of the change.

OR

5b. Click on **No**. The change will be made, but Outlook will not send a message to update the attendees of the change.

OR

5c. Click on **Cancel** to cancel any changes. The changes will be discarded.

Canceling a Meeting

When a meeting has been canceled, it is important to update your calendar so that your schedule will be accurate. Canceling the meeting will also update the calendars of the people that you invited to the meeting.

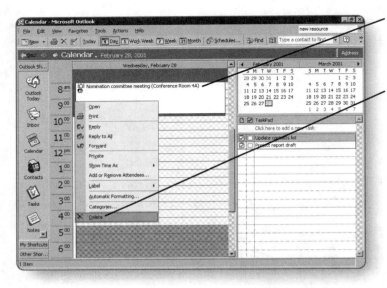

1. Right-click on the **meeting** in the calendar. A shortcut menu will appear.

2. Click on **Delete**. A confirmation message box will open.

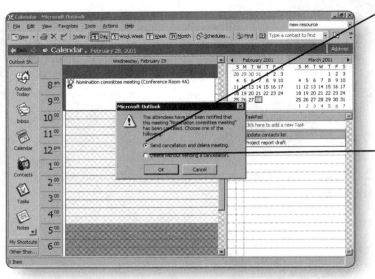

3a. Click on **Send cancellation and delete meeting** to notify the attendees. The cancellation will be sent and the meeting will be deleted from your calendar.

OR

3b. Click on **Delete without sending a cancellation** to cancel the meeting without notifying attendees. The meeting will be deleted from your calendar.

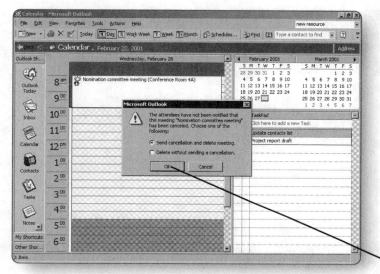

NOTE

If you send a cancellation, the attendees will be notified with an e-mail message. When they receive the message, they can click on the Remove from Calendar button to delete the canceled meeting from their calendar.

4. **Click** on **OK**. The meeting will be deleted and a cancellation may or may not be sent, depending on the choice you made in step 3.

Turning an Appointment into a Meeting

An appointment affects only your calendar, whereas a meeting involves other people. Occasionally you might have an appointment on your calendar and realize that other people need to be invited. You can easily turn the appointment into a meeting by inviting others.

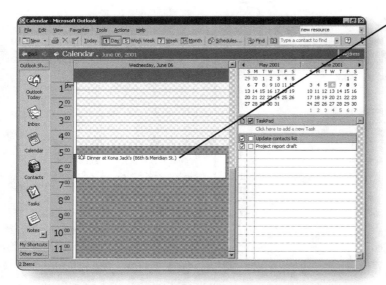

1. Double-click on the **appointment** in the calendar. The Appointment window will appear.

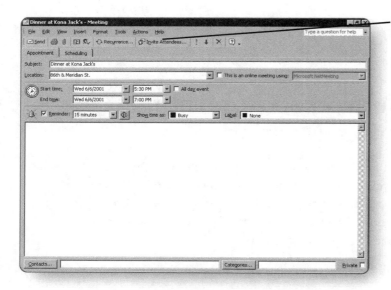

2. Click on **Invite Attendees**. A new Meeting window will appear.

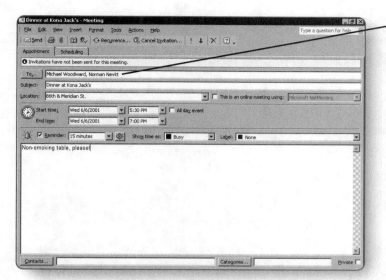

3. Type the **names** of the people whom you want to invite in the To text box.

4. Type any changes to the appointment, if desired. The changes will be made.

5. Click on **Send**. An invitation to the meeting will be sent to those people whose names you typed in the To text box.

15

Requesting an Online Meeting

If you've ever spent time in an Internet chat room, you have some idea of what an online meeting is like. Many companies are setting up online meetings to have people in different cities attend meetings without incurring the high cost of travel. During an online meeting, you can hold conversations, share documents, look at videos, and even speak to others. In this chapter, you'll learn how to:

- Request and attend an online meeting
- Make any meeting an online meeting

Requesting an Online Meeting

Filling in an online meeting request is not much different than a regular meeting request. You simply choose a convenient time for everyone and invite others to attend. The main difference is the location—instead of gathering together in a room, people can attend the meeting from their home, office, or any place they have a computer.

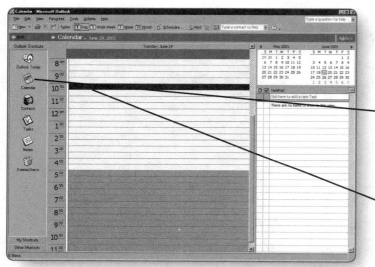

1. Click on the **Calendar icon** on the Outlook bar. The Calendar will appear in your Information viewer.

2. Right-click in a **blank area** of the calendar. A shortcut menu will appear.

3. Click on **New Meeting Request**. The Meeting window will appear.

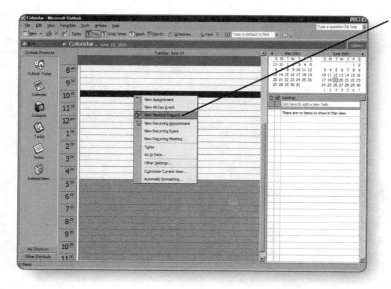

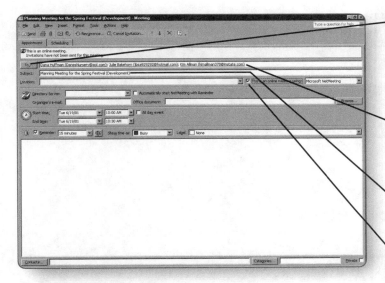

4a. **Click** on the **To: box**. A list of contacts will appear. Select your addresses from the list.

OR

4b. **Type** the **e-mail addresses** of the people you would like to invite.

5. **Type** the **subject** in the Subject: text box.

6. **Click** on the **check box** next to This is an online meeting using:, if it is not selected. A check mark will be placed in the box and the dialog box will change to present online meeting options.

7. **Click** on the **down arrow** next to This is an online meeting using: list box and select the online meeting software you want to use. The software will be selected.

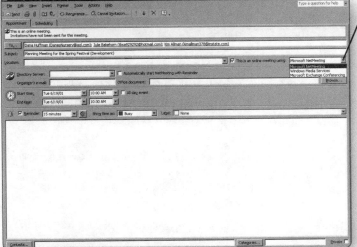

TIP

Microsoft NetMeeting, Windows Media Services. and Microsoft Exchange Conferencing are free programs. They can be downloaded from the Microsoft Web site at **http://www.microsoft. com**.

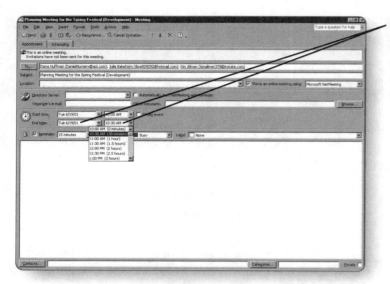

8. **Click** on the **Start time list box** and the **End time list box** to select starting and ending times for the meeting. The times will be selected.

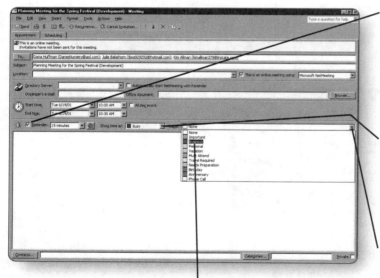

9. **Click** on the **Reminder: check box** and select the amount of time prior to the meeting for which Outlook should send a reminder. A reminder will be set.

10. **Click** on the **down arrow** next to the Show time as: list box and select how Outlook should display the time. The time will be selected.

11. **Click** on the **down arrow** next to Label. A drop-down list will appear.

12. **Select** a **label**. The label will be assigned.

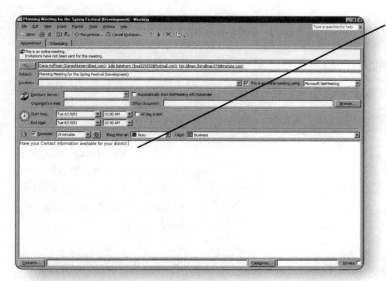

13. Click in the **text area** and **type** any **notes** regarding the meeting.

14. Click in the **Directory Server: list box** and type a directory server name.

NOTE

The directory server information is very important. All meeting attendees must be logged on to the same server in order to participate. If you are asked to attend a meeting, you will be told which directory server to use. If you are organizing the meeting, you can choose any directory server you like. Some directory servers are ils.microsoft.com, uls.microsoft.com, or ils.four11.com.

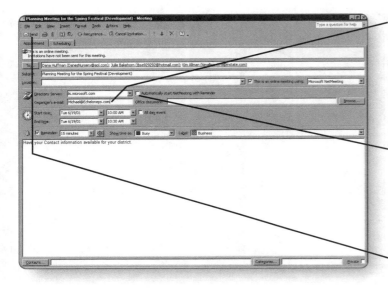

15. If you are organizing the meeting for someone else, **click** in the **text box** next to Organizer's e-mail: and type the name of the meeting organizer. The new name will appear.

16. **Click** on the **check box** next to Automatically start NetMeeting with Reminder. A check mark will be inserted into the check box.

17. **Click** on **Send**. Invitations will be sent to those invitees who are currently online.

Attending an Online Meeting

When you have been invited to an online meeting, you can respond just as you would for another meeting. An online meeting may already be in progress when you are invited, so it is a good idea to respond to the meeting organizer as quickly as possible.

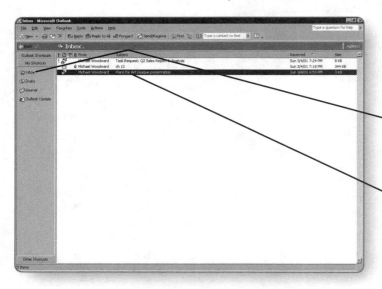

1. **Click** on the **Inbox icon** on the Outlook bar. The Inbox will appear in the Information viewer.

2. **Click twice** on the **meeting request**. The request will appear.

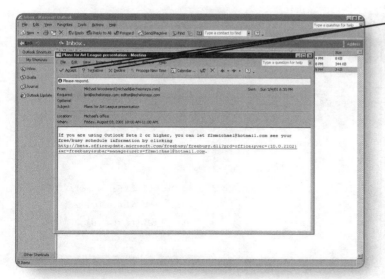

3. Click on **Accept**, **Tentative**, or **Decline** to place the meeting in your calendar. Once the meeting is on your calendar, you will be ready to join the online meeting.

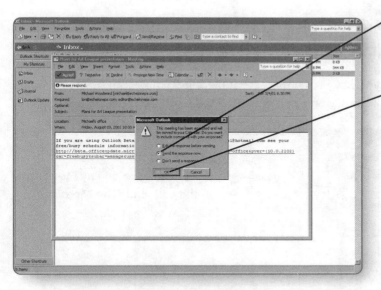

4. Select a **choice** to complete your send request. The option will be selected.

5. Click on **OK**. The dialog box will close and the message will be sent.

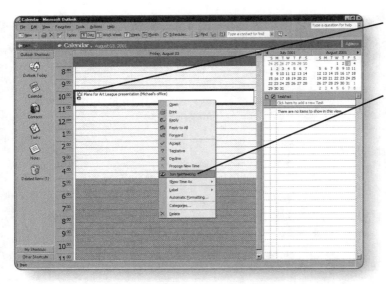

6. **Right-click** on the **meeting** in the calendar. A shortcut will appear.

7. **Click** on **Join NetMeeting**. Microsoft NetMeeting will open.

TIP

If you set a reminder, the reminder will automatically include a Join button that you can click.

Making Any Meeting an Online Meeting

If you have a meeting scheduled and your room reservation is bumped, don't panic! Once a meeting is on the calendar, it's easy to turn it into an online meeting.

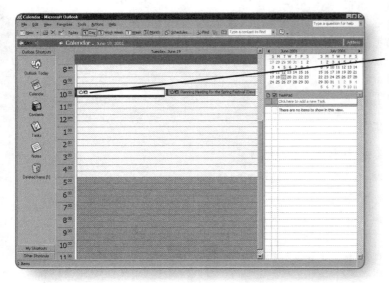

1. **Click twice** on any **meeting** in the calendar. The Meeting window will appear.

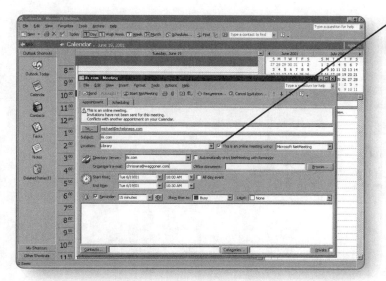

2. Click on the **check box** next to This is an online meeting using: and enter the necessary information.

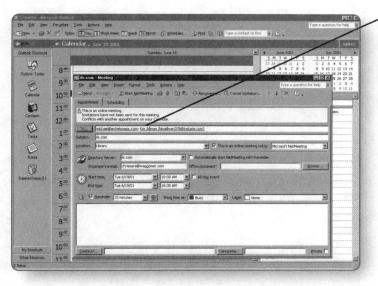

3. Click in the **To text box** and **type** the **name** or **e-mail address** of the person(s) you want to invite.

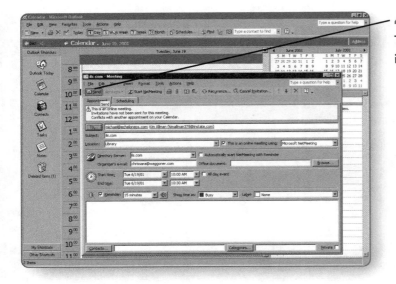

4. Click on the **Send button**. The meeting attendees will be informed of the change.

Part III Review Questions

1. What are the three primary calendar views provided by Outlook? *See "Showing Different Calendar Views" in Chapter 11*

2. In the Date Navigator, what appears around today's date? *See "Using the Date Navigator" in Chapter 11*

3. What is a recurring appointment? *See "Scheduling a Recurring Appointment" in Chapter 12*

4. What makes events different from appointments? *See "Planning an Event" in Chapter 13*

5. When making changes to a recurring event, do the changes have to affect all instances of the event? *See "Editing a Recurring Event" in Chapter 13*

6. What feature does Outlook provide to find a meeting time suitable to multiple schedules? *See "Planning a Meeting" in Chapter 14*

7. What are the three choices available when responding to a meeting request? *See "Responding to a Meeting Request" in Chapter 14*

8. If an appointment affects only *your* calendar, who does a meeting affect? *See "Turning an Appointment into a Meeting" in Chapter 14*

9. What feature does Outlook provide that allows other people to join a meeting without physically meeting together? *See "Requesting an Online Meeting" in Chapter 15*

10. When attending an online meeting, must all the attendees be logged on to the same server? *See "Requesting an Online Meeting" in Chapter 15*

PART IV

Keeping in Touch with Contacts

16

Creating New Contacts

If you've looked at any business cards recently, you've probably noticed how much information is included on them these days. Everyone seems to have multiple phone numbers, e-mail addresses, street addresses, and even a Web address! Creating contacts in Outlook is a great way to keep all this information organized and have it available when you need to get in touch with someone. In this chapter, you'll learn how to:

- Create a new contact
- View the address map
- Create a new contact from the same company
- Add a contact from an e-mail message

Creating a New Contact

It's a good idea to create a new contact record as soon as you meet someone, even if you don't have all the information that you need. You can always leave a field blank or go back later and update the contact as you receive more details.

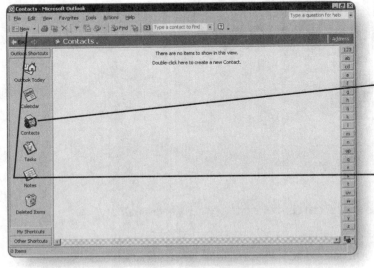

1. **Click** on the **Contacts icon** on the Outlook Shortcuts bar. Your contacts will appear in the Information viewer.

2. **Click** on the **New Contact button**. A new, blank Contact window will appear.

3. **Click** in the **Full Name text box** and **type** the **name** of the individual.

4. **Click** in the **Job title text box** and type a **job title**.

5. **Click** in the **Company text box** and **type** a **company name**.

6. **Click** on the **down arrow** next to the File as list box and **select a filing scheme** from the drop-down list.

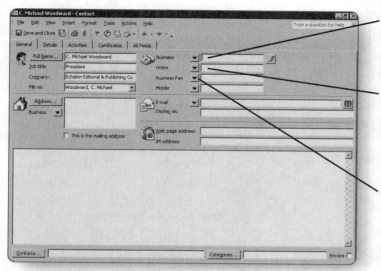

7. Click in the **text box** next to **Business** and **type** a **business telephone number**.

8a. Click in any of the other **phone number fields** and **type** a **telephone number**.

OR

8b. Click on any of the **down arrows** next to the numbers and **select** a **different type of number**.

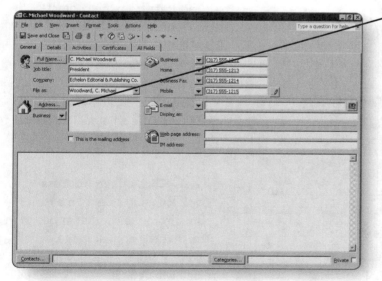

9. Click in the **Address text box** and **type the address**.

NOTE

If you do not type the address in a format that Outlook can understand, a Check Address dialog box may appear when you exit the Address field. At this point you can fill in more address information and click on OK.

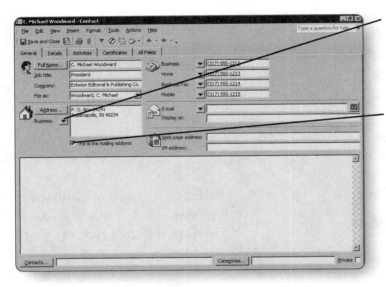

10. **Click** on the **down arrow** next to Business and **select a different type of address**, if necessary.

11. **Click** in the **check box** next to This is the mailing address. The address in the Address text box will be the default mailing address.

NOTE

Mailing addresses are used in other programs, such as Word or Access, when retrieving an address from the contact list on an envelope or shipping label.

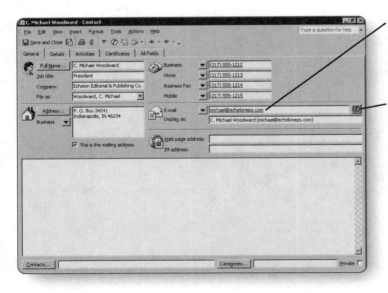

12a. **Click** in the **E-mail text box** and **type** an **e-mail address**.

OR

12b. **Click** on the **Address Book icon** and **select** an **e-mail name** from the list that appears. The text will appear in the e-mail text box and the Display as name will default.

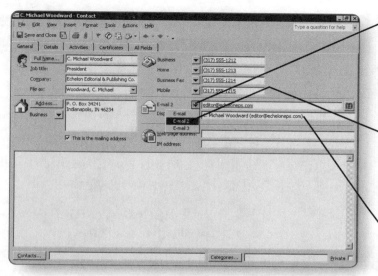

13. **Click** on the **down arrow** next to E-mail to add another e-mail address, if necessary. You can store up to three e-mail addresses for each contact.

14. **Click** on **E-mail 2** or **E-mail 3**. Your selection will appear in the list box and the insertion point will be in the text box.

15. **Type** the additional **e-mail address**. The address will appear in the text box.

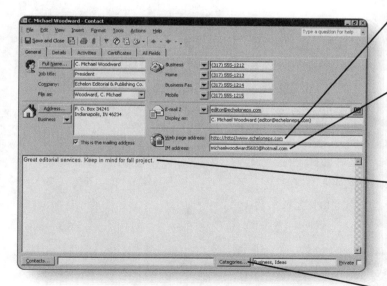

16. **Click** in the **Web page address text box** and **type** a **Web page address**.

17. **Click** in the **IM address text box** and **type** an **IM address**. The address will appear in the text box.

18. **Click** in the **comment text box** and **type** any **comments** or **notes** about the contact. The text will appear in the comments area.

19. **Click** on **Categories**. The Categories dialog box will open.

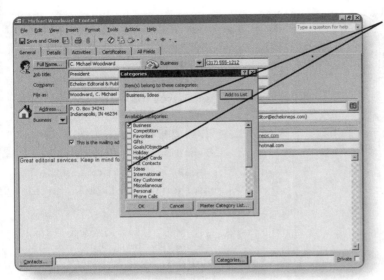

20. **Click** in the **check box** next to any category. The category will be added to the contact.

TIP

You can add multiple categories to a contact, or add your own categories. To add a new category, type a category in the Item(s) Belong to these categories text box and click on the Add to List button. You can also click on Master Category List, type a new category, and click OK.

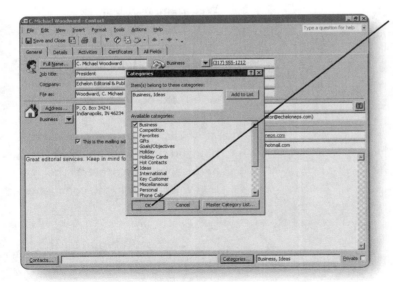

21. **Click** on **OK**. The Categories dialog box will close and you will return to the Contact window.

There are many more fields of information that can be added to the contact. Similar fields are organized together on the tabs of the Contact window.

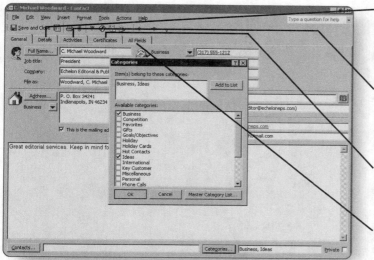

- **Details**. Enter information about the contact's birthday, anniversary, spouse's name, or department.

- **Activities**. Record details about letters, e-mails, or phone calls sent to the contact.

- **Certificates**. If you have added security, you can load security IDs in this tab.

- **All Fields**. Enter additional fields of information for the contact.

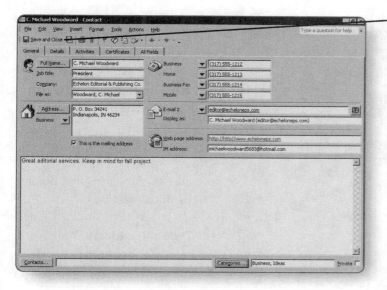

22. Click on **Save and Close.** The contact will appear in the contact list.

Viewing the Address Map

Have you ever needed quick directions to an address? Or perhaps you know where an address is, but you need to locate nearby streets or cities. The new Address Map feature allows you to do all these things and more.

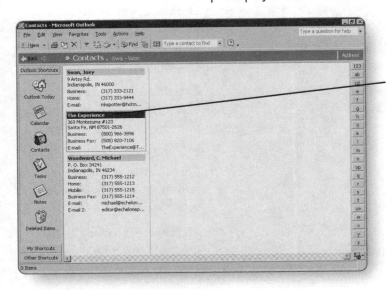

1. Double-click on a **contact** in the Information viewer. The contact will open.

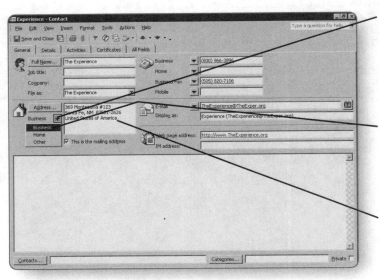

2. Click on the **down arrow** beneath the Address button. A drop-down list will appear. You can store up to three addresses for each contact.

3. Click on **Business**, **Home**, or **Other**. The option will be selected and the insertion point will be in the text box.

4. Type the **address**. The address will appear in the text box.

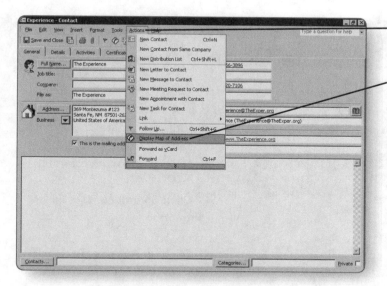

5. Click on **Actions**. The Actions menu will appear.

6. Click on **Display Map of Address**. Outlook will point your Internet browser to the page on the Outlook Web site that contains a detailed street map of the contact's address.

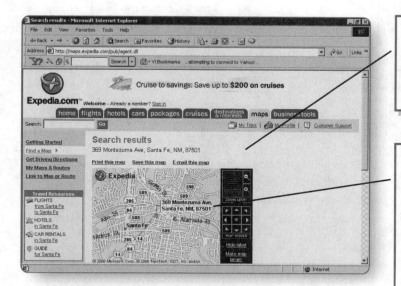

NOTE

You must be connected to the Internet to access the map.

TIP

If the address you are retrieving from the contact list has a four-digit extension on the ZIP code you will be asked to limit it to a five-digit ZIP code when the map program opens. This is best modified after the map program opens rather than modifying your contact list.

Creating a New Contact from the Same Company

Often, you will have similar information for several contacts. People who work for the same company often have the same business telephone numbers and addresses. Instead of typing repetitive information, let Outlook do the work for you!

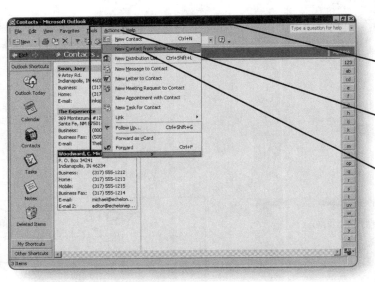

1. **Click** on **any contact** in the Information viewer.

2. **Click** on **Actions**. The Actions menu will appear.

3. **Click** on **New Contact from Same Company**. Outlook will open a new contact and fill in the address, business phone, and company name information from the original contact you selected.

NOTE

Outlook will not copy non-business information, such as home address or home phone numbers, when you create a new contact using this method.

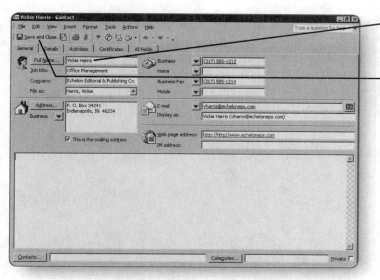

4. Type any **new contact information**.

5. Click on **Save and Close**. The contact will be saved and the window will close.

Adding a New Contact from an E-mail Message

What if you receive an e-mail message from someone and decide to add that person to the contact list? You don't have to retype the e-mail address—Outlook can take the information and create a new contact for you.

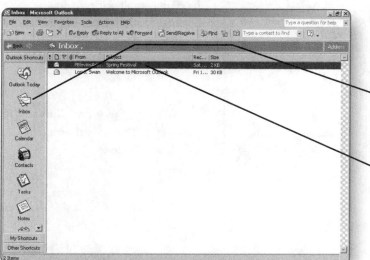

1. Click on the **Inbox icon** on the Outlook bar. Your Inbox will appear in the Information viewer.

2. Click twice on a **message**. The message will appear.

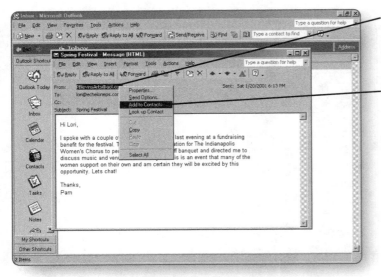

3. **Right-click** on the **e-mail address** in the From line. A shortcut menu will appear.

4. **Click** on **Add to Contacts**. The Contact window will appear.

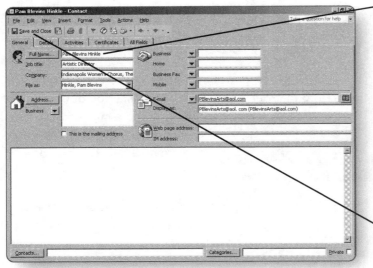

5. **Type** the **necessary information** for the contact in the appropriate text boxes.

NOTE

The e-mail address will automatically be added to the contact record.

6. **Click** on **Save and Close**. The contact will be saved and the window will close.

17

Working with Contacts

Outlook makes it fast and easy to draft a letter, send e-mail, or explore a Web page with the information stored in the contact record. In this chapter, you'll learn how to:

- Edit and print contacts
- Send an e-mail message to a contact
- Write a letter to a contact
- Explore a contact's Web page
- Dial a contact
- Track contact activities
- Use contacts for a mail merge

Editing a Contact

It's rare to have all of the data you need when you initially
create a contact. As you receive more details, you can add,
edit, or delete any information in the contact record.

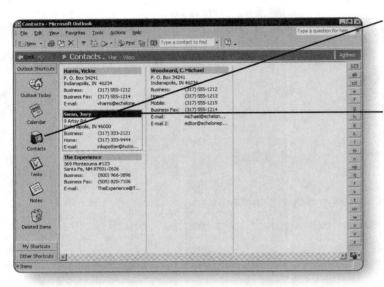

1. Click on the **Contacts icon**
on the Outlook bar. Your
Contacts will appear in the
Information viewer.

2. Click twice on any **contact**.
The contact will appear.

TIP

If your Contacts list is
lengthy, you can move
quickly to the contact you
want to edit by clicking
the alphabetical tabs at
the far right edge of the
information viewer.

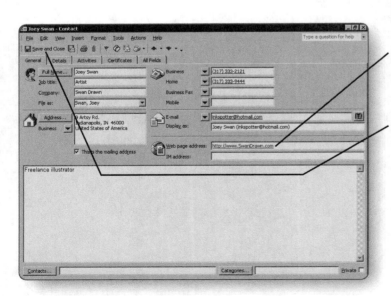

3. Type any changes to the
contact. The changes will be
made.

4. Click on **Save and Close**. The
contact will close and the
changes you've made will be
saved.

Printing a Contact

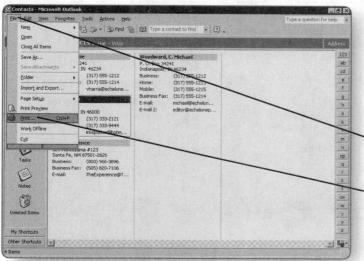

If you need a contact list, it's easy to generate a printout. Outlook gives you the option of printing one contact, selected contacts, or all the contacts in your list.

1. Click on **File**. The File menu will appear.

2. Click on **Print**. The Print dialog box will open.

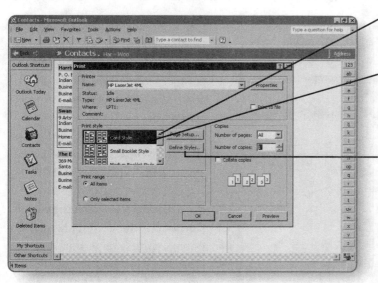

3. Scroll through the **Print style list**. Notice the available formats.

4. Select a **print style**. Your choice will be highlighted.

TIP

A print style can be edited if the style does not meet your needs. Click on Define Styles and select the print style you want to modify. Click on Edit and make any changes to the font size or style, shading, paper size, and headers or footers.

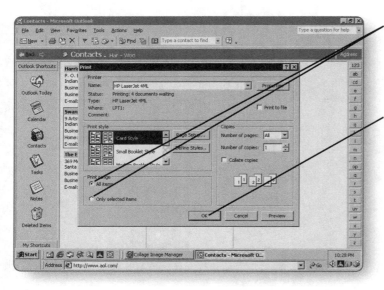

5. **Click** on the **option button** for **All items** or **Only selected items**. The option will be selected.

6. **Click** on **OK**. The Print dialog box will close and Outlook will print your option selection in step 4.

Sending an E-mail to a Contact

After you have recorded an e-mail address, it's easy to send an e-mail message to the contact. Outlook allows you to store up to three e-mail addresses for a contact, so you can easily reach someone with multiple addresses.

1. **Right-click** on a **contact**. A shortcut menu will appear.

2. **Click** on **New Message to Contact**. If the contact has an e-mail address, an e-mail message window will open already addressed to that person.

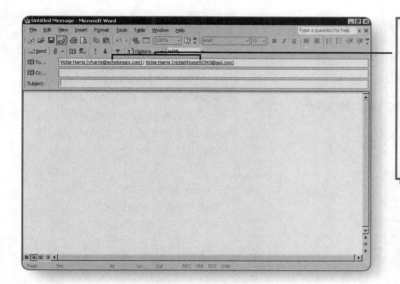

NOTE

If a contact has more than one e-mail address, all the addresses for the contact will be included in the To text box, and you can delete the addresses you don't need.

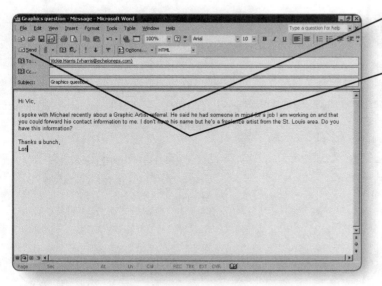

3. Type the **message**. The text will appear.

4. Click on **Send**. The message will be sent.

Writing a Letter to a Contact

After you have a postal address for a contact, you can use it to send a letter. Outlook has three addresses: Business, Home, and Other. The address that is marked as the mailing address will be used when sending a letter.

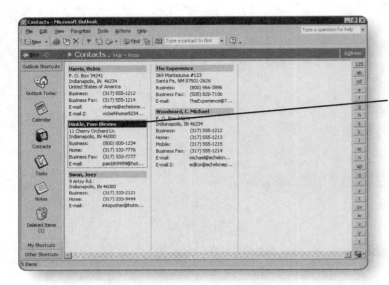

1. Click on a **contact**. The contact will be selected.

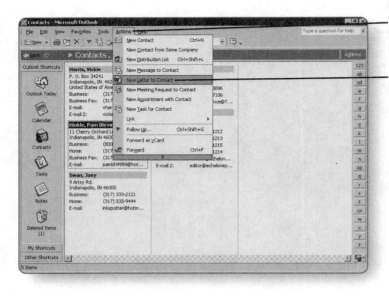

2. Click on **Actions**. The Actions menu will appear.

3. Click on **New Letter to Contact**. The Letter Wizard will open.

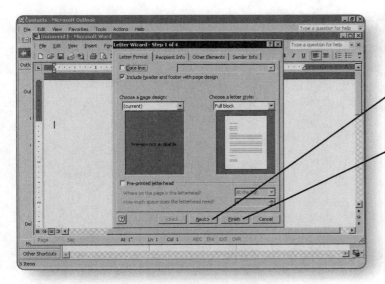

4. Click on the **desired options** for the letter. The options will be selected.

5. Click on **Next** to move through the Letter Wizard.

6. Click on **Finish** when you are finished with the Letter Wizard.

NOTE

In Word, you can access the addresses in the Contact list by clicking on the Address Book button in the Envelopes and Labels dialog box.

Creating a Mail Merge with Contacts

When you need to get the same information to a lot of people, a mail merge is often the best way to go. Outlook's Mail Merge feature makes composing form letters easier than ever.

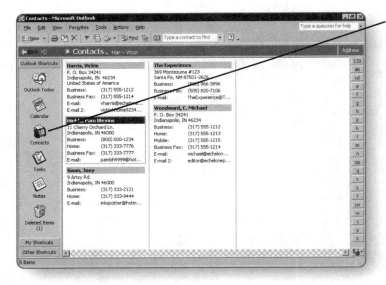

1. Click on the **Contacts icon** on the Outlook bar. Your Contacts will appear in the Information viewer.

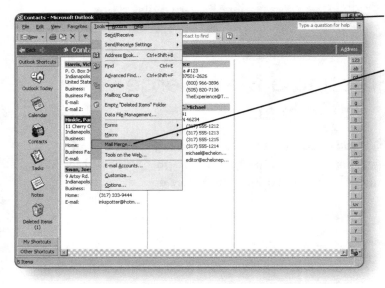

2. Click on **Tools**. The Tools menu will appear.

3. Click on **Mail Merge**. The Mail Merge Contacts dialog box will open.

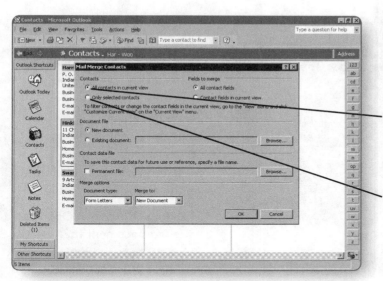

4. Click on a **selection** under Contacts to choose which contacts to include in the merge. The options include:

- **All contacts in current view**. Use all the contacts that are showing in the information viewer.

- **Only selected contacts**. Use only the contacts currently selected in the Information viewer.

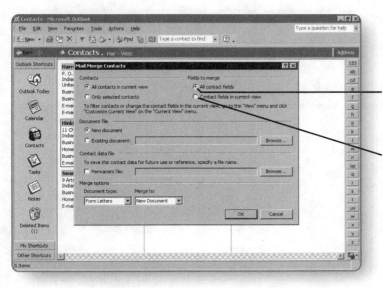

5. Click on a **selection** under Fields to Merge. The options include:

- **All contact fields**. Uses all the fields from the Outlook Contacts dialog box.

- **Contact fields in current view**. Uses only the fields that are showing in the Information viewer.

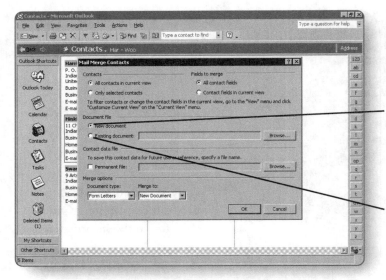

6. Click on a **selection** under Document File. The contact information will be merged into a new or existing document.

- **New document**. Creates a new document in Microsoft Word and inserts your selected Contact fields to use in the merge.

- **Existing document**. Opens an existing document that already contains the desired merge fields. Click on the Browse button to locate the document on your computer.

TIP

For detailed instructions on working with merge fields and documents, open Microsoft Word and press F1 to get help from the Office Assistant.

7. Click on a **selection** under Document Type. The options include:

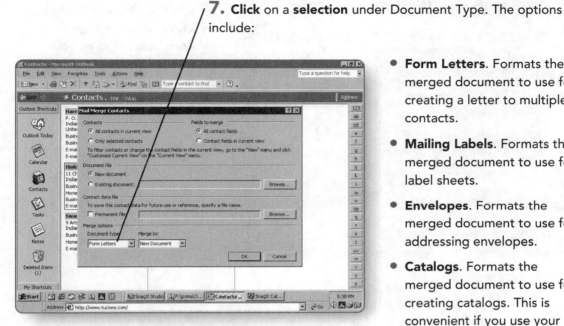

- **Form Letters**. Formats the merged document to use for creating a letter to multiple contacts.

- **Mailing Labels**. Formats the merged document to use for label sheets.

- **Envelopes**. Formats the merged document to use for addressing envelopes.

- **Catalogs**. Formats the merged document to use for creating catalogs. This is convenient if you use your Contacts list to track inventory and products.

8. Click on a **selection** under Merge To. The options include

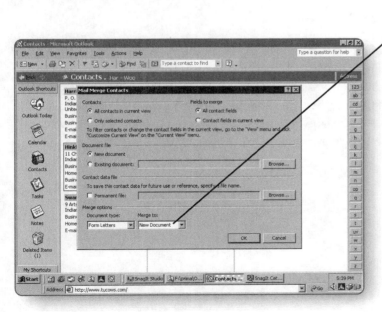

- **New Document**. Merges the information into a new document that can be saved and edited.

- **Printer**. Sends the merge directly to the printer. Does not save the merged document.

- **Fax**. Sends the merge directly to the fax modem using Outlook.

- **E-Mail**. Sends the merge directly to a new e-mail message using Outlook.

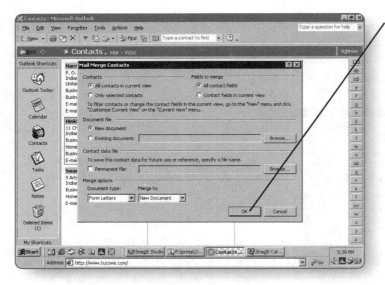

9. **Click** on **OK**. The dialog box will close and the merge will be created. Depending on your selections, Word may open and present the Office Assistant, the Mail Merge Helper, or both.

Exploring a Contact's Web Page

Many businesses have pages on the Web that people can access to quickly locate information about their company. Individuals are also creating their own pages and loading them on the Internet. Fortunately, Outlook allows you to keep a link to a Web page in the contact record, making it easy to visit a Web page at any time.

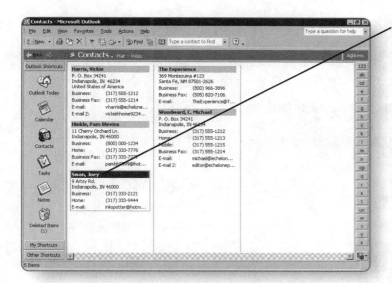

1. Double-click on a **contact** in the Information viewer. The contact will open.

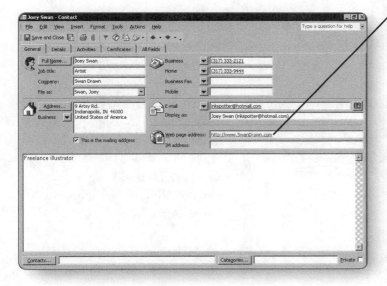

2. Click on the **hyperlink** next to Web page address. Outlook will point your Internet browser to that page.

3. Click on **Close** when you are finished exploring. The browser will close and the contact will reappear.

NOTE

You must have Internet access and a Web browser to explore a contact's Web page.

Tracking Contact Activities

Outlook can help you keep track of all the activity surrounding each person in your Contacts folder. It uses the Contacts and Journal features together to log all incoming and outgoing mail, phone calls, and related documents for each contact.

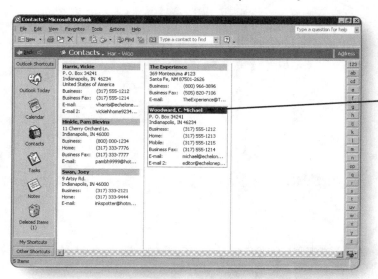

1. Double-click on the **contact** you want to track in the Information viewer. The contact will open.

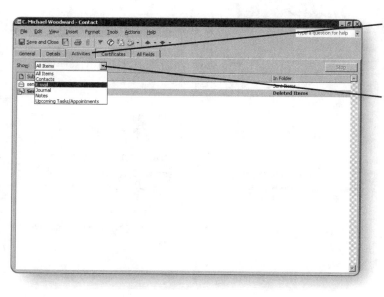

2. Click on the **Activities** tab. The contact's Activities page will appear.

3. Click on the **down arrow** next to Show. A list of activity types will appear, including:

- **All Items**. Displays all the activities related to this contact.

- **Contacts**. Displays other contacts linked to this contact.

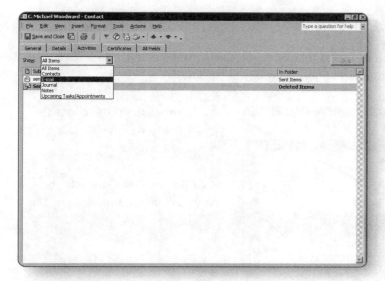

- **E-mail**. Displays all the e-mail sent to and received from the contact.

- **Journal**. Displays all the journal entries related to this contact.

- **Notes**. Displays all notes related to this contact.

- **Upcoming Tasks/ Appointments**. Displays all activities related to this contact that are currently scheduled in the calendar.

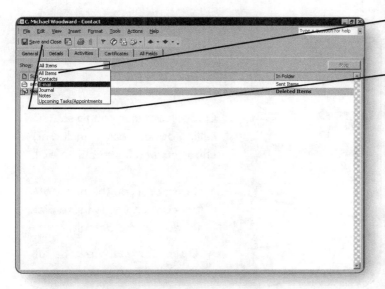

4. Click on **All Items** to see activities of all types.

5. Click on **Save and Close**. The Contacts folder will reappear in the Information viewer.

NOTE

If you've been tracking activities for this contact for awhile, it may take Outlook a moment or two to find and display all of the related activities.

Calling a Contact

You can use Outlook's AutoDialer feature to automatically dial a contact's phone number or fax line.

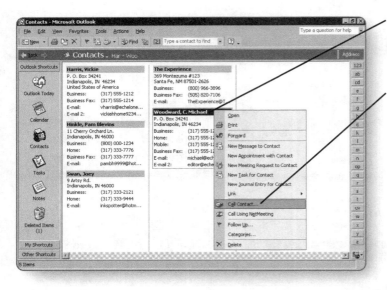

1. **Right-click** on the **contact** you want to call. A shortcut menu will appear.

2. **Click** on **Call Contact**. The New Call dialog box will appear.

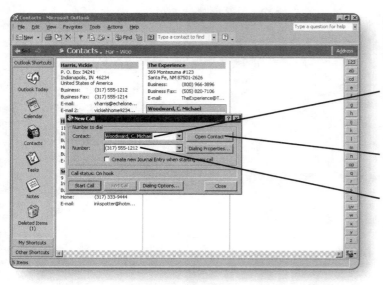

Outlook enables you to set calling options easily, including choosing which number to dial.

- **Contact**. Type the name of the contact you want to dial (or accept the default).

- **Open Contact**. View the full contact dialog box.

- **Number**. Choose which number to dial, depending on what is available in the contact's information.

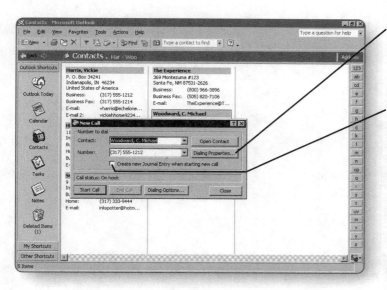

- **Dialing Properties**. Edit the dialing properties, such as long distance calling card information.

- **Create new Journal Entry when starting new call**. Log this call in the Journal for tracking purposes.

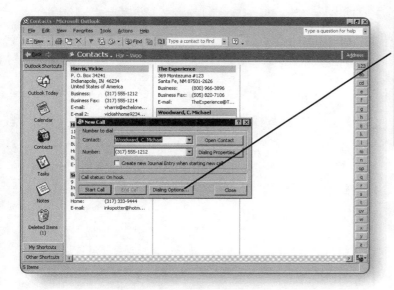

TIP

Click on Dialing Options to set advanced features for the call, such as speed dialing and modem properties.

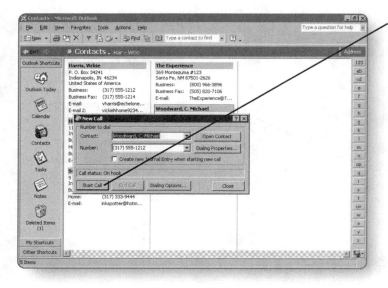

3. Click on **Start Call** to make the call. Outlook will dial the selected phone number.

4. Click on **Talk** and **pick up** the **receiver** when the phone begins to ring. Your call will be connected and you can begin talking.

18

Organizing Contacts

After you have entered numerous contact records, you may need to organize them. Contacts can be organized by categories, by names, by location, and more. You can also find a contact quickly using Outlook's Find feature. In this chapter, you'll learn how to:

- Find a contact
- Use folders, categories, and views to organize contacts
- Create and work with personal distribution lists

Finding a Contact

What if you have several thousand contacts and you need to quickly find one? Outlook has a Find feature that leads you straight to what you're looking for. You can even search all the text of the contact if you don't know the exact name or company.

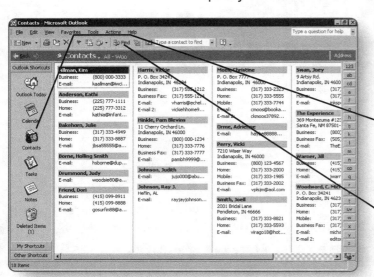

1. **Click** on the **Contacts icon** on the Outlook bar. Your contacts will appear in the Information viewer.

2. **Click** on **Find**. The Find messages in Contacts pane will appear.

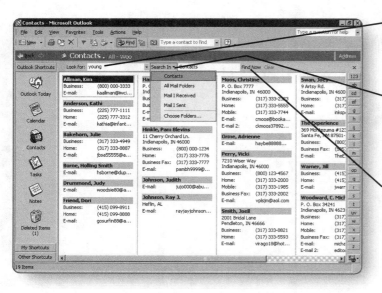

3. **Type** your **search criteria** in the Look for: text box. The text will appear.

4. **Click** on the **Search In** drop-down box and select a **search location**. Your selection will appear.

5. **Click** on the **Find Now button**. Outlook will begin the search.

If Outlook finds a contact record that matches the search criteria, it will be displayed on the screen. Click twice on the contact record to display the contact.

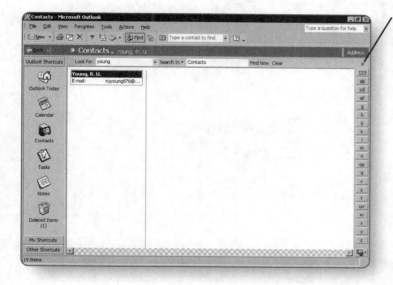

6. **Click** on **Close**. The Contacts pane with found items will close.

Using Folders to Organize Contacts

Folders are a great way to organize contacts. For example, you can create a client folder and place the client's contact record in the folder, along with e-mail messages, notes, or tasks related to the client.

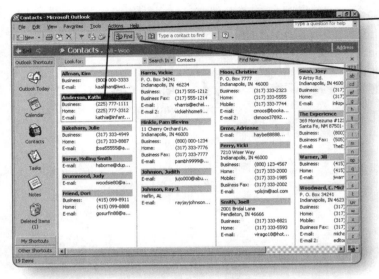

1. Click on a **contact**. The contact will be selected.

2. Click on the **Organize** icon. The Ways to Organize Contacts pane will appear.

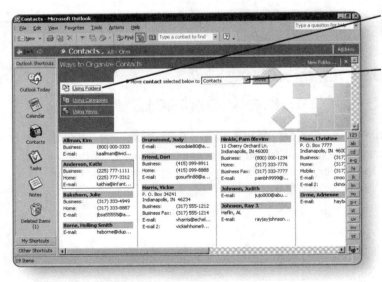

3. Click on **Using Folders**. The tab will come to the front.

4. Click on the **Down Arrow** next to the Move contact selected below to list box. The list of available folders will appear.

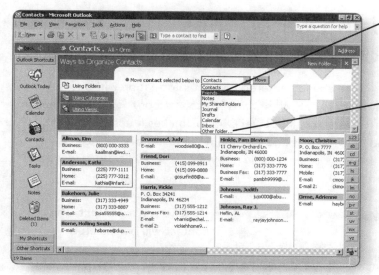

5a. **Click** on an **existing folder**. It will be highlighted.

OR

5b. **Click** on **Other folder** to create a new folder. It will be created.

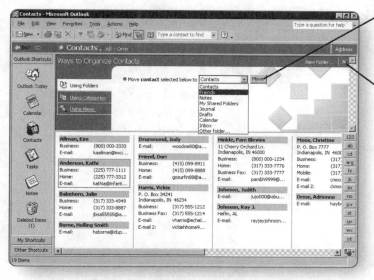

6. **Click** on the **Move button**. The contact will be moved to the new folder.

7. **Click** on **Close**. The Ways to Organize Contacts pane will close.

Using Categories to Organize Contacts

If you've already entered contact information without categories, you might think it's too late or too much bother to add them now. Not true! Outlook makes it easy to select multiple records and add them to a category. Using this method, you can quickly get your category list up to date and organized.

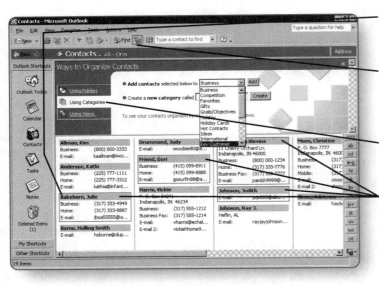

1. Click on a **contact**. The contact will be selected.

2. Click on the **Organize** icon. The Ways to Organize Contacts pane will appear.

3. Click on **Using Categories**. The tab will come to the front.

4. Click on the **contact(s)** you want to add to a particular category. Those contacts will be selected.

TIP

To select a range of contacts, click on the first contact, press the Shift key, and click on the last contact. To select non-contiguous contacts, hold down the Ctrl key and click on each contact that you want to select.

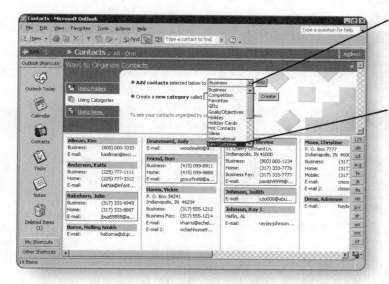

5. **Click** on the **Down Arrow** next to the Add contacts selected below to list box. The list of categories will appear.

6. **Click** on a **category**. Your selection will appear in the list box.

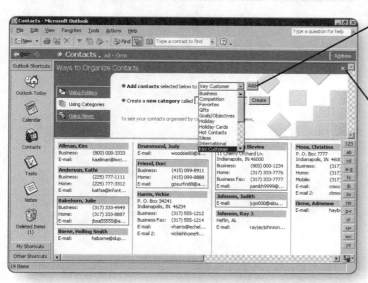

7. **Click** on the **Add button**. The contact(s) you've selected will be added to the selected category.

8. **Click** on **Close**. The Ways to Organize Contacts pane will close.

Using Views to Organize Contacts

When you have a large contact list, you may find yourself changing views frequently. Some of the available views are Categories, Company, and Location. You can edit any of the existing views or create your own.

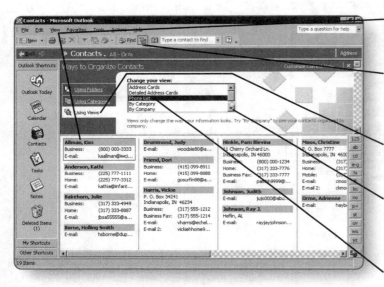

1. **Click** on a **contact**. The contact will be selected.

2. **Click** on the **Organize** icon. The Ways to Organize Contacts pane will appear.

3. **Click** on **Using Views**. The tab will come to the front.

4. **Click** on the **Up** or **Down Arrow**. You can scroll through the available views.

5. **Click** on **any view**. The view will change.

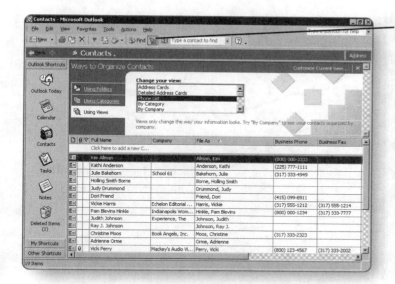

6. **Click** on the **Organize button**. The Ways to Organize Contacts pane will close.

If you frequently send messages to the same group of people, you can save time by creating a personal distribution list. When sending a message, you can simply enter the list name rather than choose all the contacts individually.

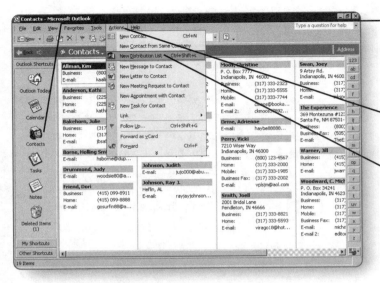

1. **Click** on the **Contacts icon** on the Outlook bar. Your contacts will appear in the Information viewer.

2. **Click** on **Actions**. The Actions menu will appear.

3. **Click** on **New Distribution List**. The Distribution List dialog box will open.

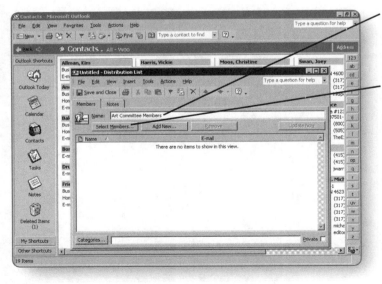

4. **Click** in the **edit box** next to the Name: text box and **type** a **name** for the list.

5. **Click** on the **Select Members button**. The Select Members dialog box will open.

6. Select the **names** on the left that you want to add to the personal distribution list. The contacts will be highlighted.

7. Click on the **Members button**. The names will appear on the right.

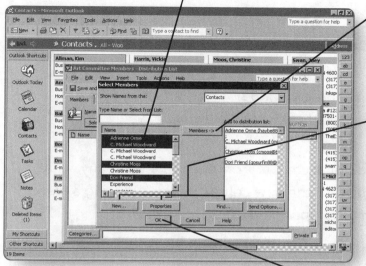

NOTE

Optionally, you can click on New to add another contact from this screen, click Properties to review content of a contact, or click Find to search the contact list for particular criteria.

8. Click on **OK**. The dialog box will close and the Distribution List dialog box will reopen.

9. Click on the **Add New button** to create a new contact for the distribution list.

10. Click on **Remove** to delete a specific contact from the list. It will be deleted.

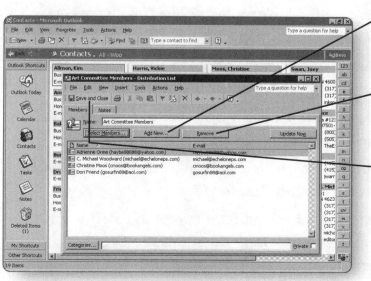

11. Click on **Save and Close**. The dialog box will close and your new distribution list will appear in the Information viewer.

Part IV Review Questions

1. What feature of Outlook helps you keep track of phone numbers, addresses, and Web addresses? *"See Creating New Contacts" in Chapter 16*

2. How does Outlook respond if you do not type an address in a format that Outlook understands? *See "Creating a New Contact" in Chapter 16*

3. When creating an additional contact from the same company, what information is not copied to the new contact? *See "Creating a New Contact from the Same Company" in Chapter 16*

4. What feature can you use to find directions to an address? *See "Viewing the Address Map" in Chapter 16*

5. How many e-mail addresses can be stored with a contact? *See "Sending E-mail to a Contact" in Chapter 17*

6. In Word, what button in the Envelopes and Labels dialog box can you click on to access your Outlook contacts? *See "Writing a Letter to a Contact" in Chapter 17*

7. Which two journals does Outlook use to track the activity surrounding a contact? *See "Tracking Contact Activities" in Chapter 17*

8. What Outlook feature can automatically dial a contact phone or fax number? *See "Calling a Contact" in Chapter 17*

9. Which types of Outlook items can you store in a folder? *See "Using Folders to Organize Contacts" in Chapter 18*

10. When selecting contacts, what key must you press to select a non-contiguous list of contacts? *See "Using Categories to Organize Contacts" in Chapter 18*

PART V

Staying on Top of Things with Tasks

19

Creating Tasks

With so much work to do, it helps to keep a list of the most important items you need to complete. The Task List in Outlook will help you keep all of these items under control, and give you a record of which tasks have been completed. In this chapter, you'll learn how to:

- Add a new task
- Set a reminder
- Update a task's status and send a status report
- Mark a task complete
- Delete a task

Adding a New Task

It's easy to add tasks to your task list. You can type directly into the list of tasks, or you can open a Task window and fill in more detail.

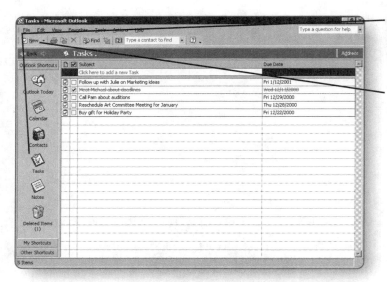

1. **Click** on the **Tasks icon** on the Outlook bar. Your tasks will appear in the Information viewer.

2. **Click** on the **New Task button**. A new Task window will appear.

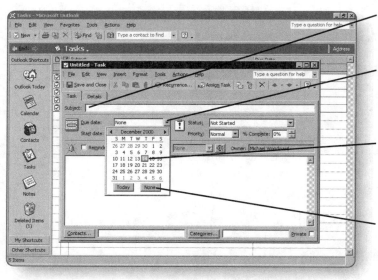

3. **Type** the **subject** of the task in the Subject: text box.

4. **Click** on the **down arrow** next to the Due date: list box. A drop-down list will appear.

5a. **Click** on a **due date**. The date will appear in the list box.

OR

5b. **Click** on **None**.

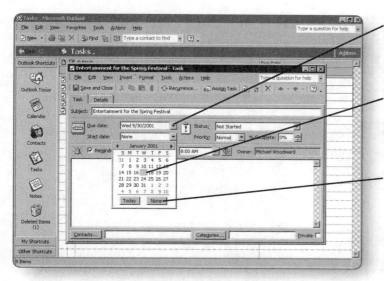

6. Click on the **down arrow** next to the Start date: list box. A drop-down list will appear.

7a. Click on a **start date**. The date will appear in the list box.

OR

7b. Click on **None**.

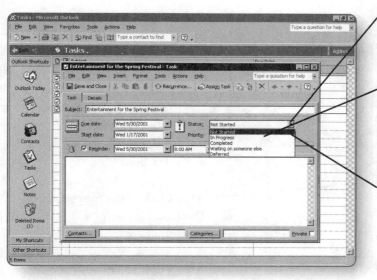

8. Click on the **down arrow** next to the Status: list box. A drop-down list will appear.

9a. Click on a **status**. The selection will appear in the list box.

OR

9b. Click on **Not Started**.

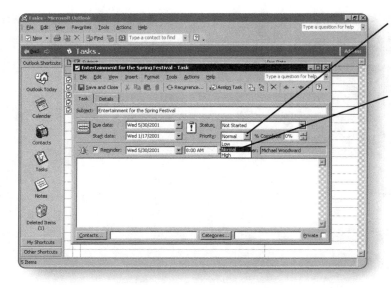

10. **Click** on the **down arrow** next to the Priority: list box. A drop-down list will appear.

11. **Click** on a **Priority**. The selection will be highlighted.

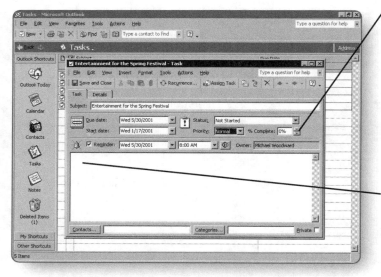

12. **Click** on the **up** or **down arrow** next to the % Complete: list box. A drop-down list will appear.

13. **Click** on a **percentage complete**. The amount of increase or decrease will appear in the list box.

14. **Click** in the **message box**. The insertion point will be in the message box.

15. **Type** any **notes** regarding the task. The text will be inserted into the message box.

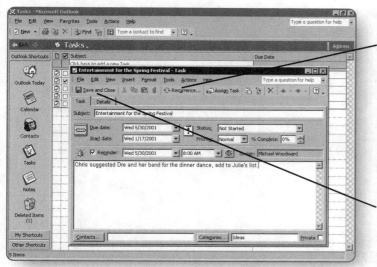

NOTE

You can make any task a recurring event, such as a quarterly tax payment or a monthly status report. Click on Recurrence on the Outlook toolbar to schedule a recurring task.

16. **Click** on **Save and Close**. The task will be saved and the Task window will close.

Setting a Reminder

If a task is important, you may want to set a reminder. A reminder will pop up and let you know that the task is due. You can postpone or dismiss the task when you are reminded.

1. **Double-click** on the **task**. The details of the task will appear.

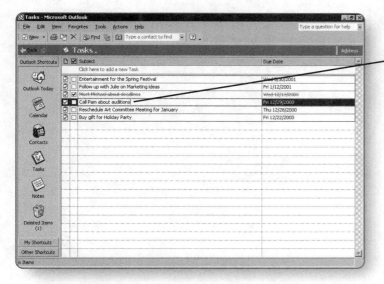

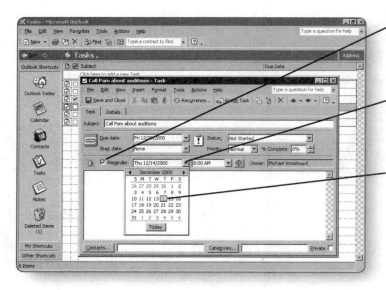

2. **Click** on the **Reminder check box**. A check mark will be placed in the box.

3. **Click** on the **down arrow** next to the Reminder: list box. A drop-down list will appear.

4. **Click** on a **date** to be reminded. The date will show in the list box.

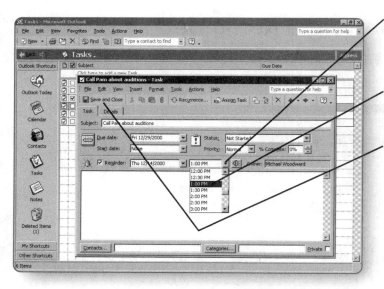

5. **Click** on the **down arrow** next to the time text box. A drop-down list will appear.

6. **Click** on a **time**. The time will show in the list box.

7. **Click** on **Save and Close**. The task window will close and any changes you've made will be saved.

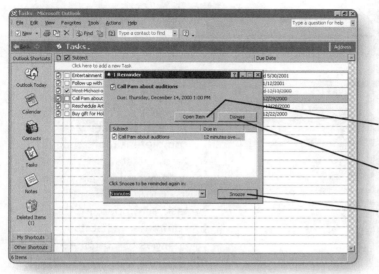

Reminders will only pop up while Outlook is running. When a reminder appears, you can respond with one of three actions:

- **Open Item**. Click on Open Item to open the task.

- **Dismiss**. Click on Dismiss to close the reminder.

- **Snooze**. Click on Snooze to delay the reminder. Select a time in the Click Snooze to be reminded again: list box.

Updating Tasks with Status Information

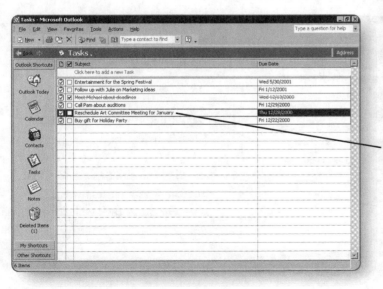

When a task is on your task list, you can update the task by changing the percentage complete detail. This will help you keep your task list up to date.

1. Double-click on the **task**. The details of the task will appear.

2. **Click up** or **down** on the **spin button** next to the % Complete: list box to increase or decrease the percentage complete. The change will appear.

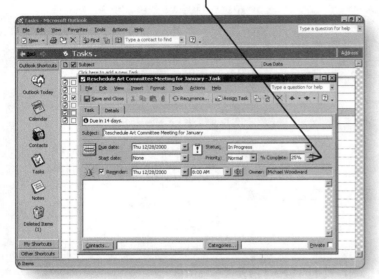

NOTE

When the percentage complete is more than zero, the status automatically changes to In Progress. When the task is 100 percent complete, the status changes to Completed.

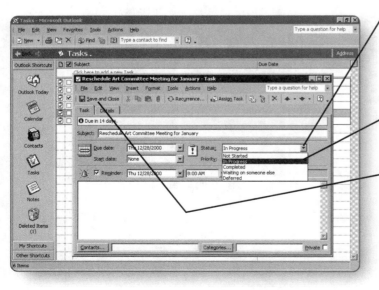

3a. **Click** on the **down arrow** next to the Status: list box. A list of status options will appear.

OR

3b. **Click** on a **status option**. The status will be updated.

4. **Click** on the **Save and Close** button. The changes will be saved and the task will close.

Sending Status Reports

You can send a status report to inform parties of the status of the task.

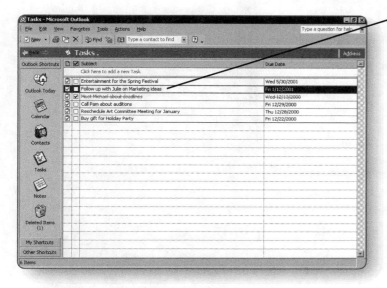

1. Double-click on a **task** in the task list. The task will open.

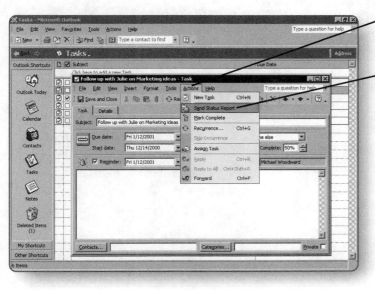

2. Click on **Actions**. The Actions menu will appear.

3. Click on **Send Status Report**. A new Task Status Report window will appear.

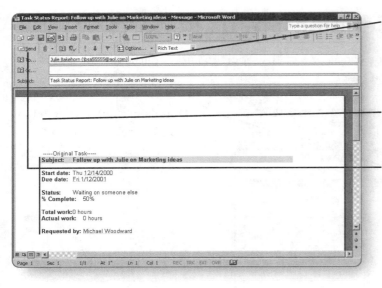

4. Type the **e-mail address** in the To: text box of the person to whom you want to send a status report. The address will appear.

5. Type any **message** in the message text box.

6. Click on **Send**. A status report will be sent.

Marking a Task as Complete

When you are finished with a task, you can mark it as complete. A completed task does not disappear completely. It remains on your task list, and you can choose to display the task or not.

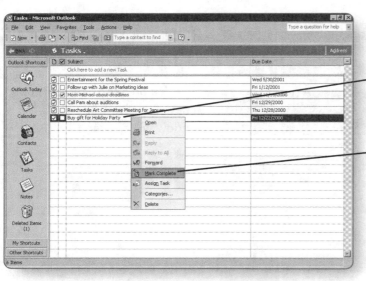

1. Right-click on a **task** in the task list. A shortcut menu will appear.

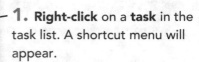

2. Click on **Mark Complete**. A check mark will appear next to the task in the task list.

TIP

Another quick way to mark a task as complete is to click on the Complete check box on the task list. You also can double-click on the task and choose Mark Complete from the Action menu.

Deleting a Task

Occasionally a task may need to be deleted. If the task is no longer necessary, you can delete the task to clean up your task list.

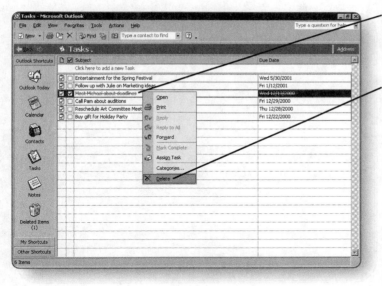

1. Right-click on a **task** in the task list. A shortcut menu will appear.

2. Click on **Delete**. The task will be deleted.

20

Assigning Tasks

If you are lucky, you will not have to handle all your tasks alone. Outlook has a feature called Task Request that lets you assign tasks to other people. They can accept, reject, or assign the task to someone else. In this chapter, you'll learn how to:

- Create a task request
- Respond to a task

Creating a Task Request

A Task Request is a task that you create and then assign to someone else. You can receive status reports so that you know the status of the task and when it has been marked complete.

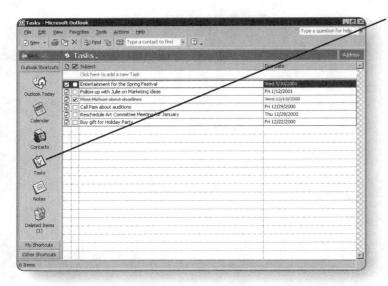

1. **Click** on the **Tasks icon** on the Outlook bar. Your tasks will appear in the Information viewer.

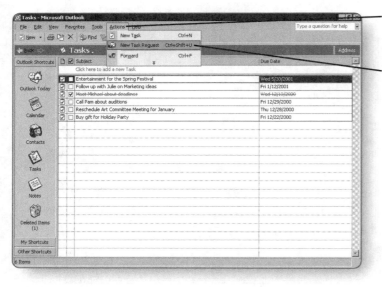

2. **Click** on **Actions**. The Actions menu will appear.

3. **Click** on **New Task Request**. A new Task window will appear.

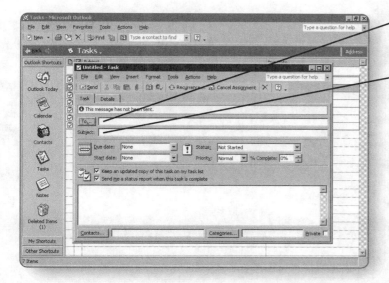

4. Type the **recipient's name** in the To text box.

5. Type the **subject** in the Subject: text box.

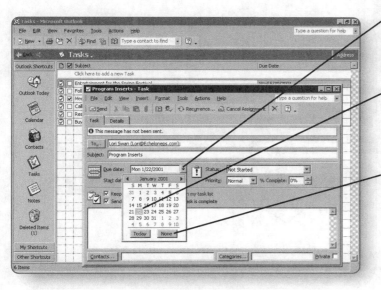

6. Click on the **down arrow** next to the Due date: list box. A drop-down list will appear.

7a. Click on a **due date**. The date will appear in the list box.

OR

7b. Click on **None**.

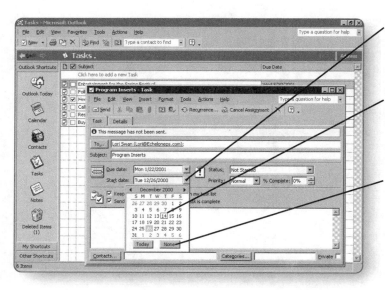

8. Click on the **down arrow** next to the Start date: list box. A drop-down list will appear.

9a. Click on a **start date**. The date will appear in the list box.

OR

9b. Click on **None**.

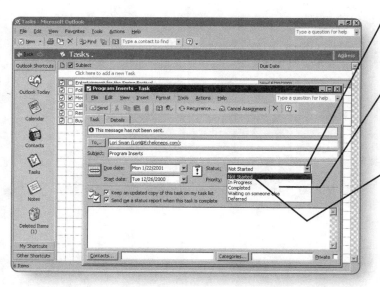

10. Click on the **down arrow** next to the Status: list box. A drop-down list will appear.

11a. Click on a **status**. The status will appear in the list box.

OR

11b. Click on **Not Started**.

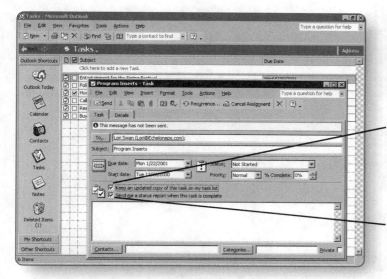

You have some tracking options available when assigning a task, which allow you to receive notification or automatic updates as progress is made:

- **Keep an updated copy of this task on my task list**. A copy of the task will stay on your task list and will be updated automatically.

- **Send me a status report when this task is complete**. You will receive a message when the task is marked complete.

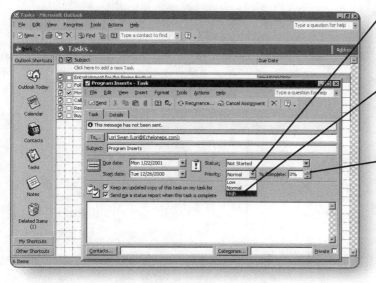

12. **Click** on the **down arrow** next to the Priority: list box. A drop-down list will appear.

13. **Click** on a **priority**. The selection will appear in the list box.

14. **Click** on the **up or down arrow** next to the % Complete: list box. The percent complete will increase or decrease.

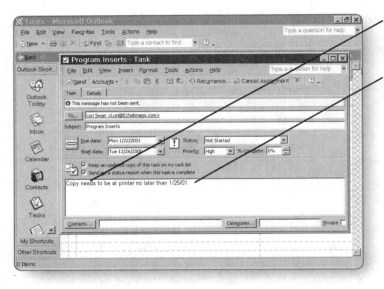

15. **Click** in the **message text box**.

16. **Type** any **notes** regarding the task. The note will appear in the message area.

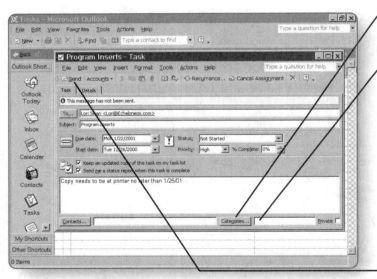

17. **Click** on the **Categories button**.

18. **Type** any **categories** you want to add. The categories will be added.

NOTE

You may need to maximize the Task Request to see the Categories text box.

19. **Click** on **Send**. The task will be sent to the recipient.

Task Requests will remain on your task list if you have selected the option to keep an updated copy on your task list.

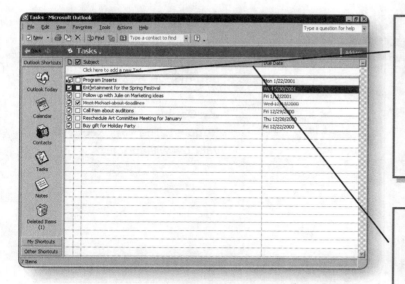

TIP

In the task list, you can distinguish a task from a Task Request by the difference in the icons. (Task requests are indicated with two small hands "holding" the task.)

TIP

You can sort your task list by clicking on the Icon button, Complete button, Subject, or Date on the toolbar. Clicking a second time will toggle your view from ascending to descending order.

Responding to a Task

If you receive a Task Request, you have several choices. You can accept the task, reject the task, or assign the task to someone else. Outlook makes any of these options easy to choose.

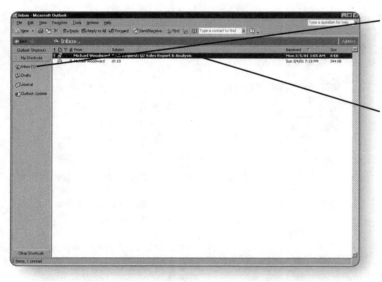

1. **Click** on the **Inbox icon** on the Outlook bar. The contents of your Inbox will appear in the Information viewer.

2. **Double-click** on the **Task Request**. The Task Request window will appear.

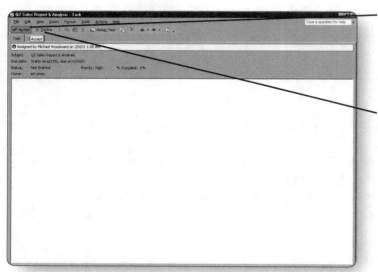

3a. **Click** on **Accept** to accept the task. The task will be added to your task list.

OR

3b. **Click** on **Decline** to decline the task. The task won't be added to your task list.

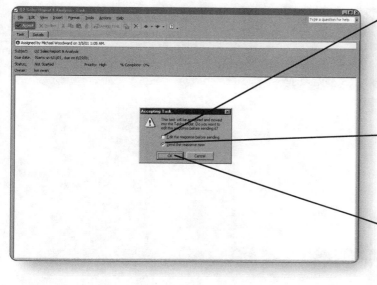

4a. Click on the **Edit the response before sending option button** to send a response.

OR

4b. Click on the **Send the response now option button** to accept or decline the task without sending a response.

5. Click on **OK**. Outlook will either send your response or allow you to edit it, depending on the option you chose in step 4.

Delegating Tasks

If you are unable to complete the task but can delegate the task to someone else, you can reassign the task. When you reassign the task, you give up ownership of the task; however, you can still keep an updated copy of the task on your task list.

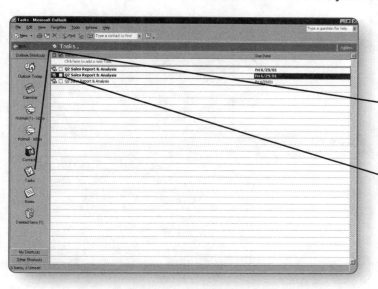

1. Click on the **Tasks icon** on the Outlook bar. Your tasks will appear in the Information viewer.

2. Double-click on the **Task Request** in the task list. The Task Request window will appear.

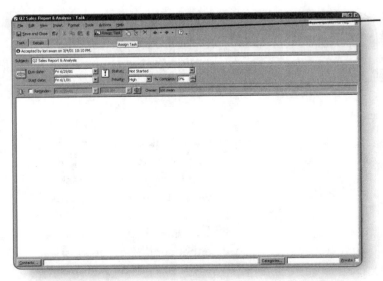

3. Click on the **Assign Task button**. A new Task window will open.

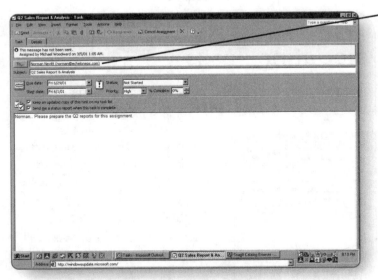

4. Type the **name** of the person in the To: text box to whom you are sending the task.

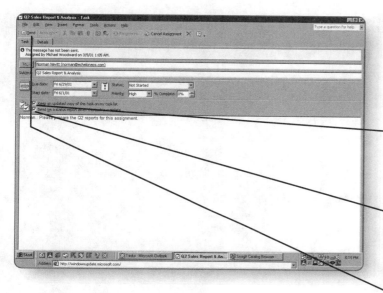

You have some tracking options available when assigning a task, which allow you to receive notification or updates as progress is made:

- **Keep an updated copy of this task on my task list**. A copy of the task will stay on your task list and be updated.

- **Send me a status report when this task is complete**. You will receive a message when the task is complete.

5. **Click** on **Send**. The task will be delegated to the person indicated in step 4.

Declining a Task after You Have Accepted It

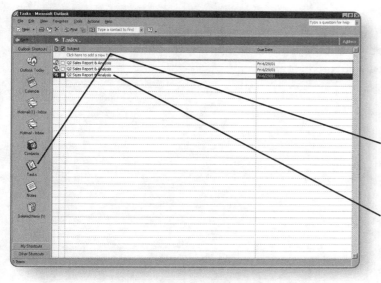

Have you ever bitten off more than you can chew with pending projects? Outlook can help you out of a sticky situation by allowing you to decline a task you had previously accepted.

1. **Click** on the **Tasks icon** on the Outlook bar. Your tasks will appear in the Information viewer.

2. **Double-click** on the **task** in the task list. The task will appear.

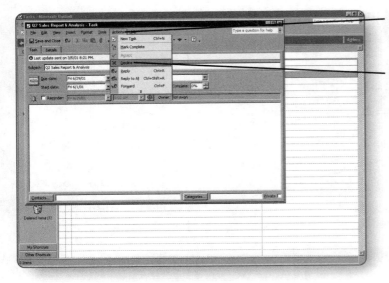

3. Click on **Actions**. The Actions menu will appear.

4. Click on **Decline**. The Declining Task dialog box will open.

5a. Click on the Edit the response before sending option button to decline the task and add a response.

OR

5b. Click on the Send the response now option button to decline the task without sending a response.

6. Click on OK. Outlook will allow you to edit the task before you send it, or send it immediately, depending on the option you selected in step 5.

21

Organizing Tasks

If you have a long list of tasks, you will need a few tricks so you can see the most important tasks, or the tasks that are due first. Changing views and sorting the task list are fast and easy ways to keep tasks under control. In this chapter, you'll learn how to:

● Use folders and categories to organize tasks

● Change the task list view

● Sort and print the task list

Using Folders to Organize Tasks

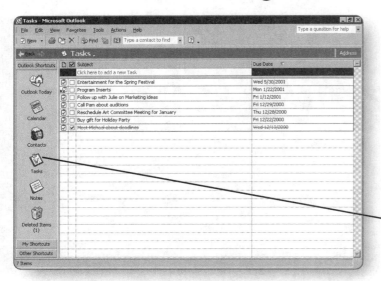

Outlook automatically stores tasks in the Tasks folder. After you have used Outlook for a while, the Tasks folder may grow to contain an enormous amount of tasks. Instead of scrolling through a long list of tasks, you can create subfolders under the Task folder, and view tasks by folder.

1. **Click** on the **Tasks icon** in the Outlook bar. Your tasks will appear in the Information viewer.

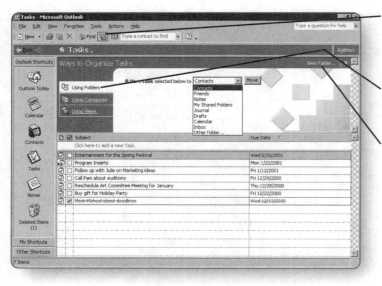

2. **Click** on the **Organize icon**. The Ways to Organize Tasks pane will open.

3. **Click** on **Using Folders**. The tab will come to the front.

4. **Click** on **New Folder**. The Create New Folder dialog box will open.

5. Type a **folder name** in the Name: text box.

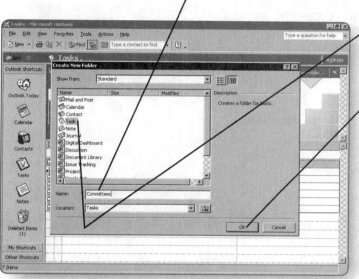

6. Click on the **Task folder**. The new folder will be a subfolder of the Tasks folder.

7. Click on **OK**. The new folder will be created.

NOTE

You may receive a message asking if you want a shortcut to the new folder placed on the Outlook toolbar. If you do, click on Yes; otherwise, click on No.

NOTE

A Folder List may appear on your window. Your new folder will appear in this list. You can close the Folder List by clicking the X.

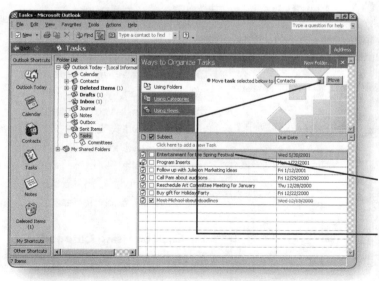

8. Click on **any task** in the Task list. The task will be selected.

9. Click on the **down arrow** next to the Move task selected below to list box. A drop-down list will appear.

10. Click on a **folder**. The folder will be selected.

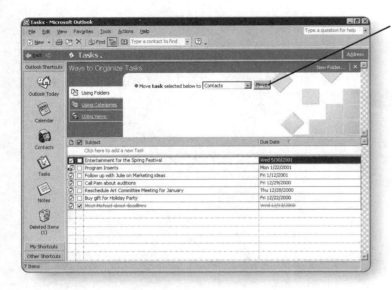

11. **Click** on the **Move button**. The task will be moved to the folder you selected in step 10. Leave the Organize window open for the next section.

Using Categories to Organize Tasks

Categories are words or phrases that can be applied to any Outlook item, such as an e-mail message, a note, or a task. Outlook comes with numerous categories, and you can add more categories to customize the category list. Using categories will keep all the tasks for a particular client or project tied together, and make sorting and viewing much easier.

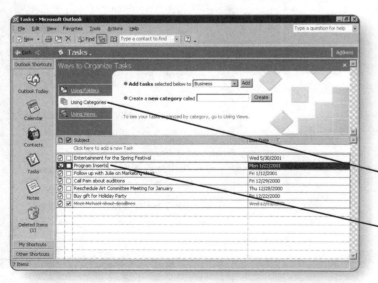

1. **Click** on **Using Categories**. The tab will come to the front.

2. **Click** on a **task(s)** in the task list. The task(s) will be selected.

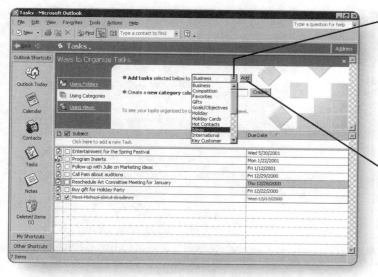

3. Click on the **down arrow** next to Add tasks selected below to list box. A drop-down list will appear.

4. Click on a **category**. It will be selected.

5. Click on **Add**. The category will be added to the selected tasks. Leave the Organize window open for the next section.

Using Views to Organize Tasks

Now that you have explored categories, you may be wondering how they will be used to organize the task list. It's easy! Changing the task list view is one quick way to organize the task list.

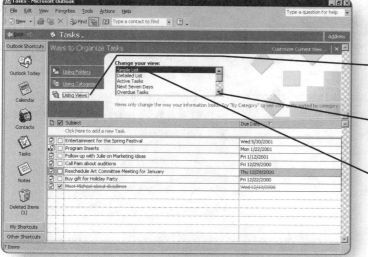

1. Click on **Using Views**. The tab will come to the front.

2. Scroll through the **list of views** to find your selection.

3. Click on **any view**. The task list view will change.

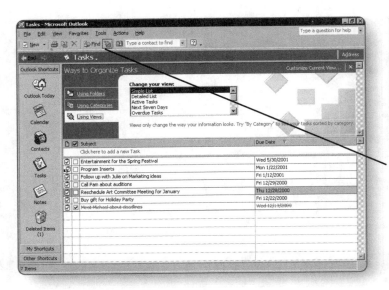

TIP

To view the tasks organized by categories, choose the By Category view.

4. Click on **Organize**. The Ways to Organize Tasks pane will close.

Remember that changing the task view does not delete any existing tasks; it simply removes them from view. To see all tasks, choose the Simple List view.

Sorting the Task List

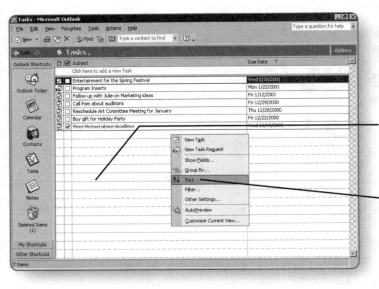

Some people prefer to sort their task lists instead of using views. You can sort by any field in a task, such as priority, due date, or subject.

1. Right-click on a **blank area** of the task list. A shortcut menu will appear.

2. Click on **Sort**. The Sort dialog box will open.

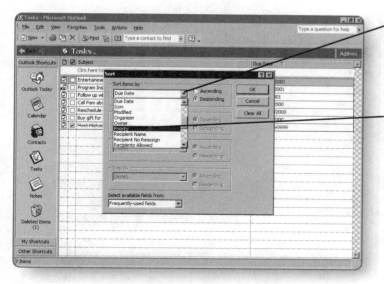

3. **Click** on the **down arrow** to the right of the Sort items by list box. A drop-down list will appear.

4. **Click** on a **field selection**. The selection will be highlighted.

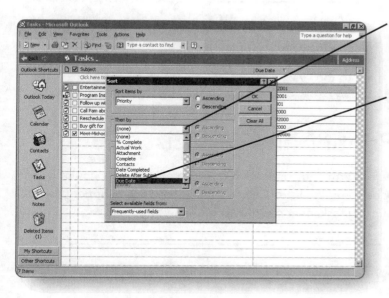

5. Optionally, **click** on the **down arrow** under Then by. A drop-down list will appear.

6. **Click** on a **field selection** to sort by multiple criteria.

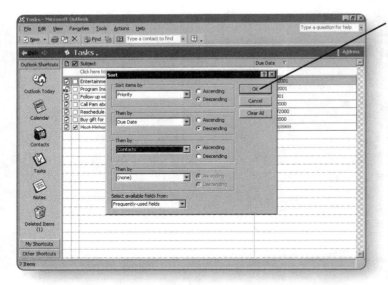

7. Click on **OK**. Your tasks will be sorted according to the criteria you've chosen in steps 4 and 6.

TIP

Click on a column head in the information viewer to quickly sort your task list by that field. Click on it again to sort in reverse order.

NOTE

If you select a sort field that is not currently displayed on the task list view, a message will open. To add the sort field to the view, click on OK; otherwise, click on No.

Printing the Task List

Before attending a meeting or going out of town, you may need to print a list of tasks. Outlook has several options for printing tasks that can give you exactly what you need.

TIP

You can select individual tasks on the task list by holding down the Ctrl key as you click on the desired tasks.

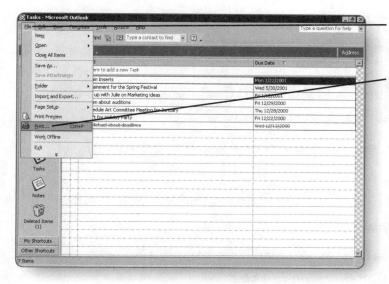

1. **Click** on **File**. The File menu will appear.

2. **Click** on **Print**. The Print dialog box will open.

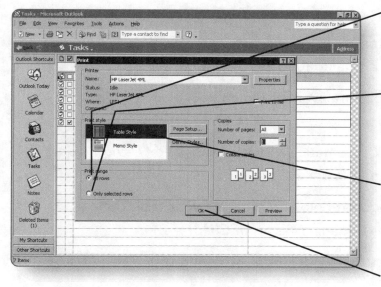

3a. **Click** on **All rows** to print all tasks. All tasks will print.

OR

3b. **Click** on **Only selected rows** to print only the selected tasks. Only selected tasks will print.

4. **Click** on the **desired Print Style**. The output will be formatted according to your selection.

5. **Click** on **OK**. Outlook will print all your tasks, or just the ones you've selected, depending on which option you chose in step 3.

Part V Review Questions

1. Which Outlook feature would you use to track items you need to complete? *See "Creating Tasks" in Chapter 19*

2. Can tasks be scheduled as recurring? *See "Adding a New Task" in Chapter 19*

3. Does Outlook need to be running to see a reminder? *See "Setting a Reminder" in Chapter 19*

4. What happens to a task after you mark it as complete? *See "Marking a Task as Complete" in Chapter 19*

5. What is a Task Request? *See "Creating a Task Request" in Chapter 20*

6. When delegating a task to someone else, can you keep an updated copy of the task? *See "Delegating Tasks" in Chapter 20*

7. What response options are available when you receive a Task Request? *See "Responding to a Task" in Chapter 20*

8. Where does Outlook automatically store tasks? *See "Using Folders to Organize Tasks" in Chapter 21*

9. How can using Categories help you organize your tasks? *See "Using Categories to Organize Tasks" in Chapter 21*

10. Does changing the task view delete any existing tasks? *See "Using Views to Organize Tasks" in Chapter 21*

PART VI

Tracking Your Time with the Journal

22

Working with Journal Entries

The Journal is a feature that allows you to keep track of all the activities that you perform in the course of a day—whether it's responding to a meeting request, sending an e-mail, or opening a document. This feature is essential when billing time to clients or maintaining an accurate record of your daily activities. In this chapter, you'll learn how to:

- Automatically track Journal activities
- Create a new journal entry
- Modify a journal entry
- Delete a journal entry

Tracking Journal Activities Automatically

The easiest way to start using the Journal is to set up Outlook to automatically record certain types of activities. Some examples of the types of activities that you can record are e-mail messages, meeting responses, and task requests.

1. Click on the **Journal icon** on the Outlook bar. The Journal will appear in the Information viewer.

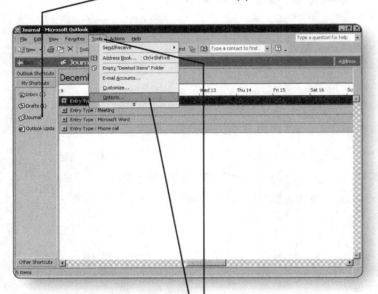

NOTE

If this is the first time you've opened the Journal, you may see a dialog box asking if you want to turn on the Journal. If you click on Yes in this dialog box, you can skip the rest of the steps in this section; however, you may want to use these steps to change the types of items the Journal tracks.

NOTE

You may need to click on the My Shortcuts group on the Outlook bar to find the Journal icon.

2. Click on **Tools**. The Tools menu will appear.

3. Click on **Options**. The Options dialog box will open.

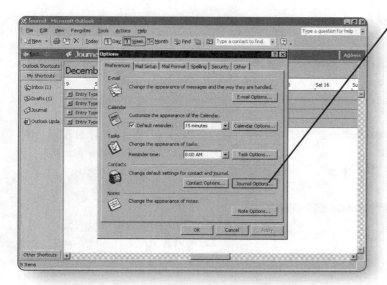

4. Click on the **Journal Options button**. The Journal Options dialog box will open.

5. Click on the **check box** next to each item you want to record automatically. A check mark will be placed in the box.

6. Click on **OK** until all open dialog boxes are closed.

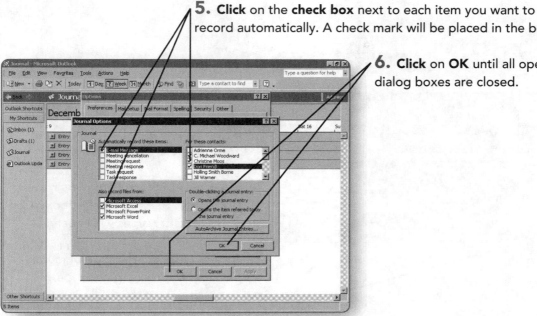

Creating a New Journal Entry

You may have noticed that some activities are not automatically recorded, such as phone calls. Don't worry, there are quick and easy ways to create a journal entry for these activities.

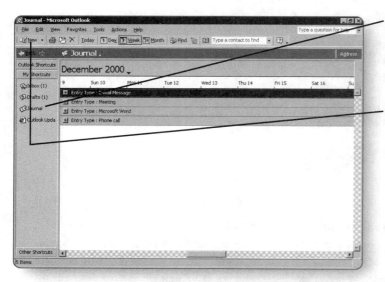

1. Click on the **Journal icon** on the Outlook bar. Your journal entries will appear in the Information viewer.

2. Click on **New**. The Journal Entry dialog box will open.

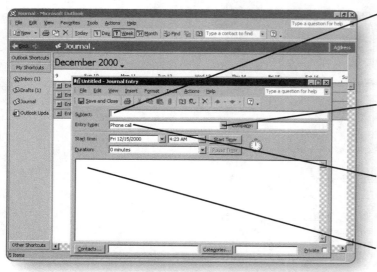

3. Click in the **Subject text box** and **type** the **subject** of the journal entry. The subject will appear in the text box.

4. Click on the **down arrow** next to Entry type list box. A list of entry types will appear.

5. Select the **type** of journal entry. The selected type will appear in the list box.

6. Type any **notes** regarding the journal entry. The note will appear in the message area.

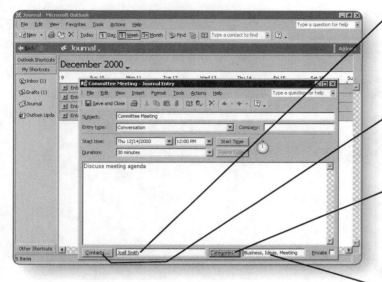

7a. **Type** the **name** of the contact in the Contacts text box.

OR

7b. **Click** on the **Contacts button** to access your Contact list.

8a. Optionally, **click** on the **Categories** button to access the Categories list.

OR

8b. Optionally, **type** the **name** of the category or categories in the Categories text box.

9. **Type** the **company name** in the Company text box.

10. **Click** on the **down arrow** next to the Start time list box. A calendar will appear.

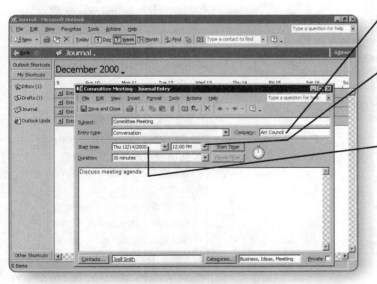

11. **Click** on a **date** to **establish** the **starting date**.

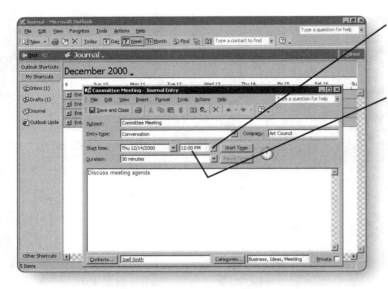

12. **Click** on the **down arrow** next to the time text box. A list of times will appear.

13. **Click** on a **time** to establish the **starting time**.

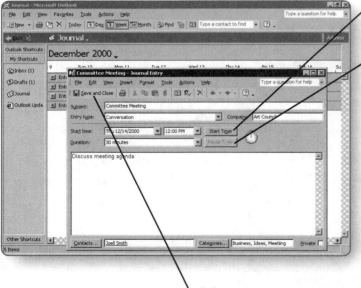

14. **Click** on the **Start Timer button**. The timer will start.

15. **Click** on the **Pause Timer button**. The timer will pause.

NOTE

To keep accurate records, pause the timer when you are interrupted or have to temporarily stop recording the activity. Click on the Start Timer button again to resume the timer.

---

16. **Click** on the **Save and Close button**. The timer will stop and the journal entry will be saved and closed.

Modifying a Journal Entry

What happens if you start recording a journal entry and forget to stop the timer when the activity is finished? Don't worry; it's easy to modify journal entries to change inaccurate information, or to add additional information to the entry.

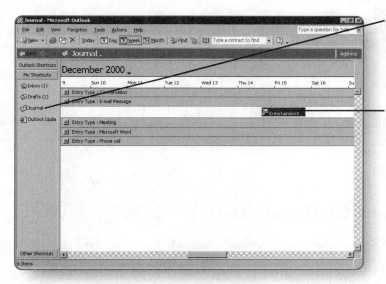

1. **Click** on the **Journal icon** on the Outlook bar. Your journal entries will appear in the Information viewer.

2. **Click twice** on any **entry**. The entry will appear.

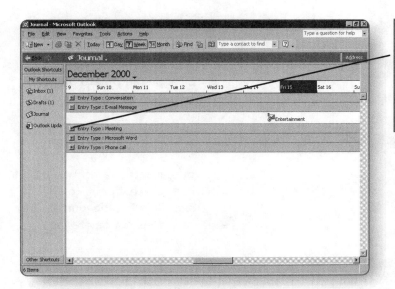

NOTE

To view a particular entry, you may need to click on the plus (+) sign to expand the list of entries.

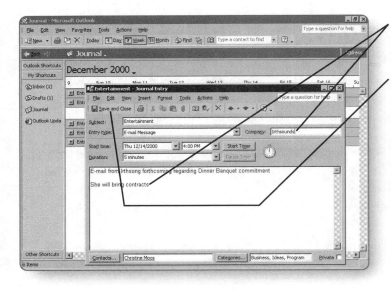

3. Type any **changes** to the entry. The changes will appear.

4. Click on the **Save and Close button**. The journal entry will close and any changes you've made will be saved.

Deleting a Journal Entry

When journal entries are automatically recorded, you may end up with some unneeded entries. Deleting a journal entry is very easy with Outlook.

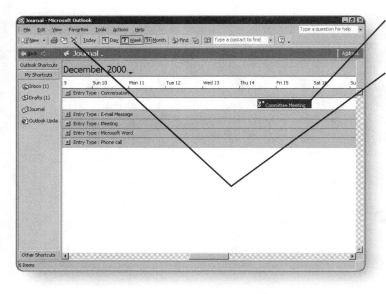

1. Click on any **journal entry**. The entry will be selected.

2. Click on the **Delete button**. The entry will be deleted.

NOTE

Journal entries are shortcuts that point to an item. Deleting the journal entry does not delete the actual item.

23

Changing the Journal View

In the previous chapter, you learned how to create, modify, delete, and automatically track journal entries. Now you can customize your Journal view to make it easier to find and change entries. Also, you'll learn how to tie journal entries to your contacts and organize journal entries by changing category assignments and view settings. In this chapter, you'll learn how to:

- View the Journal
- View the Journal entries for a contact
- Use categories and views to organize the Journal
- Customize Journal views
- Customize Journal entry actions

Viewing the Journal

There are several ways to view the Journal. You can display the entries by type, contact, category, or by looking at the last seven days. In some views, the Journal appears as a timeline—you can scroll through the days to see the recorded activities.

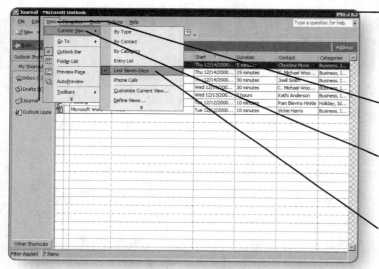

1. **Click** on the **Journal icon** on the Outlook toolbar. The Journal will appear in the Information viewer.

2. **Click** on **View**. The View menu will appear.

3. **Click** on **Current View**. The Current View submenu will appear.

4. **Click** on **any view**. The view will be selected.

If you select the By Type, By Contact, or By Category view, a timeline will appear at the top of the Information viewer.

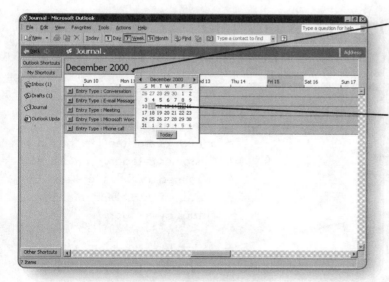

5. Click on the **down arrow** next to the month name in the banner. A Date Navigator will appear.

6. Click on **any date**. The Journal view will change to focus on the date you've chosen.

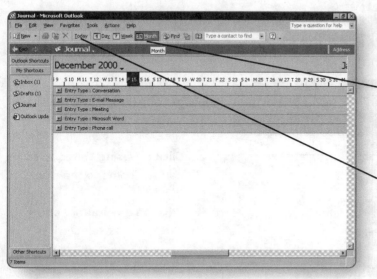

You can also change views with any of the buttons on the Standard toolbar.

7. Click on any of the **View buttons** to switch to day, week, or month view. You will be switched to that view.

8. Click on the **Today button** to return to today's date. You will go back to today's date.

Using Categories to Organize the Journal

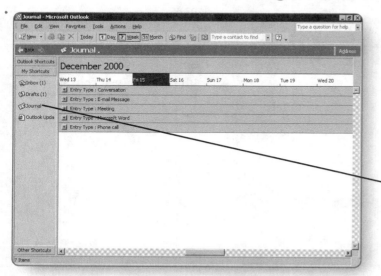

One of the best ways to organize the Journal is by using categories. After you have added several items to the Key Customer category, you can view all related activities for Key Customer by viewing journal entries by category.

1. **Click** on the **Journal icon** on the Outlook bar. Your journal entries will appear in the Information viewer.

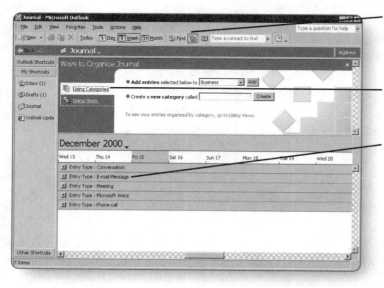

2. **Click** on the **Organize button**. The Ways to Organize Journal pane will appear.

3. **Click** on **Using Categories**. The tab will come to the front.

4. **Click** on **any journal entry**. The entry will be selected.

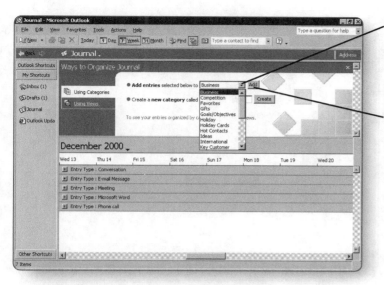

5. Click on the **down arrow** next to the Add entries selected below to list box and **select** a **category**.

6. Click on the **Add button**. The journal entry will be added to the category selected in step 5.

Displaying Journal Entries by Category

After the selected items have been added to a category, you can use views to display journal entries by category.

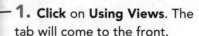

1. Click on **Using Views**. The tab will come to the front.

2. Click on the **scroll arrows** of the Change your view: scroll box. The available views will appear.

3. Click on **one of the views**. The Journal entries will appear in the selected view format.

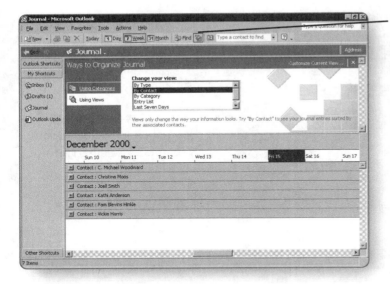

4. Click on the **Organize button**. The Ways to Organize Journal pane will close.

Customizing Views

Each of the views in the Journal has predefined settings that can easily be changed. Some of the items you can change are including or excluding labels on the journal icons, showing week numbers, or changing the font of the view.

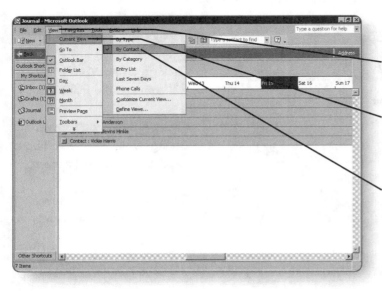

1. Click on **View**. The View menu will appear.

2. Click on **Current View**. The Current View submenu will appear.

3. Click on **the view you want to customize**. The Information viewer will change to reflect your selection.

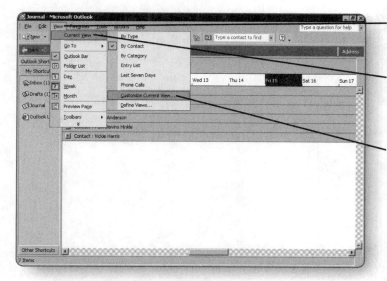

4. Click on **View**. The View menu will appear.

5. Click on **Current View**. The Current View submenu will appear.

6. Click on **Customize Current View**. The View Summary dialog box will open.

NOTE

Some options are available only for particular view formats. Depending on the current view you've selected, the options discussed in this section might not be available.

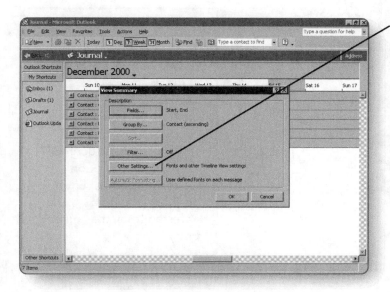

7. Click on the **Other Settings button**. The Format Timeline View dialog box will open.

NOTE

The customization options will vary depending on which view you selected.

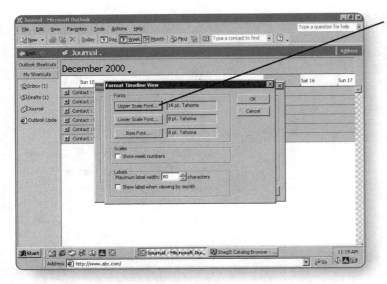

8. Click on any of the **buttons** in the Fonts area and make the desired changes. Your updates will appear in the dialog box.

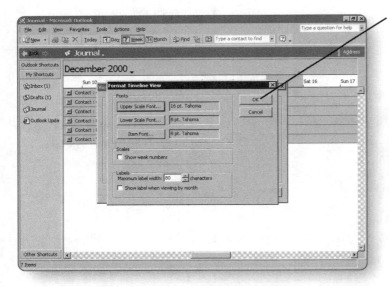

9. Click on **OK** until all open dialog boxes are closed. The Journal will reappear in the Information viewer.

TIP

You can change the default behavior of Outlook and journal entries. Click on Tools, Options, and then click on Journal Options. In the Double-clicking a Journal Entry section, click on Opens the Journal Entry or Opens the Item Referred to by the Journal Entry.

Part VI Review Questions

1. Can Outlook automatically record Journal entries? *See "Tracking Journal Activities Automatically" in Chapter 22*

2. How can you manually create a Journal entry? *See "Creating a New Journal Entry" in Chapter 22*

3. How do you temporarily stop the timer? *See "Creating a New Journal Entry" in Chapter 22*

4. What must you click on to expand a list of Journal entries? *See "Modifying a Journal Entry" in Chapter 22*

5. Does deleting a Journal entry delete the item to which the entry refers? *See "Deleting a Journal Entry" in Chapter 22*

6. Which three Journal views display a timeline? *See "Viewing the Journal" in Chapter 23*

7. What Outlook feature helps you organize the Journal? *See "Using Categories to Organize the Journal" in Chapter 23*

8. How can you view all Journal entries by category? *See "Displaying Journal Entries by Category" in Chapter 23*

9. How can you display a label next to the Journal entry icons? *See "Customizing Views" in Chapter 23*

10. Where do you set the default behavior for Outlook journal entries? *See "Customizing Views" in Chapter 23*

PART VII

Capturing Your Thoughts with Notes

24

Working with Notes

The Notes feature in Outlook lets you quickly jot down any important thoughts, reminders, or other information. Use notes in Outlook instead of grabbing the closest scrap of paper around you. In this chapter, you'll learn how to:

- Create, edit, and delete a note
- Add a category to notes
- Turn a note into an e-mail or task

Creating a Note

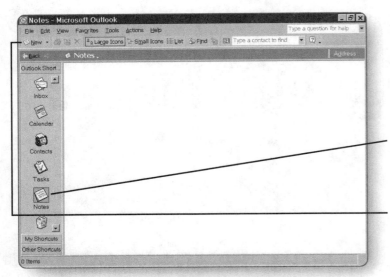

Creating an electronic note in Outlook is easier than reaching for a pen and paper. Creating notes electronically guarantees that you won't have to transfer them to your computer later on.

1. Click on the **Notes icon** on the Outlook bar. Your notes will appear in the Information viewer.

2. Click on the **New Note button**. A new note window will appear.

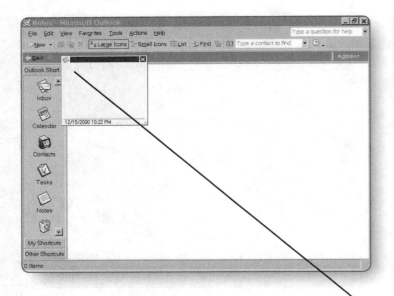

NOTE

If you don't see the date and time at the bottom of the note window, go to the Tools menu and select Options. Select the Other tab and click on the Advanced Options button. From the Advanced Options window, click in the check box labeled When viewing Notes, show time and date in the Appearance options section.

3. Type the **note**.

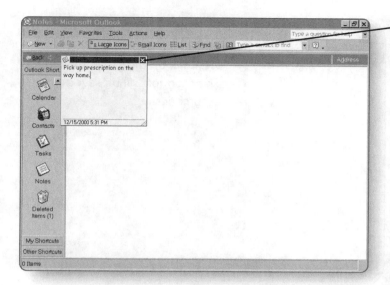

4. Click on the **Close button**. The note will be saved automatically.

TIP

You can press the Esc key to close a note.

NOTE

Only the first several words of the note will appear in the note preview in the Information viewer.

Editing a Note

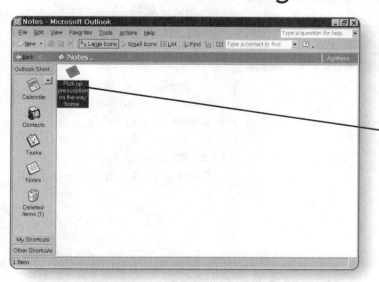

If you gather more information or need to make a change after creating a note, don't worry—you can update the note even after you have closed it.

1. Double-click on any **note**. The note will open.

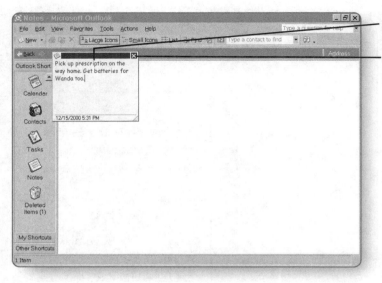

2. Type any **changes**.

3. Click on the **Close button**. The changes will be saved automatically.

Categorizing a Note

It's far easier to organize electronic notes than a stack of phone messages on your desk. You can use Categories in Outlook to group notes into subjects for easy identification and organization.

1. Right-click on any **note** in the Information viewer. A shortcut menu will appear.

2. Click on **Categories**. The Categories dialog box will open.

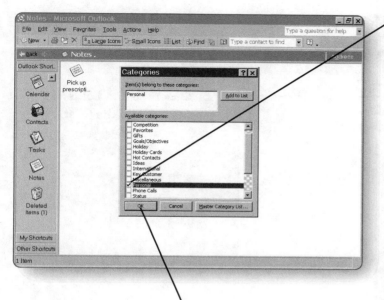

3. Click in any **check box** in the Available categories: scroll box. A check mark will be placed in the box.

NOTE

Notes can be added to multiple categories, or you can add your own categories. Click in the Item(s) belong to these categories text box, type the name of the new category, and click on the Add to List button.

4. Click on **OK**. Your note will be added to the categories you've selected.

Turning a Note into Another Outlook Item

Do you want more from your notes? You can send the note content to another person, create a task from the note, or add an item to the calendar by dragging the note into another Outlook folder.

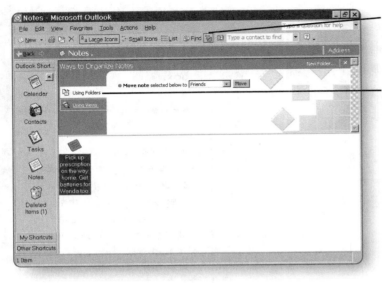

1. **Click** on **Organize**. The Ways to Organize Notes pane will open.

2. **Click** on **Using Folders**. The tab will come to the front.

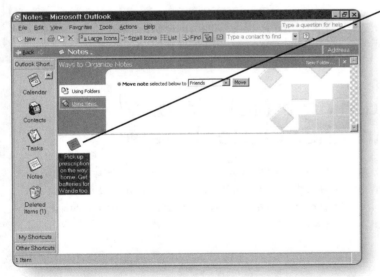

3. **Click** on any **note** in the note pane. The note will be selected.

TIP

You can select multiple notes by holding down the Ctrl key and clicking on a note.

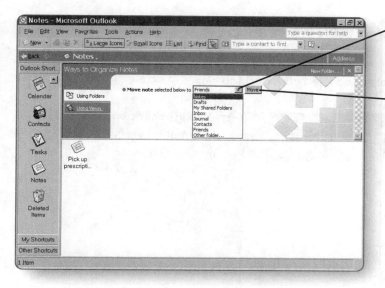

4. **Click** on the **down arrow** next to Move note selected below to and **select** a **folder**.

5. **Click** on the **Move button**. The selected note(s) will be moved to a new folder.

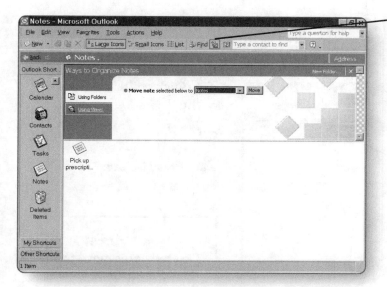

6. **Click** on **Organize**. The Ways to Organize Notes pane will close.

NOTE

Another way to move a note to a folder is to click on the note and drag it onto another folder icon on the Outlook bar or folder list.

Deleting a Note

No longer need your note? Outlook makes it easy to delete notes and keep your desktop clean.

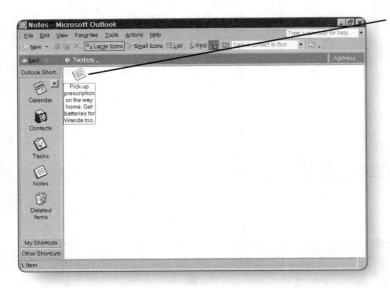

1. **Right-click** on a **note** in the Information viewer. A shortcut menu will appear.

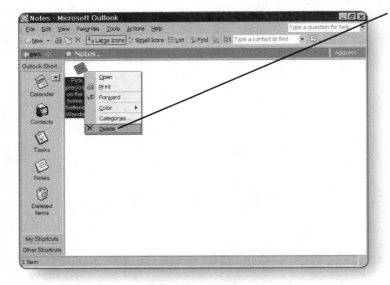

2a. **Click** on **Delete**. The note will be deleted.

OR

2b. **Press Delete**. The note will be deleted.

NOTE

Deleted notes move to the Deleted Items folder. If you later realize you need a deleted note, you can open the Deleted Items folder and drag the note back to the Notes folder.

25

Changing the Look of Notes

Using the Notes feature in Outlook, you can quickly jot down any important thoughts, reminders, or other information. You can change the appearance of notes so you can easily find and identify the note for which you are looking. In this chapter, you'll learn how to:

- Change note colors and displays
- Use views to organize notes
- Sort or filter views

Changing Note Colors

If you are visually oriented, Outlook has a great feature that will allow you to organize your notes by color.

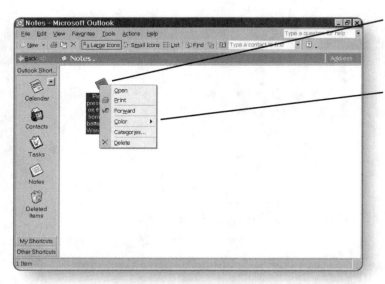

1. Click on the **Note icon** in the Outlook bar. Your notes will appear in the Information viewer.

2. Right-click on any **note**. A shortcut menu will appear.

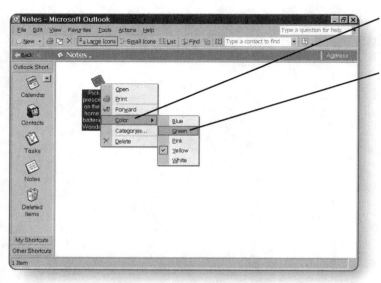

3. Click on **Color**. The Color submenu will appear.

4. Click on any **color**. The color will be applied to the note.

TIP

Colors can be used to organize notes into visual categories. For example, make personal items blue and important items pink.

Changing Note Defaults

By default, notes are yellow and medium in size. You can change these defaults for any new notes added to the Notes folder.

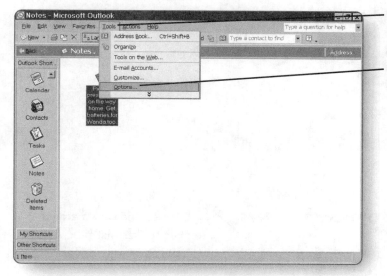

1. **Click** on **Tools**. The Tools menu will appear.

2. **Click** on **Options**. The Options dialog box will open.

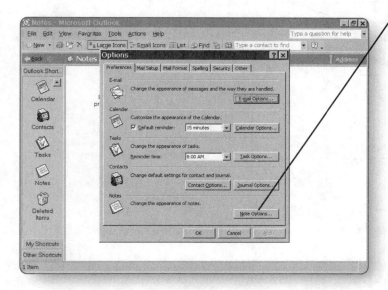

3. **Click** on the **Note Options button**. The Notes Options dialog box will open.

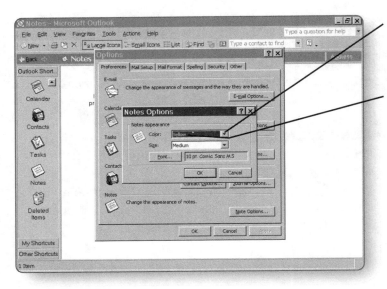

4. **Click** on the **down arrow** next to the Color: list box. A list of available colors will appear.

5. **Click** on a **color**. Your choice will appear in the list box.

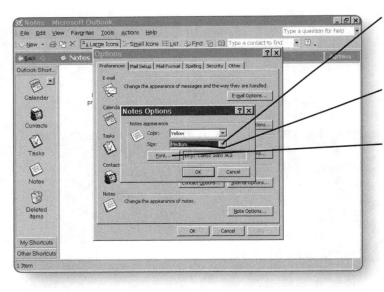

6. **Click** on the **down arrow** next to the Size: list box. A list of available sizes will appear.

7. **Click** on a **size**. Your choice will appear in the list box.

8. **Click** on the **Font button**. The Font dialog box will open.

9. Click on a **font**, **font style**, and **size**. Your selections will be highlighted.

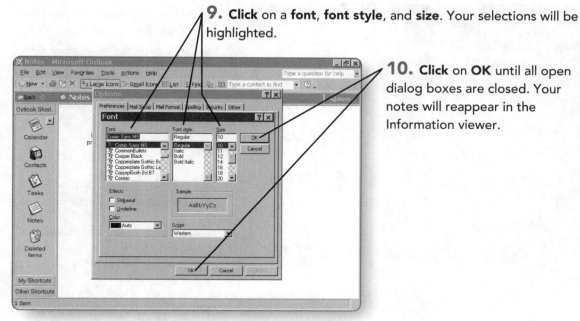

10. Click on **OK** until all open dialog boxes are closed. Your notes will reappear in the Information viewer.

Changing the Notes Display

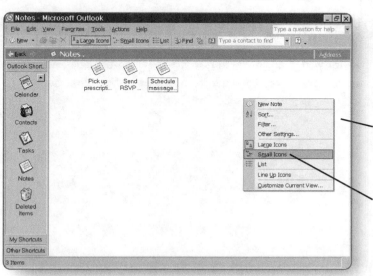

Notes are displayed in the Information viewer as icons. You can change the size of the icon or display a simple list of notes instead.

1. Right-click on a **blank area** in the Information viewer. A shortcut menu will appear.

2a. Click on **Small Icons**. Your notes will be displayed as smaller icons. You will be able to see more notes in the Information viewer, but you won't be able to see as much detail on each one.

OR

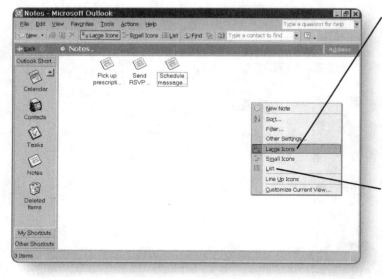

2b. Click on **Large Icons**. Your notes will be displayed as larger icons. You won't be able to see as many notes in your Information viewer, but you'll be able to see more details about each one.

OR

2c. Click on **List**. Your notes will be visible in a list format.

TIP

Use the Large Icons, Small Icons, and List buttons on the Standard toolbar to quickly change the list type.

Changing the Notes View

Views let you change which notes appear on the screen. Using views is a great way to organize notes or to find the notes you need.

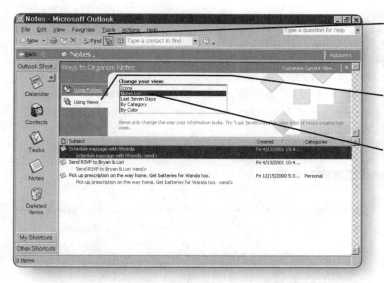

1. Click on **Organize**. The Ways to Organize Notes pane will open.

2. Click on **Using Views**. The tab will come to the front.

3. Click on any **view**. The view will change.

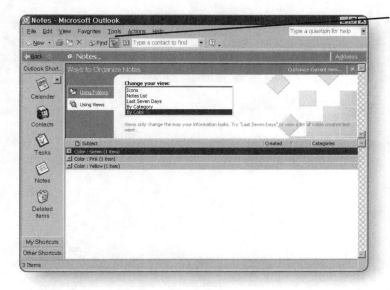

4. Click on **Organize**. The Ways to Organize Notes pane will close.

Sorting and Filtering Notes

Sorting notes will group together similar notes. After you've sorted your notes, you can scroll through all the notes to find the ones you want. Filtering notes allows you to show only the notes you need. The other notes are not deleted; they simply do not display onscreen.

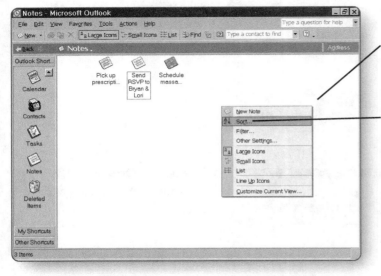

Sorting Notes

1. **Right-click** on any **blank area** of the Information viewer. A shortcut menu will appear.

2. **Click** on **Sort**. The Sort dialog box will open.

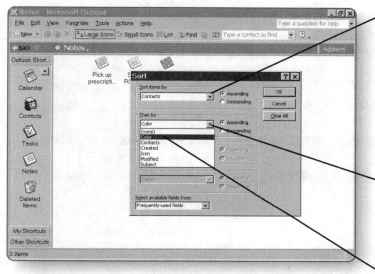

3. Click on the **down arrow** next to the Sort items by list box. A list of available sorting criteria will appear.

4. Click on a **sorting criteria**. Your choice will appear in the list box.

5. Optionally, **click** on the **down arrow** next to the Then by list box. A list of available sorting criteria will appear.

6. Click on a **sorting criteria** to create a second-level sort. Your second-level criteria choice will appear in the list box.

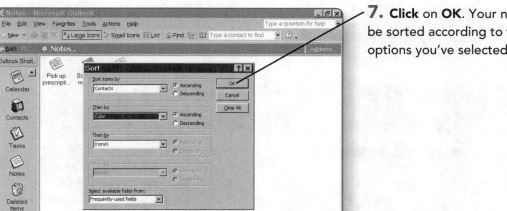

7. Click on **OK**. Your notes will be sorted according to the options you've selected.

Filtering Notes

Maybe you only want to see a particular type of note, such as all personal notes, or all notes created on a certain date. Filtering will get to the notes you want while skipping over all of the others.

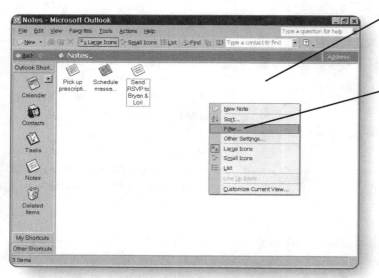

1. Right-click on any **blank area** of the Information viewer. A shortcut menu will appear.

2. Click on **Filter**. The Filter dialog box will open.

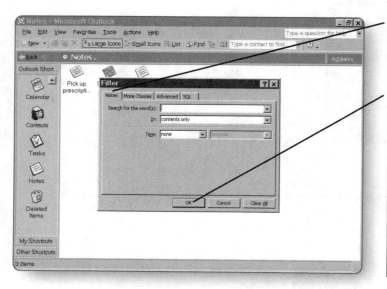

3. Click on any **tab** and select the desired filter criteria. Your choices will be selected.

4. Click on **OK**. Your notes will be filtered according to the criteria you've selected.

NOTE

To remove filter criteria and display all notes, click on the Clear All button on the Filter dialog box.

Part VII Review Questions

1. Why would you add a note? *See "Creating a Note" in Chapter 24*

2. How much of the note will appear in the note preview of the Information viewer? *See "Creating a Note" in Chapter 24*

3. Can a note be edited after closing it? *See "Editing a Note" in Chapter 24*

4. Why might you add a category to a note? *See "Categorizing a Note" in Chapter 24*

5. Can you place the contents of a note in an e-mail message? *See "Turning a Note into Another Outlook Item" in Chapter 24*

6. Where do deleted notes go? *See "Deleting a Note" in Chapter 24*

7. Why might you change the color of a note? *See "Changing Note Colors" in Chapter 25*

8. What is the default size and color assigned to a note? *See "Changing Note Defaults" in Chapter 25*

9. How are notes displayed in the Information viewer? *See "Changing the Notes Display" in Chapter 25*

10. Does applying a filter delete notes? *See "Filtering Notes" in Chapter 25*

PART VIII

Customizing Outlook

26

Accessing Frequently Used Commands

Most common Outlook commands appear on the toolbars at the top edge of the screen. If there is a command you use that does not appear on the screen as a toolbar button, don't worry! Outlook allows you to completely customize the toolbars and the Outlook bar, providing you with one-click access to the tasks or folders you need. In this chapter, you'll learn how to:

- Add commands to toolbars
- Delete commands from toolbars
- Reset toolbars
- Add groups and shortcuts to the Outlook bar
- Add shortcuts to the Outlook bar

Adding Commands to Toolbars

Do you want to click on a button and have an often-performed task occur? You can add any Outlook command to the toolbars.

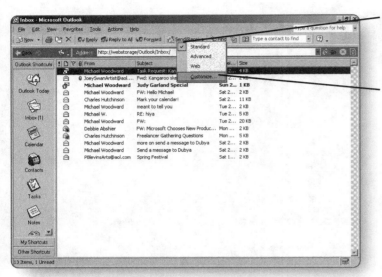

1. **Right-click** on any **toolbar button**. A shortcut menu will appear.

2. **Click** on **Customize**. The Customize dialog box will open.

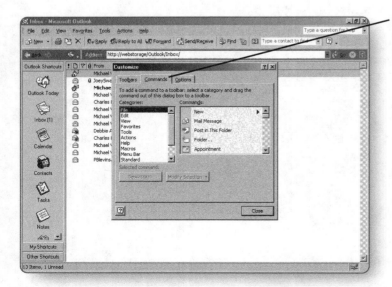

3. **Click** on the **Commands tab**. The tab will come to the front.

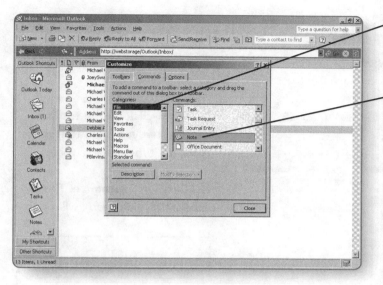

4. Click on any **category**. You will see the commands associated with the category.

5. Click on any **command**. The command will be selected.

NOTE

As you drag the command, there will be a small X attached to the mouse pointer. When the pointer changes to a plus (+) sign, release the mouse button to place the command on the toolbar.

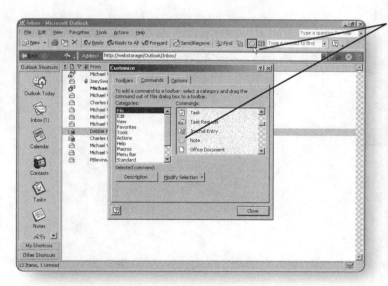

6. Click and **drag** the **command** to an existing toolbar. The command will be added.

TIP

Click on a command in the Customize dialog box, and then click on the Description button to see a description of how the command works.

Deleting Toolbar Buttons

Want a more streamlined toolbar? You can remove any toolbar button via the Customize dialog box.

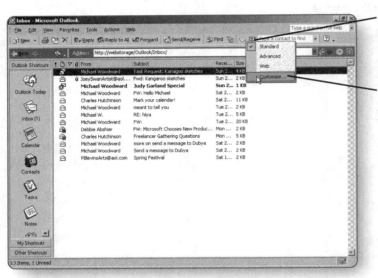

1. Right-click on the **toolbar button** that you want to remove. A shortcut menu will appear.

2. Click on **Customize**. The Customize dialog box will open.

NOTE

The Customize dialog box must be open to add or delete buttons from the toolbars.

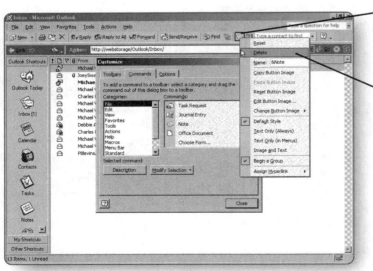

3. Right-click again on the **toolbar icon**. A drop-down list will appear.

4. Click on **Delete**. The selected icon will be removed from the toolbar.

Resetting Toolbars

Whoops! Did you delete a toolbar button by accident? If you've changed a toolbar, Outlook allows you to quickly restore toolbar buttons to their original settings.

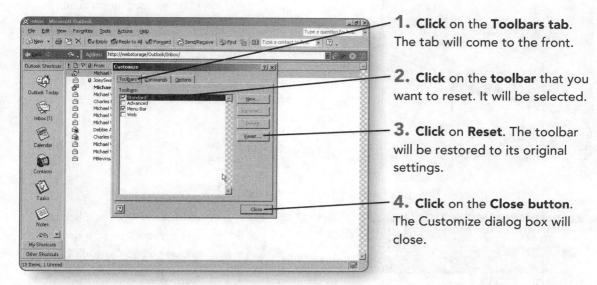

1. **Click** on the **Toolbars tab**. The tab will come to the front.

2. **Click** on the **toolbar** that you want to reset. It will be selected.

3. **Click** on **Reset**. The toolbar will be restored to its original settings.

4. **Click** on the **Close button**. The Customize dialog box will close.

Adding Groups to the Outlook Bar

A quick way to access the folders you need is by clicking on the Outlook bar. Folders on the Outlook bar are arranged into groups, and you can add or delete any group.

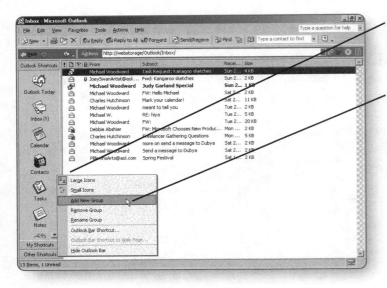

1. Right-click on any **blank area** of the Outlook Shortcuts bar. A shortcut menu will appear.

2. Click on a **Group command** on the shortcut menu. The available commands include:

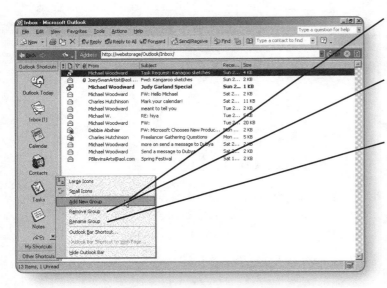

● **Add New Group**. Click on this option to add a new group to the Outlook bar.

● **Remove Group**. Click on this option to remove a group from the Outlook bar.

● **Rename Group**. Click on this option to rename any group on the Outlook bar with a new name.

NOTE

Deleting a group from the Outlook bar will not remove the folders or their contents from Outlook. The icons on the Outlook bar are merely shortcuts that point to the actual items.

Adding Shortcuts to the Outlook Bar

Shortcuts are pointers to frequently used folders. For example, if there is a client folder on the network, you may want to create a shortcut pointing to the folder so that you can access its files quickly. Once you have a shortcut on the Outlook bar, all you have to do is point and click to navigate to a new location.

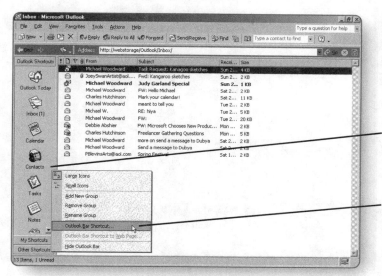

1. Right-click on a **blank area** of the Outlook bar. A shortcut menu will appear.

2. Click on **Outlook Bar Shortcut**. The Add to Outlook Bar dialog box will open.

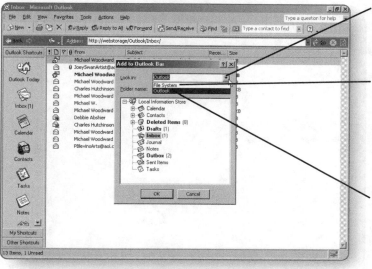

3. Click on the **down arrow** next to the Look in: list box. Two choices will appear.

4a. Click on **File System**. Shortcuts to any folders on your computer or network will appear.

OR

4b. Click on **Outlook**. Shortcuts to all Outlook folders will appear.

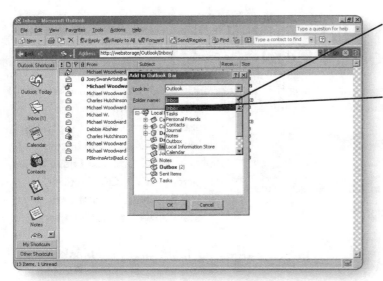

5. Click on the **arrow** next to Folder name. A drop-down list will appear.

6. Click on the **folder** to which you want to add a shortcut. It will be selected.

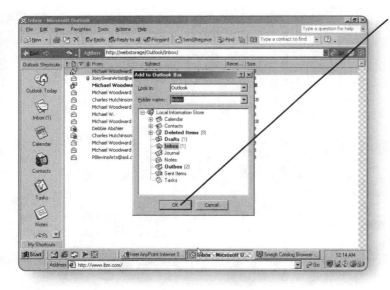

7. Click on **OK**. The shortcut will be added.

27

Customizing Your Messages

Are you tired of plain e-mail messages? The white background, the gray headers—maybe it's a little too dull. Don't spend hours trying to spruce up your e-mail messages—let Outlook do it for you! In this chapter, you'll learn how to:

- Send mail messages with stationery
- Use Microsoft Word as your e-mail editor

Sending Mail Messages Using Stationery

If you want a new look for your electronic correspondence, you can use stationery to brighten up your messages. But before you can use stationery, Outlook needs to change the format of the e-mail messages to HTML. This is a one-time procedure.

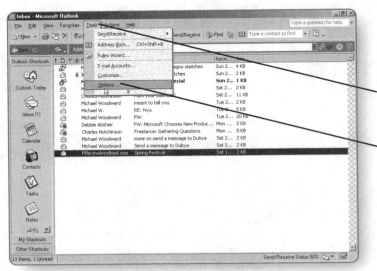

1. Click on **Tools**. The Tools menu will appear.

2. Click on **Options**. The Options dialog box will open.

3. Click on the **Mail Format tab**. The tab will come to the front.

4. Click on the **down arrow** next to the Compose in this message format: list box. A drop-down list will appear.

5. Click on **HTML**. It will be selected.

Now that Outlook knows that you want to use HTML, you can set a default stationery, change the font, or edit the stationery.

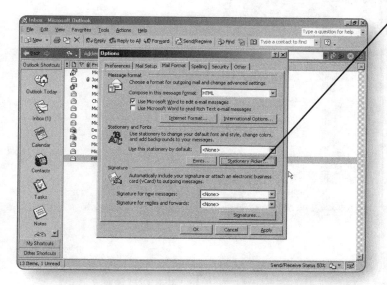

6. Click on **Stationery Picker**. The Stationery Picker dialog box will open.

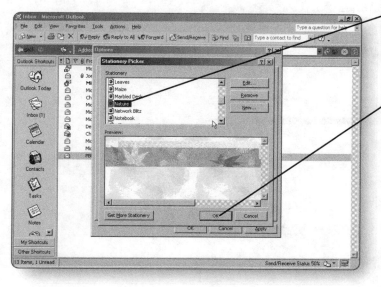

7. Click on any **stationery type** in the Stationery list box. You will see a preview of the stationery.

8. Click on **OK**. The stationery you chose will be the default for all new messages.

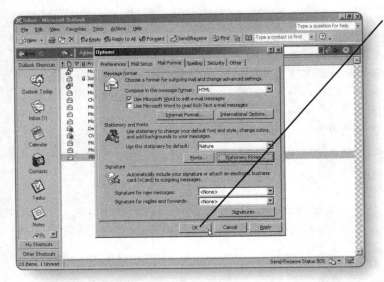

9. Click on **OK**. The Options dialog box will close.

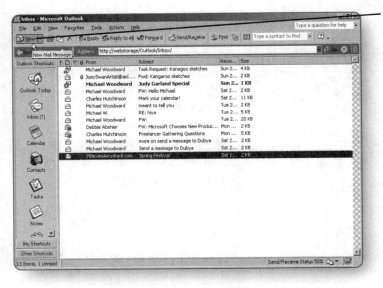

10. Click on **New**. A new message will appear, using the default stationery.

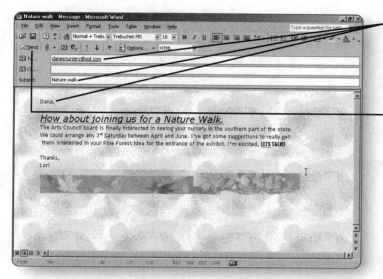

11. **Type** the **required information** for the message in the To:, Subject:, and message text boxes. The text will appear.

12. **Click** on **Send**. The message will be sent on the stationery that you've selected.

NOTE

Some e-mail users cannot properly view messages in HTML format. For those recipients, the message text can be read, but it may contain miscellaneous codes or characters, and the stationery you select may instead be received as an attached file. To avoid this problem, select Send Using Plain Text in that contact's settings.

Using Other Stationery Patterns

Once you've selected your default stationery, you can still use other stationery patterns or send a plain e-mail message.

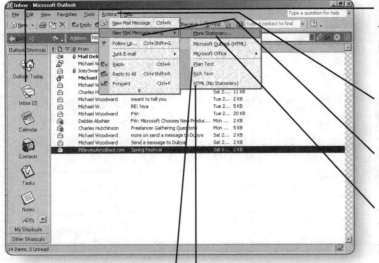

1. **Click** on the **Inbox icon** on the Outlook bar. Your e-mail messages will appear in the Information viewer.

2. **Click** on **Actions**. The Actions menu will appear.

3. **Click** on **New Mail Message Using**. A submenu will appear.

4a. **Click** on **More Stationery**. You will be able to access all of the stationery.

OR

4b. **Click** on **HTML (No Stationery)**. Your original, default message background will be used.

OR

4c. **Click** on **Plain Text**. Your message will be sent with no formatting features.

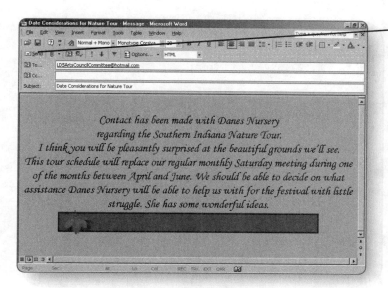

5. Click on **Send** when you're finished addressing and composing the message. The message will be sent with the stationery setting you've chosen.

Using Microsoft Word as Your E-mail Editor

If you have used Microsoft Word, you know how many formatting options are available in the application. Microsoft Word is by default set as your e-mail editor. Its full range of formatting options, as in other Microsoft applications, become available to you in Outlook.

1. Click on **Tools**. The Tools menu will appear.

2. Click on **Options**. The Options dialog box will open.

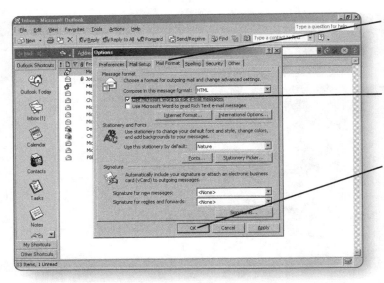

3. Click on the **Mail Format tab**. The tab will come to the front.

4. Click on **Use Microsoft Word to edit e-mail messages**. It will be selected.

5. Click on **OK**. Microsoft Word will now be your e-mail editor.

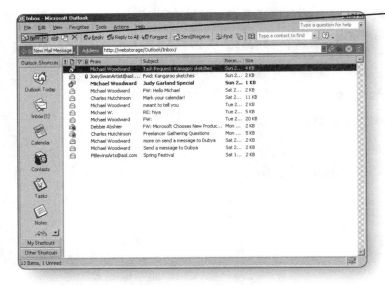

6. Click on **New**. A new message will appear, using the default WordMail template.

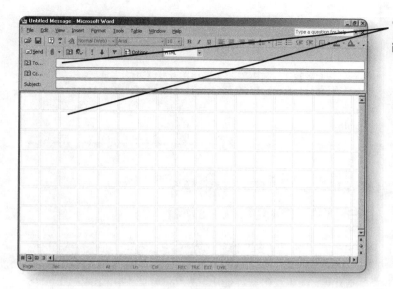

7. **Type** the required **information** for the message.

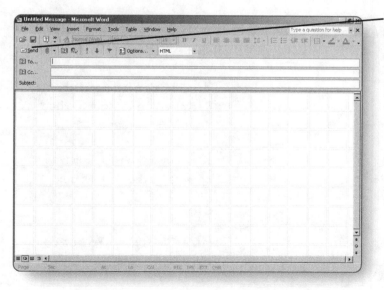

8. **Click** on **Send**. The message will be sent.

TIP

To change WordMail's default template, open Word, click on Tools, and choose Options. In the Options dialog box, click on E-mail Options and choose the theme or stationery that you want to use as the standard template.

Sending Messages Directly from Word

If you have a document in Word that you want to use as an e-mail message, you don't have to create a message in Outlook first and then attach the document. Instead, Outlook can help you send your Word document directly from Microsoft Word in a few simple steps.

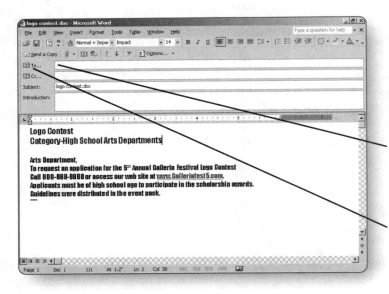

1. **Open** or **create** the **Word document.**

2. **Click** on **File, Send to, Mail Recipient** on Word's toolbar. WordMail will appear.

3a. **Type** the **recipient's name(s)** in the To text box.

OR

3b. **Click** on the **To button** to select recipients from your Contacts list.

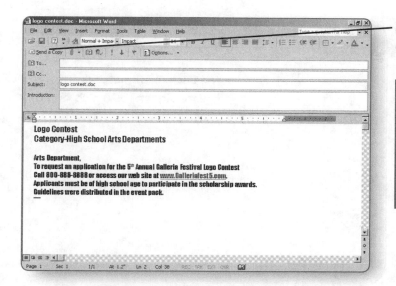

4. **Click** on **Send a Copy**.
Outlook will send the message.

NOTE

If the recipient does not
use Microsoft Office, the
Word document will be
received as an
attachment.

Adding Signatures
to Messages

You can create a signature in Outlook that will automatically or
manually post to your messages. Signatures can be created
with flair when adding different
font selections.

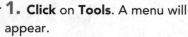

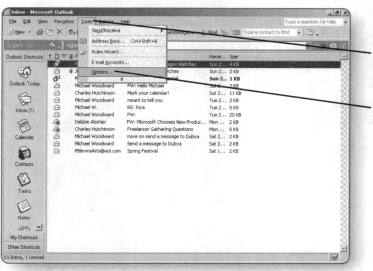

1. **Click** on **Tools**. A menu will
appear.

2. **Click** on **Options**. The
Options dialog box will open.

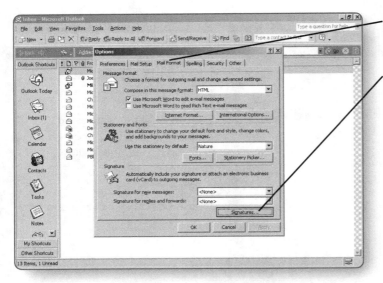

3. Click on the **Mail Format** tab. The tab will come into view.

4. Click on **Signatures**. The Create Signatures dialog box will open.

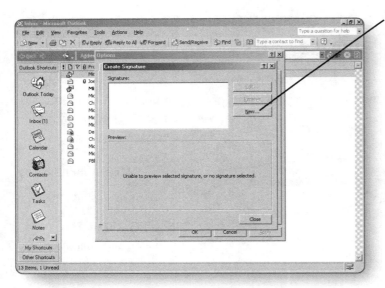

5. Click on **New**. The Create New Signature dialog box will open.

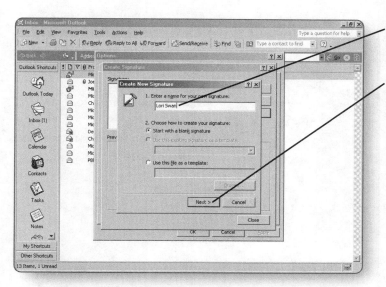

6. **Type** a **file name** for your signature.

7. **Click** on **Next**. The Edit Signature dialog box will appear.

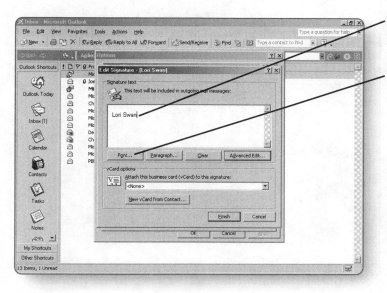

8. **Type** the **signature**. The signature will appear.

9. **Click** on **Font**.

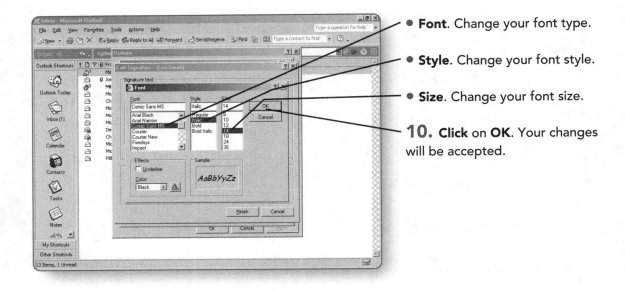

● **Font**. Change your font type.

● **Style**. Change your font style.

● **Size**. Change your font size.

10. **Click** on **OK**. Your changes will be accepted.

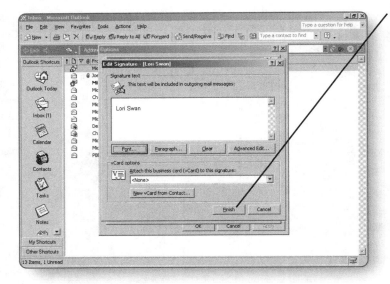

11. **Click** on **Finish**. Your signature will be saved.

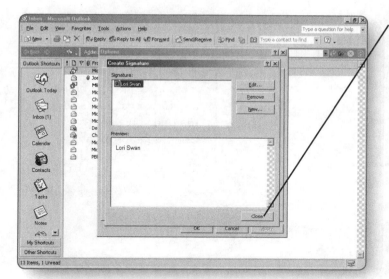

12. Click on **Close**. The Create Signature dialog box will close.

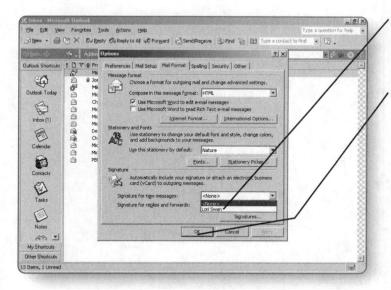

13. Click on the **new signature**. The selection will be accepted.

14. Click on **OK**.

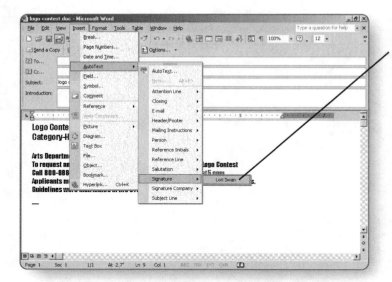

NOTE

You can choose a different default signature for new messages and for replies and forwards. Just select the one you want to use from the appropriate drop-down lists at the bottom of the dialog box.

28

Changing Preferences and Options

One of the most powerful features of Outlook is its ability to adapt to your preferences. If you don't like the way your mail, calendar, or other folders operate, you can change your environment easily. In this chapter, you'll learn how to:

- Customize e-mail options
- Customize preferences

Customizing E-mail Options

You may have noticed that there are numerous default e-mail settings in Outlook. If you don't like the way Outlook e-mail works, you can change it! For example, you can specify what occurs when you close an e-mail message or receive a new e-mail message, and what to do with items in the Deleted Items folder when you exit Outlook.

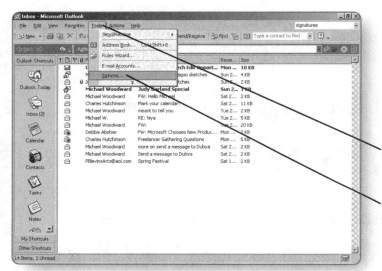

1. Click on **Tools**. The Tools menu will appear.

2. Click on **Options**. The Options dialog box will open.

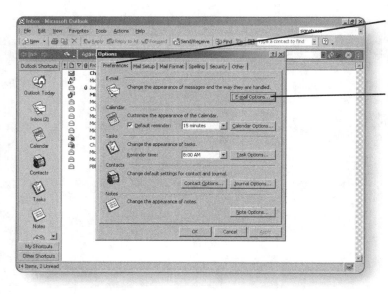

3. Click on the **Preferences tab**. The tab will come to the front.

4. Click on the **E-mail Options button**. The E-mail Options dialog box will open.

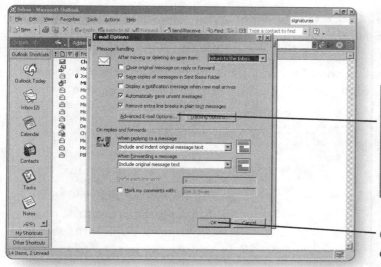

5. Select the **options** you would like to change. The new settings will appear.

TIP

Click on Advanced E-mail Options for additional saving, sending, and other options.

6. Click on **OK** until all open dialog boxes are closed.

Customizing Preferences

The Inbox is not the only folder you can customize in your Outlook environment. The Calendar, Notes, Journal, and Tasks can all be tailored to fit your needs.

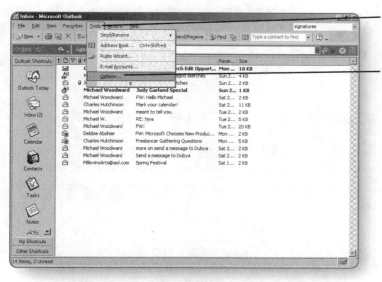

1. Click on **Tools**. The Tools menu will appear.

2. Click on **Options**. The Options dialog box will open.

3. **Click** on the **Preferences tab**. The tab will come to the front. You can define options for the following items:

- **Calendar**. Click on Calendar Options to change the dates displayed on the calendar, to add holidays or time zones, and more.

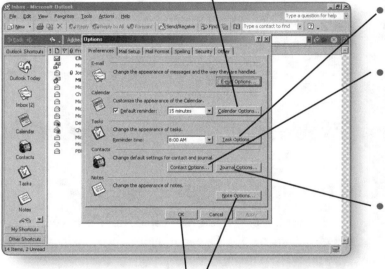

- **Tasks**. Click on Task Options to change the color of overdue or completed tasks.

- **Contacts**. Click on Contact Options to determine how Outlook displays the names in you Contacts list or to detect duplicate contacts when importing them from other sources.

- **Journal**. Click on Journal Options to select which contacts and activities should be recorded in the Journal.

- **Notes**. Click on Note Options to change the default appearance of notes.

4. **Click** on **OK** until all open dialog boxes are closed.

Additional Preferences

Still don't have exactly what you want? In addition to the feature-specific preferences you learned about earlier in this book, there are some additional preferences you can change in Outlook.

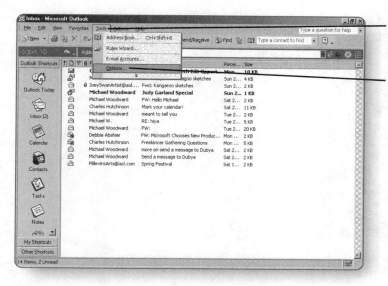

1. Click on **Tools**. The Tools menu will appear.

2. Click on **Options**. The Options dialog box will open.

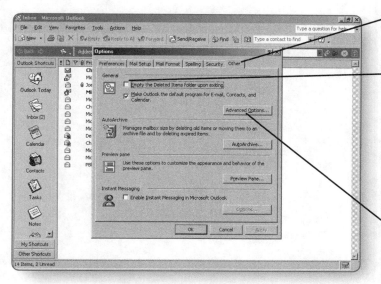

3. Click on the **Other tab**. The tab will come to the front.

4. Click on the **check box** next to Empty the Deleted Items folder upon exiting. A check mark will appear in the box and the deleted items will be emptied every time you exit the program.

5. Click on the **Advanced Options button**. The Advanced Options dialog box will open.

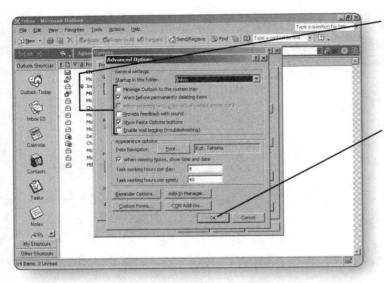

6. Click on the **check boxes** next to the options you want to select. A check mark will appear next to those options that you select.

7. Click on **OK** until all open dialog boxes are closed.

Part IX Review Questions

1. When adding commands to a toolbar, what two symbols appear at the mouse pointer? *See "Adding Commands to Toolbars" in Chapter 26*

2. Which dialog box must be opened to add or delete buttons from the toolbars? *See "Deleting Toolbar Buttons" in Chapter 26*

3. What happens to folders and their contents when you delete a group from the Outlook bar? *See "Adding Groups to the Outlook Bar" in Chapter 26*

4. What are shortcuts? *See "Adding Shortcuts to the Outlook Bar" in Chapter 26*

5. What happens to an HTML e-mail message when a user cannot properly view HTML format messages? *See "Sending Mail Messages Using Stationary" in Chapter 27*

6. What Office application is, by default, set as your e-mail editor? *See "Using Microsoft Word as Your E-mail Editor" in Chapter 27*

7. When you send a document in Word as an e-mail message, how will the recipient see the Word document if they do not use Microsoft Office? *See "Sending Messages Directly from Word" in Chapter 27*

8. Can new messages, replies and forwards have different default signatures? *See "Adding Signatures to Messages" in Chapter 27*

9. Is the Inbox the only folder you can customize? *See "Customizing Preferences" in Chapter 28*

10. How do you tell Outlook to automatically empty the Deleted Items folder every time you exit Outlook? *See "Additional Preferences" in Chapter 28*

PART IX

Appendix

A

Using Keyboard Shortcuts

You may have noticed the keyboard shortcuts listed on the right side of several of the menus. You can use these shortcuts to execute commands without using the mouse to activate menus. You may want to memorize these keyboard shortcuts. Not only will they speed your productivity, but they will also help decrease wrist strain caused by excessive mouse usage. In this appendix you'll learn how to:

 Get up to speed with frequently used keyboard shortcuts

 Use keyboard combinations to work with e-mail messages

 Use keyboard combinations to work with the calendar, contacts, and other Outlook features.

Top 10 Keyboard Shortcuts in Microsoft Outlook 2002

1. Use Outlook Help   Press F1

2. Send/receive mail on default accounts   Press F5

3. Go to the Inbox   Press Ctrl+Shift+I

4. Create a new message   Press Ctrl+Shift+M

5. Create a new contact   Press Ctrl+Shift+C

6. Create a new appointment   Press Ctrl+Shift+A

7. Print the selected item(s)   Press Ctrl+P (open the Print dialog box)

8. Reply to message   Press Ctrl+R

9. Forward message   Press Ctrl+F

10. Send the message   Press Ctrl+S

Learning the Basic Shortcuts

Trying to memorize all these keyboard shortcuts isn't as hard as you may think. Windows applications all share the same keyboard combinations to execute common commands. Once you get accustomed to using some of these keyboard shortcuts in Outlook, try them out on some of the other Microsoft Office programs.

Using Menu Item Hot Keys

You can execute any menu command in a Windows application by pressing Alt, and then pressing the command's *hot key*, the key underlined in the menu command's name (such as File or Format). In Outlook, for example, you can send items in your Outbox from your default mail account(s) using only the keyboard. Go to the Inbox and follow these steps:

1. Press the **Alt** key. The first menu name on the menu bar, **File**, will be highlighted.

2. Press **T** for **Tools**. The Tools menu opens.

3. Press **E** for **Send/Receive**. The Send/Receive submenu opens.

You can also use the arrow keys to navigate menus, open submenus, and highlight menu items. If the menu item does not have a hot key, press the Up or Down arrow until the item is highlighted, and then press Enter to execute. (To complete the preceding example, highlight which account to use and press Enter to send the messages waiting in that account.)

> ### NOTE
> Remember that Outlook 2002's menus expand and reveal additional commands after they are open for a moment. If you have a command's hot key memorized, you don't have to wait for the menu item to appear before you can execute the command. Just press the shortcut key combination—Outlook will know what to do.

Hot key shortcuts are notated in this appendix as **Alt+x+y**, where x and y are the underlined key on a menu name or command. For example, the previous steps would be shown as **Alt+T+E**.

You might want to use some commands no matter where you are in Outlook, such as composing mail or getting help. The following table includes some keyboard shortcuts that you can use anywhere in Outlook.

To Execute This Command	Do This
Use Outlook Help	Press the F1 key
Use the What's This? button	Press the Shift and F1 keys simultaneously (Shift+F1)
Select all items or text	Press Ctrl+A
Copy selected text or item	Press Ctrl+C
Cut selected text or item	Press Ctrl+X
Paste selected text or item	Press Ctrl+V
Delete selected text or item	Press Ctrl+D
Undo last edit or action	Press Ctrl+Z
Move selected items to a different folder	Press Ctrl+Shift+V
View the contents of another folder	Press Ctrl+Y
Open the Go to Folder dialog box	Press Ctrl+G
Work Offline	Press Alt+F+K
Close Outlook	Press Alt+F+X

Working with Messages

You probably use Outlook's e-mail features more than anything else. The following table shows you a few of the more common keyboard shortcuts that can save you time when working with your messages.

Receiving and Reading Messages

You can download, open, and read your mail without ever touching the mouse. The following table shows you some of the keyboard shortcuts you can use when reading and replying to your e-mail.

> **NOTE**
> You must be in Inbox view to use these shortcuts.

To Execute This Command	Do This
Switch to the Inbox	Press Ctrl+Shift+I
Send and receive mail from all default accounts	Press F5
Open or close the Preview Pane	Press Alt+V+N
Open the selected message(s)	Press Ctrl+O
Mark the selected message(s) as Read	Press Ctrl+Q
Switch to next open message	Press Ctrl+>
Switch to previous open message	Press Ctrl+<
Find text in current message	Press Ctrl+F
Save a message's attachments	Press Alt+F+N
Flag a message for follow-up	Press Ctrl+Shift+G
Reply to the current message	Press Ctrl+R
Reply to all recipients of the current message	Press Ctrl+Shift+R
Forward the current message	Press Ctrl+F
Print a message	Press Ctrl+P
Move current message to another folder	Press Ctrl+Shift+V
Close the current message	Press Alt+F4

Composing and Sending Messages

When you're composing new messages, it's often more convenient to use a keyboard shortcut than to dig through the Outlook menu structure. The following table lists a few of the common keyboard shortcuts for creating and sending messages.

> **NOTE**
>
> You must be in Inbox view to use these shortcuts.

To Execute This Command	Do This
Create a new message	Press Ctrl+Shift+M
Open the Address Book	Press Ctrl+Shift+B
Display the Bcc field in the message header	Press Alt+V+B
Format the selected text (open the Text dialog box)	Press Alt+O+F
Format the selected paragraph	Press Alt+O+P
Insert an attachment or file	Press Alt+I+F
Insert a hyperlink	Press Alt+I+H
Check the spelling of a message	Press F7
Save the message to the Drafts folder	Press Ctrl+S
Send the message using the default account	Press Alt+S
Close the current message without saving	Press Alt+F4

Working with Other Outlook Features

Outlook's Calendar, Contacts, and other features also support keyboard shortcuts. The shortcuts in this section will help you work with those features more efficiently and effectively.

Calendar

You can use keyboard shortcuts to navigate the Calendar and create and edit appointments, meetings, and events. The following table lists some shortcuts for the commands you're most likely to use with the Calendar:

NOTE
You must be in Inbox view to use these shortcuts.

To Execute This Command	Do This
Switch to the Calendar folder	Press Alt+G+F+C
View the five-day work week calendar	Press Alt+R
Go to Today	Press Alt+D
Find text in appointments	Press Alt+I
Plan a meeting	Press Alt+A+P
Create a new appointment	Press Ctrl+N
Create a new meeting request	Press Ctrl+Shift+Q
Create a new recurring appointment	Press Alt+A+A
Create a new recurring meeting	Press Alt+A+C

Contacts

Once you have selected the text to which you want to make the editing changes, apply one of the combinations in the following table.

NOTE

You must be in Inbox view to use these shortcuts.

To Execute This Command	Do This
Switch to the Contacts folder	Press Alt+G+F+O
Create a new contact	Press Ctrl+Shift+N
Create a new distribution list	Press Ctrl+Shift+L
Create a new message to the selected contact	Press Alt+A+M
Start a mail merge	Press Alt+T+G
Start a new call	Press Ctrl+Shift+D

Notes and Tasks

How many times have you been working diligently on something when another thought pops into your head that you need to write down? Using Outlook's keyboard shortcuts, you can pop up a new note or task instantly, capture the thought, and go right back to what you were working on without skipping a beat. The following table lists a few common keyboard shortcuts for working with notes and tasks. You can use these commands from anywhere in Outlook.

To Execute This Command	Do This
Create a new task	Press Ctrl+Shift+K
Create a new task request	Press Ctrl+Shift+U
Create a new note	Press Ctrl+Shift+N
Save and close a task	Press Alt+S
Save and close a note	Press Alt+Spacebar+C
Forward the selected note(s) or task(s)	Press Ctrl+F

Glossary

A

Account. Personal access information allowing users to utilize e-mail and internet features.

Address Book. An electronic file that allows you to store e-mail addresses and other information. An address book may be global or personal.

Address Map. A way to view the location of an address on a map via the Internet.

Adult Content Mail. Mail that would not be suitable for individuals under the age of 18.

Appointment. A scheduled block of time on the calendar. Appointments can contain information about the purpose, location, and duration of the engagement.

Archive. A process of retrieving dated information and placing it into another location. Archived information is still available; it is simply located in another folder.

Attachment. A document or file that is a part of an e-mail message.

AutoArchive. A process of automatically retrieving dated information and placing it into another folder. AutoArchiving will reduce the size of the folders and keep Outlook operating optimally. By default, Outlook will prompt you to AutoArchive items older than 14 days.

AutoDialer. A feature, once set, that will automatically dial preset numbers using your computer's modem.

Automatic Signature. A way to include your name and other information automatically at the bottom of every e-mail message.

AutoPick. AutoPick allows Outlook to search for a mutually available meeting time for all meeting attendees.

AutoPreview. An Inbox view that allows you to display the first three lines of text in the e-mail message.

B

Browser or Web Browser. A computer program you can use to view and interact with pages and sites on the World Wide Web. The most popular browsers are Microsoft Internet Explorer and Netscape Navigator. Outlook can act as a browser, but that is not its primary function.

Bullets. Symbols that precede an item in a list.

C

Calendar. An Outlook folder that displays meetings, appointments, and events.

Categories. Words or phrases used to group together similar Outlook items.

Certificates. Companion files that contain digital identification codes (also known as Digital IDs).

Contacts. An electronic Rolodex. May include information such as addresses, phone numbers, e-mail addresses, and Web pages.

Current View. An option on the View menu that allows you to control the display of items on the screen. You can choose one of Outlook's standard views, or you can design your own.

D

Date Navigator. A thumbnail picture of a month. The Date Navigator is a quick way to change the day, week, or month displayed on the screen.

Delegate. A person to whom you give the authority to reply to incoming mail for you, such as your assistant or your boss.

Desktop. When you start your computer, the large area on your screen is called the desktop.

Dialog Box. A box that appears onscreen and presents settings that can be selected and activated.

Directory Service. An e-mail address lookup service that you can add to your accounts list.

Draft Message. A message that has not yet been sent. If you don't have time to complete a message and would like to return to it, saving the message will place it in the Drafts folder for later retrieval.

E

E-mail Address. A unique identifier that allows others to deliver electronic messages. An individual may have more than one e-mail address. An example is elvis@graceland.com.

E-mail Editor. The interface used to compose e-mail messages.

Event. Any appointment that lasts 24 hours or longer.

Exchange Server. A computer that processes messages and other Outlook items. Think of it as your electronic post office.

Export. The ability to send or export files and folders to other users or file locations.

Extended Menus. A menu command that has a right-pointing arrow. When you click on an extended menu, another menu appears next to it.

F

Field. A space in which information is entered. Some examples of fields in e-mail messages are Subject and Date Received.

Filter. A filter excludes certain types of items. For example, you can filter your e-mail to include only those messages received in the last seven days.

Flag. Use a flag to mark an item for special attention. For example, a flag can indicate that an item needs further review.

Folder. In Outlook, folders store items. Folders include the Inbox, Calendar, Tasks, Contacts, Journal, and Notes.

Forward. When you receive an e-mail message that you think others would like to read, but they are not on the original distribution list, you can click on Forward to send it to them.

Free/Busy Service. A feature enabling you to share your published calendar schedules with others. This feature requires access to the Microsoft Office Internet Free/Busy Service or another Internet or intranet location. Other users can tell only if you are busy or available, not the details of your calendar.

G

Global Address List. A place to keep addresses that can be accessed by many people.

Groups. A set of items (messages, tasks, and so on) with a common element, such as messages of high priority or contacts from the same company. Groups can be sorted, expanded, and collapsed.

H

HTML. HyperText Markup Language. Used for composing e-mail messages with stationery.

HTTP (Hypertext Transfer Protocol) Mail. Outlook XP supports Web-based e-mail services such as Hotmail or Yahoo mail, which you also can access directly from any web browser when you're not working on your usual computer.

I

Icon. A picture that represents a command or folder.

Import. The ability to transfer a file from another user to your account.

Inbox. The Inbox stores all of your incoming e-mail messages.

Information Viewer. The display area for e-mail messages, calendar items, contacts, tasks, journal items, or notes.

Internet Explorer. A Web browsing application.

ISP. Internet Service Provider. A company that provides dial-up access to the Internet, and often gives you an e-mail address and other services as well.

J

Journal. The Journal is an Outlook folder that stores records of phone calls, meetings, meeting responses, and other activities.

Journal Entry. An individual record of a single activity, such as a phone call.

Junk Mail. Unsolicited e-mail.

M

Meeting Request. Outlook feature allowing users to propose a meeting with others, whether or not they are on your corporate network.

Menu Commands. Options that appear on the menu bar that will perform a function.

Message Recall. A method for retrieving an e-mail message from the recipient's Inbox before he or she is able to read the item.

Microsoft NetMeeting. Free, downloadable software from Microsoft that allows you to conduct an online meeting.

Microsoft Office. A suite of software applications from Microsoft Corporation. It includes Word, Outlook, Excel, PowerPoint, and Access.

Microsoft Passport. A user account required to access a number of Microsoft's online services, including the Microsoft Free/Busy service.

N

Netscape Navigator. A Web-browsing application.

News Server. A server specifically geared toward providing access to newsgroups.

Newsgroups. Newsgroups are monitored collections of messages written and posted by individuals and stored in a news server. Access to read and post messages requires permission through a newsreader.

Newsreader. An application used to read and reply to newsgroup messages.

Notes. An Outlook folder that allows you to post ideas, thoughts, or quick bits of information on electronic sticky notes.

O

Office Assistant. A Help system from Microsoft that allows you to ask questions and receive answers regarding Outlook.

Offline. Working in Outlook without a live Internet connection. You can use most Outlook features offline, but your outgoing messages and requests won't be sent until you connect.

Online Meeting. A method of communicating with others simultaneously across the Internet. Online meetings can contain typed discussions, real-time video, and spoken conversation.

Online Meeting Request. The command used to invite other individuals to an online meeting and to give them the information they need to join the meeting.

Organize. An Outlook feature that presents different ways of arranging items in the Information viewer.

Outbox. An Outlook folder in which outgoing e-mail messages are stored. This is a temporary holding bin; once the items are sent, they are moved from the Outbox to the Sent Items folder.

Outlook Bar. The gray column on the left of the screen that contains shortcuts to the Outlook folders.

Outlook Symbols. Flags, objects, and symbols within Outlook that designate particular messages at a glance.

Outlook Today. A snapshot preview of the day's activities, e-mail messages, and tasks.

P

PDL. Personal Distribution List. A PDL is a list of e-mail addresses that you create and maintain. The name of the PDL can be entered on the To line of a message, instead of typing each individual address.

Personal Address Book. A storage location for personal e-mail addresses—sometimes referred to as a PAB file.

Personal Distribution List. See PDL.

Plain-Text Format. A basic text format that displays messages without creative formatting features.

Plan a Meeting. An option that allows you to review the meeting attendees' schedules before requesting a meeting time.

POP Mail. A protocol used to accept and deliver e-mail from an Internet e-mail server.

Preview Pane. A viewing option that displays the content of whichever message is selected, enabling you to quickly scan your incoming messages without opening them.

Print Style. The print style consists of the predefined font, page setup, and header and footer settings for a print job. You can create new print styles or modify existing ones.

Priority. A flag that can be attached to important tasks and messages.

Profile. A setting that tells Outlook who you are. Profiles allow more than one person to access Outlook at each computer.

Properties. Settings assigned to each folder that determine permissions, synchronization, and more. Properties are accessed by right-clicking on a folder in the Outlook bar.

R

Read Receipt. An Outlook option that, when attached to a message, will notify sender that sent messages have been received.

Recurrence Pattern. The specified schedule of recurring events.

Recurring Appointment. An appointment that occurs more than once, such as a daily, weekly, or monthly meeting.

Recurring Event. A calendar option in Outlook allowing users to automatically calculate and schedule recurring meetings and events.

Reminder. An electronic update that will notify you a certain time before an appointment, meeting, or task due date.

Reply. An electronic response to the sender of an e-mail message.

Reply to All. An electronic response to the sender and all other recipients of an e-mail message.

Resource. A resource can be a conference room or a piece of audiovisual equipment. Resources appear in the Location box in the Meeting Request.

Right Mouse Click. Moving the mouse pointer over an item and clicking the button located on the right side of the mouse to display a shortcut menu. Sometimes referred to as an alternate click.

Rules Wizard. A step-by-step guide for creating rules that manage your incoming messages.

S

ScreenTip. A box that pops up on the screen when the mouse pointer is held over a toolbar button.

Scroll Bar. The horizontal or vertical bar used to navigate through numerous items. Clicking on the scroll arrows, or clicking and dragging the box on the scroll bar, will change the items displayed.

Scroll. The action of clicking on scroll arrows on a list box to display more of the item on the screen.

Secure Password Authentication. A special security feature required by some ISPs in order for you to access your account.

Sensitivity. A level of privacy attached to a mail item. Items can be set to Normal, Personal, Private, or Confidential sensitivity.

Sent Items Folder. An Outlook folder that contains all sent items, such as e-mail messages, meeting requests, and task requests.

Shortcut. A pointer to an item or folder that provides one-click access. Deleting a shortcut does not delete the actual item or folder.

Snooze. Temporarily suspending a reminder. Similar to a snooze button on an alarm clock.

Sort. A method of displaying items in a certain order in the Information viewer.

Start Page. The default display of Outlook when the application is started. Any Outlook folder, including Outlook Today, can be set as a start page.

Stationery. A background for e-mail messages.

Stationery Picker. A method for choosing or designing stationery.

Status Report. An update on the progress of a task.

Synchronize. The ability to synchronize your offline folders automatically or manually when working from a remote location.

T

Task Request. A task sent to another person. An individual receiving a task request can accept, tentatively accept, or decline the task.

Tasks. An Outlook folder that contains items in your task list. Tasks are useful for recording a to-do list and prioritizing assignments.

Toolbar. A bar at the top of the screen that contains Outlook commands. Toolbars can display toolbar buttons or drop-down menus. Outlook toolbars can be customized.

Toolbar Button. A button on a toolbar allows one-click access to perform a command.

Tracking Options. A method for tracing the progress of an item as it is sent and read by the recipient.

V

View. The display for the Information viewer. The view can be changed to any of several other Outlook views, or new views can be created.

W

Web Page Address. The location of a Web page, usually starting with http://www.

Index